P9-CAF-847

The New Authoritarians

The New Authoritarians

Convergence on the Right

David Renton

Haymarket Books
Chicago, Illinois

© 2019 David Renton. Originally published in 2019 by Pluto Press, London.

This edition published in 2019 by
Haymarket Books
P.O. Box 180165
Chicago, IL 60618
773-583-7884
www.haymarketbooks.org
info@haymarketbooks.org

ISBN: 978-1-60846-908-6

Distributed to the trade in the US through Consortium Book Sales and
Distribution (www.cbsd.com) and internationally through Ingram Publisher
Services International (www.ingramcontent.com).

This book was published with the generous support of Lannan Foundation
and Wallace Action Fund.

Special discounts are available for bulk purchases by organizations and
institutions. Please call 773-583-7884 or email info@haymarketbooks.org
for more information.

Printed in Canada by union labor.

Library of Congress Cataloging-in-Publication data is available.

10 9 8 7 6 5 4 3 2 1

Contents

Acknowledgements

I am grateful to all the friends with whom I have discussed the ideas here: Anne Alexander, Joe Allen, Jon Anderson, Kate Bradley, David Broder, Sasha Das Gupta, Neil Davidson, Alex Etches, Phil Gasper, Jules Gleeson, Daniel Gordon, Elane Heffernan, Charlie Hore, Brendan McGeever, Gary McNally, Joe Mulhall, Bill Mullen, Dave Pinnock, Charlie Powell, Joe Ruffell, Sue Sparks, Dan Trilling and Satnam Virdee. My thanks also to David Castle who commissioned this book, and to everyone at Pluto Press.

Convergence on the right

The right has changed; it has embraced the ideas of its outliers. In the US and Europe, conservatives have made alliances with those previously consigned to the margins. Ten years ago, the centre right had lesser ambitions. Its priority was to cut taxes and reduce welfare. Today's right seeks to restrict welfare benefits to members of the national community, excluding migrants and Muslims. Its new politics address both the apparent shrinking of public finances and the desire on the part of some of the public to exclude foreigners. While the right has developed, large parts of the left are still arguing for positions which were at their most popular more than 20 years ago. The left has allowed itself to seem the party of unreformed capitalism, neither acknowledging that the economy has failed to deliver for tens of millions of people, nor daring to confront the right's myth-making around immigration.

The new character of our recent moment was at its clearest between June 2016 and May 2017. In less than a year, the right enjoyed three significant victories: the Brexit referendum in the United Kingdom, the election of Donald Trump, and Marine Le Pen's second place in the French Presidential elections.

The campaign for a British departure from the European Union began at the end of the 1980s among Margaret Thatcher's keenest admirers and was shaped by the anger they felt at their fellow Conservatives for removing her. Privatisers and flat-taxers, they saw the referendum as a chance to change Britain and to abolish the numerous EU Regulations which protected the environment, or which made it more expensive for businesses to employ workers. The Conservative leaders who dominated the Remain campaign were incapable of saying clearly that inequality or pollution were in themselves wrong. Taking their cue from Cameron and Osborne's inability to answer the arguments for Leave in the referendum, a majority of Tory voters supported Leave. Even this, however, was not enough to win the referendum. To achieve its victory, the Leave camp also had to convince a minority of Labour voters, which it did by persuading them that immigration represented a threat to their pensions and benefits. Theresa May's post-referendum government has deferred at least until 2020 any attempt to solve the problems facing education, health or housing. In prioritising Brexit over everything else, it has not appeased the advocates of British independence. Rather, they have made Theresa May the prisoner of her most recalcitrant backbenchers. The Britain that is emerging from the referendum has not solved the problems of Europe or of immigration. It has made them central, unavoidable questions of our politics for years to come.

In the United States, the events that were to lead to the election of Donald Trump in November 2016 began five years earlier with Trump's decision to court the conspiracy-theory right. In 2011, he made himself seem a plausible challenger for the Presidency by claiming that Barack Obama was not an American citizen, but a Muslim from Kenya. From 2014, Trump kept in the headlines through the support of the website Breitbart which thrived on an audience of online

Islamophobes and misogynists. The alliance between Trump and his base continued after his election to the Presidency with his decision to appoint Breitbart's Steve Bannon as the administration's Chief Strategist. This grim alliance of the centre and far right shaped Trump's inauguration speech, his choice of international allies, and his visa ban on seven majority-Muslim countries. It continued until the events at Charlottesville in August 2017, which compelled Trump to choose between his mainstream right and far right supporters. Threatened by a revolt of mainstream businessmen and Republicans, Trump had no choice but to dismiss Bannon. Even afterwards, however, Trump's instincts did not alter. Threatening trade wars against the EU and China, promoting the online supporters of the alt right, he has straddled the mainstream and the far right.

In France, the main political parties have for years played a dual game with the Front National (FN) (now renamed the Rassemblement National), dismissing its leaders as extremists who had to be kept from power while at the same time appealing to Front National voters and promising to introduce FN policies. In government, both Socialists and Republicans insisted that by banning the veil and encouraging the police to harass young Muslims, they would separate FN votes from their party. The result has been a sustained hypocrisy, with the centre simultaneously denouncing the ideas of the margins as offensive and yet promising to implement them. The courting of the Front's electorate has not drawn their voters away from their leaders, rather it has confirmed them in their authoritarianism and racism. In 2017, it was the Front and not the Republicans who made it to the second round of the Presidential elections. The Front's success caused the Republicans to fracture with one of the two previous centre-right candidates, Nicolas Dupont-Aignan, endorsing Marine Le Pen for the Presidency. Parts of the mainstream right were willing to ally with the Front, while their endorsement of her pushed Le Pen's vote to a new height of 33 per cent. Meanwhile those who continued to reject the Front seemingly had little better to offer, with Emmanuel Macron promising to reduce the power of the Parliament and rule through an executive Presidency. Even where convergence was checked, the rise of the Front has had a continuing effect on mainstream politics, pulling it ever further to the right.

Because of their history of wars and colonial power, and their place in global institutions such as the United Nations, the IMF and the World Bank; Britain, the United States and France have a capacity to encourage the far right in many other countries. In 1979 and 1980, victories for the right in Britain and the US helped change politics in both western and Eastern Europe. Brexit and Trump have had something of the same character: their impact has been felt far beyond their own borders.

In Holland, Geert Wilders' Party for Freedom (PVV) had previously swapped neoliberal for racial welfarist politics. Wilders has argued that, 'It's one or the other, either a welfare state or an immigration country.'[1] In spring 2017 (following the victories of Brexit and Trump), the centre-right People's Party sought to copy Wilders' success, saying that if re-elected they would double the period of time migrants had to live in Holland before they could acquire Dutch citizenship. People's Party leader Mark Rutte published an open letter to migrants saying, 'Act normal or go away.' He told interviewers that Islamic immigration threatened Dutch traditions such as giving children eggs at Easter. Halbe Zijlstra, the chair of the People's Party in the Dutch parliament, also accused Muslims of conspiring against Easter, saying, 'We have been tolerant to intolerance for far too long.' These claims were not intended to engage with anything Muslims had done, they were a decision to flatter those voters who shared lurid fantasies about foreigners. The result of the elections was that the PVV's party vote held steady while Rutte's vote rose. Through the mainstream rather than the far right, racism and conspiratorial thinking have infected the government.[2]

During elections in Austria in autumn 2017, the centre-right attempted a similar move. Newspaper reports in Germany revealed that the leader of Austria's far-right Freedom Party (FPÖ), Heinz-Christian Strache, had taken part in military exercises as a member of a far-right group Wiking-Jugend. He was not the only member of that party with explaining to do; other press reports found FPÖ members trading photographs and quotes from Hitler, publishing songbooks joking about the Holocaust and being photographed in t-shirts with the names of Nazi tank divisions. In response to the FPÖ, Sebastian Kurtz's centre-right People's Party (ÖVP) promised to reduce benefits for refugees and to criminalise the wearing of the Islamic niqab. These policies did not damage the FPÖ, whose vote rose. The result was a coalition agreement between conservatives and the far right.[3]

Even before the 2016–17 political crisis, separate dynamics had emboldened the autocrats and those seeking to move their countries in that direction. These processes include the defeat of the Arab Spring, and of democratic social movements in countries such as Bahrain, Egypt, Libya, Syria and Yemen, and the defeat of a series of relatively liberal but pro-austerity parties in Hungary, Lithuania and Poland.[4] In the Middle East and in large parts of Eastern Europe, the victories of Trump and Brexit have served to further boost what was already a confident right.

The recipients of Donald Trump's support have included Egypt's General Sisi, the butcher of his country's 2011 uprising, and the first foreign leader approached by Trump after his election. Trump described Sisi as 'fantastic'. He also used social media to congratulate the Philippines' Rodrigo Duterte, who has likened himself to Adolf Hitler in boasting of his willingness to kill millions of drug addicts.[5]

Similar processes could be seen in Turkey, whose 2017 referendum replaced a parliamentary system of government with one based on Presidential rule. The President acquired the power to appoint senior judges, to control the budget and to appoint state officials and ministers. The vote was proposed by a coalition of conservative Islamist (AKP: Justice and Development) and far-right (MHP: Nationalist Action) parties. In the days leading up to the vote, the media broadcast incessant messages in favour of a Yes vote, and scores of journalists associated with the independent press were jailed. In the aftermath of the vote, Donald Trump telephoned Turkish President Recep Tayyip Erdoğan to congratulate him.[6]

Meanwhile, in Brazil, Jair Bolsonaro won the Presidential elections on the basis of his support for the military dictatorship which had ruled the country between 1964 and 1985, and by eulogising all aspects of that regime including its use of torture against left-wing critics. Trump promised to 'work closely together' with him.

In much of Eastern Europe, right-wing parties have radicalised in office, normalising politics which once were restricted to the margins. In Poland, the centre-right Law and Justice Party (PiS), has passed laws giving Parliament the power to restrict judicial terms and replace judges with political appointees. Over 100 journalists have been removed from positions in state-owned media. The government has given civil service posts to supporters of the far-right 'patriot' movement.[7] As with the Western far right, Law and Justice has maintained welfare benefits while racialising them and excluding foreigners. Law and Justice has increased pensions for Polish citizens, child benefit and the minimum wage, while its leader Jarosław Kaczyński has warned that the European Union seeks to compel Poland to accept 100,000 Muslim refugees and promised to restrict the rights of any such arrivals that bring cholera, dysentery and 'other, even more severe diseases'.[8]

Hungary's governing right-wing Civic Alliance party (Fidesz) has dismissed critical voices from the state-financed TV and radio channels,[9] and forced out the independent Central European University, a base of the opposition.[10] At the end of 2017, Fidesz began campaigning for fresh elections, with the message that there were millions of Muslim migrants willing to enter the country from Africa and that they would bring terror to Hungary. The party claimed that mass migration could be stopped only by a wall across the country's southern border. In the words of Prime Minister Viktor Orbán, 'If the levee breaks, if they open the borders, if migrants enter the country, there is no way back.' This was accompanied by attacks on the 'political empire' of George Soros the octogenarian banker who had donated some $4 million to pro-democracy NGOs. If re-elected, Fidesz promised to introduce an anti-Soros law, allowing the government to ban organisations which campaigned for the free movement of people. During the election, giant posters were put up all over the country insisting 'Let's not allow Soros to have the last laugh!' Making explicit what the official campaign was happy to leave implied, thousands of these posters were then covered in graffiti denouncing Soros as a Jew. The Fidesz campaign was then taken up by far-right politicians in the United States and the UK, who claimed that Soros was on a mission to 'breed out' white people until they were a minority in Europe.[11]

In India, the rise of the ruling Bharatiya Janata Party (BJP) has been punctuated by episodes of anti-Muslim violence, including in Bombay in 1992–3, in which around 1,000 people were killed and in Gujarat in 2002 when supporters of the BJP gathered at the site of the Babri Mosque and began building a temple to the Hindu god Ram. There followed days of anti-Muslim riots, during which 2,000 people were killed and tens of thousands of Muslims were forced to flee into temporary refugee camps.[12] The riots threatened to undermine the national government, led by Atal Vajpayee, a BJP member. Vajpayee was no moderate; he blamed the crisis on its Muslim victims, accusing them of not mingling with the Hindu majority. Yet even he realised that violence on this scale was unacceptable. Accordingly, Vajpayee travelled to Gujarat with the intention of dismissing Narendra Modi, the Chief Minister of Gujarat who was widely blamed for the killings. When Vajpayee arrived, there was a revolt by local BJP's members and by supporters of the anti-Muslim RSS cadre organisation which dominates the BJP. During the interwar years, the RSS had been influenced by Italian and German fascism. In 1939, the RSS's theorist M. S. Golwalkar even praised Hitler for 'purging' his country of Jews, calling the steps taken to that point in preparation for genocide 'a good lesson for us in Hindustan'. The RSS retains the trappings of fascism including a bent-arm salute, and parades in white shirts with sticks held like rifles.[13] Vajpayee failed to dismiss Modi in 2002, and in the months that followed the BJP was rebuilt, with its militant wing overtaking its previously more cautious leadership. Modi was not punished for his involvement. Instead he was promoted, becoming the BJP candidate for Prime Minister. Since 2014, the BJP government has closed 11,000 NGOs, accusing them of receiving foreign funding. It has criminalised anti-BJP protests. In 2017, BJP proposed to introduce a 'right of return' modelled on Israel's citizenship laws, for Hindus and other non-Muslims living in neighbouring Afghanistan, Bangladesh and Nepal, to entrench the non-Muslim character of the Indian state. It has been a repressive, authoritarian government, is hostile to opposition and distrustful of democracy.[14]

The changing nature of the right can also be seen in Russia, whose authoritarian government has taken over independent media, subjected opposition parties to harassment and thrived on a language of ultra-nationalism. The country has gone to war in the Chechen republic, in eastern Ukraine and in Syria, where its bombs have enabled the Assad dictatorship to win back control of most of the country from a democratic uprising and over half a million people have been killed.[15] Meanwhile Russia justifies its war against the Syria revolution by saying that it is doing no more than contributing to the war against Islamic terror; an excuse which brings it into alliance with the likes of Trump and Modi. Russia relies on a mixture of military and cultural power to advance its interests, on state-controlled propaganda channels such as Russia Today, on cyber-attacks and on the use of social media to boost the far-right in every country.[16] President Putin's role as a patron of convergence precedes the victories of Brexit or of Trump, but these events have served to encourage what was an existing strategy for building soft power. In 2017, for example, he sought to intervene in the French elections, by providing funds for Marine Le Pen's candidacy, a gift which she was required to acknowledge by travelling to meet him four weeks before the election.

The Russian state works through political structures which are top down and inimical to liberal democracy. But the economic character of the regime, with its low taxes on businesses and high taxes on personal consumption is close to what a British conservative or American libertarian would consider good stewardship if introduced anywhere else. For that reason, Putin's regime has been popular beyond its borders, and among wider groups than the far right. A Conservative Friends of Russia was set up in 2012 by Sergey Nalobin, who was outed in the British press as a spy. Malcolm Rifkind, a former Foreign Secretary and in 2012 the secretary of the Commons intelligence and security committee, became the group's honorary Chair, a role he was later forced to resign. Between 2016 and 2017, Russian oligarchs gave some £820,000 to the Conservative Party, with donors including Lubov Chernukhin, the wife of the former chairman of Russia's state development bank.[17]

The alliance of conservatives and the far right is unwelcome to everyone else. In the US, the Anti-Defamation League has estimated that 2.6 million anti-Jewish tweets were sent between summer 2015 and summer 2016. The ADL was especially interested in tweets directed at anti-Trump journalists, who were accused of being unpatriotic Jews. Some 800 journalists were targeted in this way, with some 45 million people reading the anti-semitic messages. Two-thirds came from just 1,600 twitter accounts. The Southern Poverty Law Center estimates the size of the largest far-right network, the Ku Klux Klan, as less than 6,000 people.[18] If we treat these two figures, 1,600 and 6,000, as boundary estimates of the size of the US far right, either figure is eclipsed by the 60 million people who voted for Trump in 2016. Without his presidential campaign, the conspiracy theorists would have had little influence over the larger number of conservatives. Co-operation between the mainstream and the extreme right has given the latter an influence out of all proportion to their support.

This is not the first time in history when the mainstream has lurched to the right, leaving socialists, feminists and other anti-racists struggling to respond. Subsequent chapters of this book engage with what it means to speak of a moment of far right advance, comparing 2016–17 to previous periods when the right has become radicalised across borders (including 1922–39 and 1979–80). These are the most notorious available comparisons; not all short moments of right-wing success have ended this badly. The late 1890s and early 1900s, for example, saw popular anti-migrant and anti-semitic campaigns in each of the United States, Britain and France, fuelled by a similar combination of economic crisis and fears of migration. Here too there was a relationship between movements of the street (the British Brothers' League, the anti-semitic campaign against Albert Dreyfus in France) and governments led by William Jennings Bryan, Jules Méline and Lord Salisbury. As the decade wore on, however, the left responded with a combination of trade union struggles and political opposition to the right, including the successful campaign in support of Dreyfus. Where their campaigns were both militant and principled, socialists were able to recover and by 1906 in many countries it seemed that racists were once more in retreat.

The question of how long this epoch of right-wing success lasts will be shaped in part by how their opponents respond and whether the left takes the opportunities available to us. The point of this book is to encourage readers to see our enemies clearly, without fear, and to focus on where they are now in the hope that by understanding them better, we can more effectively challenge them.

The mainstream right, the far right, fascism

The argument of this book rests on certain definitions. One is the distinction between left and right. The two terms have an essential difference. As Norberto Bobbio argues, they can be distinguished by their attitude towards equality.[19] The left believes that most inequalities are capable of reduction or eradication. The right, by contrast, exists to oppose 'the liberation of men and women from the fetters of their superiors, particularly in the private sphere.'[20] The distinction between left and right dates to the early days of the French revolution, when the Constituent Assembly debated whether the King should have a veto over its decisions and parliamentarians were asked to stand to the left or the right. It has recurred through global politics ever since.

The difference between left and right works to simplify political debate. Because of it, voters expect left-wing parties to prioritise health and welfare and to promote access to secondary and university education, as these are levelling policies and promote equality. Where the left enforces lower taxes, cuts welfare, or reduces access to education, it is punished at the polls. The right, too, has its own obligations. Its electorate expects the right to administer the economy in an inegalitarian fashion. A right which does not cut taxes will be punished by voters. Further, the right also argues for inegalitarian solutions in culture and society as well as economics: its voters expect right-wing administrations to promote social policies which favour men over women, whites over migrants or Muslims. Where right wing parties forget their supporters or threaten to remove property from those who hold it, their voters punish them.

The contrast between the political left and right is an abstraction, and yet it has a reality. Politics is tribal; the left is in a structured relationship, in antagonism with the right. How people position themselves disciplines how they act. This process is easiest to see with those figures who came over to the right having been closer to the centre or the left. In November 1914, Benito Mussolini, on renouncing his position as editor of the Italian socialist newspaper *Avanti!* to campaign for Italian participation in the First World War, had not envisaged the later stages of his career. He said that he was still a socialist, if perhaps of a new sort. He claimed that his differences with his former comrades were restricted to the war. Yet by approaching industrialists for funding and by promising to fight the left for influence, he transformed himself into an anti-socialist. Within months, Mussolini's direction of travel had been fixed and by May 1915 he was calling for a popular counter-revolution against the liberal state if Italy failed to join the war.[21] His future politics were already in place.

Within the right, it is possible to distinguish between conservatism, the non-fascist far right and fascism. The Scottish left-wing historian Neil Davidson distinguishes between these right-wing traditions in terms of how far they are willing to go in the defence of capitalism. For conservatives, the best means are to maintain social relationships which already exist; for the far right the task is to restore relationships which are perceived to have been lost; for fascists the task is counter-revolution, the nation must be purged of its enemies.[22]

Yet while the contrast between left and right is an essential difference between two recurring forms which can be traced over time, the distinction between the centre right and the far right is relational, a distinction of degree. In the words of one political scientist Aurélien Mondon, 'The classification "extreme right" ... holds no practical value and is only relevant if it is inscribed into a precise time and space.'[23]

The far right takes up ideas which are already present within conservatism. So, at different times, the far right has supported policies of state spending or their opposite, policies of privatisation. Neither is inherent to the far right. The Latin American military dictatorships of the 1950s and 1960s were advocates of state-led development, as was the mainstream right in the US and Europe during that period. A decade ago, the Tea Party and the Dutch PVV demanded low taxes and budget cuts, taking their cue from the majority of post-Thatcherite conservatives. Even the philosophical defence of destructive change is not the sole preserve of the far right but is a recurring theme of mainstream right-wing thought.[24]

Like the conservative right, the far right seeks to conserve the nation in the face of the threat provided by redistribution, cosmopolitanism and migration. Unlike the mainstream right, the far right sees the nation as under immediate attack from alien influences, to which a militant response is needed. In consequence the far right is more open than standard conservatism to conspiracy theories.[25]

The moment when the difference between the mainstream right and the margins is clearest is when the former indulges in 'gatekeeping,' to prevent marginal figures from capturing power.[26] The centre right can do so for reasons of long-term strategy, as when the Conservatives turned against the British fascist Oswald Mosley in 1934 after Olympia and called on Mosley's backers at the *Daily Mail* to drop him. There were strategic differences beneath this move, with Mosley's critics judging that his methods of violence were incompatible with how the right should rule. A similar refusal to adopt marginal opinions could be seen in 1968 with Ted Heath's dismissal of his main challenger for the Conservative leadership, Enoch Powell.

In the United States, perhaps the clearest recent example of gatekeeping was the way in which the Republican Party responded to David Duke, previously the Grand Wizard of the Knights of the Ku Klux Klan. In 1990, Duke campaigned for the Republican nomination for the US senate in Louisiana. Polling showed that he was likely to win the nomination against the party's preferred candidate, Ben Bagert. In the final days of the campaign, Bagert withdrew, but GOP leaders called on his supporters to vote for the Democratic candidate J. Bennett Johnston Jr., who went on to win the primary, albeit narrowly. The Republican Party of the 1990s was content to concede a seat in the US Senate rather than have it occupied by Duke.

A feature of the crisis of 2016–17 was the collapse of old methods by which centrist leaders kept themselves in power: the inability of David Cameron to persuade his own members during the Brexit referendum, the failure of the Republican grandees to keep Donald Trump out, the willingness of parts of the French right to seek office beneath Le Pen. The role of the left is not to mourn the death of gatekeeping on the right. 'Project fear,' as it became known during the Scottish and Brexit referendums, was a mechanism of ideological control and a license for widespread deceit. The methods of gatekeeping have been used most often by conventional media in discrediting movements of the centre- or far-left, or by centre-left parliamentarians in disciplining challengers to the left. We do however need a new terminology to capture the politics of the past few years, in which the centre-left has fought to protect its privileges from its own outliers, while the centre-right has handed power to those on its right. The determination of the centre-left to police its own side has made it weaker; the lethargy of the centre-right has been rewarded with a new period in power.

If the boundary between the mainstream and the far right is protean and changeable, parts of the far right are amenable to a more precise definition. In a previous book on fascism, I argued that fascism is best understood as a specific form of reactionary mass movement.[27] The specificity is fascism's leadership cult, its party form, its ideology of anti-socialism and anti-liberalism. At its heart, fascism is reactionary; it desires to advance capitalist technology while restoring society to the class peace it wrongly associates with the years prior to 1789. Fascism does not want the advance of technology to be reversed. Rather, it sees the reforms that have developed under capitalism, the emergence of universal healthcare and other non-market rights. It seeks to extinguish them and to defeat for all time any possibility of capitalism's replacement by a more egalitarian order.[28] Fascism is also a form of mass politics, characterised by rallies, marches and violence against its opponents, reflecting a fascist goal to purge the existing state. It was in this sense that the Italian Marxist Antonio Gramsci once defined fascism as an attempt 'to resolve the problems of production and exchange with machine guns and pistol shots'.[29]

Fascism's reactionary commitment runs kilter to its need for mass support. If fascism is going to succeed in rooting out political and social democracy, it needs the support of millions of people, and yet the transformation which fascism offers its supporters is no more than cultural or spiritual; it fights any measures to redistribute wealth downwards. It has to mobilise, in other words, the very people whose social advancement it exists to oppose. This contradiction enables fascism to grow during periods of crisis but also makes it unstable, since the millions whose support brings fascism to power have more egalitarian ambitions than their leaders. This constant need to win back a divergent social base drives the radicalism of fascist parties, which is expressed not in pulling down the homes of the rich, but in the purging of political and racial enemies. Where fascism has established a mass base, history has so far provided just two outcomes: either a political defeat by domestic rivals better skilled at popular mobilisation, or a cycle of re-radicalisation ultimately culminating in the involvement of fascist states in all-out racial and military war.

The non-fascist far right has different goals. In Davidson's terms, the non-fascists of the far right, '1) are electoral and seek to attain office through the democratic means at local, national and European levels; 2) they do not worship the state and, while they seek to use the state for welfare purposes for their client groups, some have embraced neoliberal small-state rhetoric; 3) they do not seek to "transcend" class.[30]

The difference between the right and the far right, being relational, is not easy to map and the content of the distinction changes over time. And yet the far right is coherent. An analogy may be drawn with how the far left has imagined its place in history. At the start of the twentieth century, the history of the left was often conceived as a sort of genealogical tree. In the lower branches, it contained such utopians from the distant past as Thomas More,[31] or the Levellers or Diggers, above them the utopian socialists Henri de Saint-Simon, Charles Fourier and Robert Owen, near the middle of the trunk the Chartists, in the higher branches Marx and Engels and among the top branches the early socialist parties. This metaphor connected the political figures who at any moment stood for the greatest equality and for a transformation of the state. If you were to ask what ideas these people had in common, there would be radical discontinuities. Thomas More was a Catholic and an opponent of the Reformation; the Levellers and the Diggers came from a milieu of Protestant sects; Saint-Simon was an atheist. Despite these differences, it was possible to speak of a tradition based around the desire for rapid democratisation, for much greater equality.

A family tree of the counter-revolutionary right would contain in its lower roots the French opponents of 1789, such as Joseph de Maistre or Louis de Bonald, the America Nativists, the Ku Klux Klan, anti-Dreyfusards Édouard Drumont and Maurice Barrès, advocates of Imperial social reform such as Joseph Chamberlain and the Edwardian Die-Hards, the British Brothers League and Action Française. The far right of the past 20 years has included a very wide range of forces: backwards-looking fascist groups seeking to imitate the political forms of the 1930s (e.g. Golden Dawn in Greece), parties of fascist origin but later at some distance from their starting point (e.g. the Italian Social Movement, the Swedish Democrats),[32] post-9/11 anti-Muslim street racists of non-fascist origin but capable of evolving in the direction of either electoralism or anti-electoralism (e.g. the English Defence League, Pegida in Germany), electoral politicians raging at the limits of conservatism (e.g. Donald Trump or Steve Bannon in the US), any number of authoritarian state regimes (e.g. Putin's Russia, Modi's India, the ruling parties in Hungary and Poland).

This book follows Davidson's approach save for one significant refinement. What he describes is a series of typical forms in the language of Weberian sociology: 'ideal types'. When writing about the far-right, he is trying to capture the recurring nature of its politics without needing to focus on its specific development at any time. The subject of this book is, by contrast, movement within the left and the right.

What happens when the boundaries move and the component parts of the right are reordered? What happens when parts of the right, which are usually distinct and hostile, begin to co-operate? What kinds of left-wing strategy will be most effective against today's aggressive and authoritarian but non-fascist right?

Convergence in context

The first chapter of this book argues that the transformation of the right has been eased by the way in which the legacy of 1939–45 has been diminished in our collective memory and been replaced by the legacy of September 11. The Second

World War has ceased to play the part it did for years after the war ended, in providing a structure and justification to the clash between conservatism and social democracy. The legacy of the war has been subordinated, to a considerable extent, by the events of 9/11. The effect of the War on Terror has been to change the boundaries of normal politics. Countries which became inured to mass deportation (Britain), to indefinite states of emergency (France) or the widespread use of imprisonment without trial (the US) have found it easier to adopt other measures of racialised exclusion.

The second chapter addresses the attempts by the far right after 1945 to find a way to reinvent itself without the stigma of fascism. Conservatives would not be willing to engage with others further to their right were it not for the lengthy process by which the post-war far right has broken from its predecessors. Some of these processes have been superficial, while others have been more significant. The chapter focuses on the figure of Julius Evola, an inspiration to post-war fascists in Italy, to the Front National in France and cited by Steve Bannon in the United States. Evola, the chapter argues, criticised the Italian fascist regime for its caution and wanted it to be more like Hitler's Germany. Yet, in the last 20 years, the main parties of the Italian far right have moved away from the likes of Evola. The Italian Social Movement under the leadership of Gianfranco Fini is cited as an example of the far right reinventing itself as a conventional electoral party. By ridding itself of its previous apologetic relationship to the past, the MSI and the other more recent parties of the Italian right created the conditions to win new generations of supporters.

The next three chapters are studies of convergence and how the process played out in Britain, the United States and France in 2016–17.

The sixth chapter addresses the internationalism of the new right, the ways in which the alliance of the centre and far right takes place across borders and the difficulty this poses to the right's conception of itself as a national movement. It argues that the crisis of 2016–17 is best understood not by a series of unconnected national crises all determined solely by domestic factors but as a moment of reactionary change comparable to the British and American elections of 1979 and 1980 and the impact they had on electoral politics elsewhere in Europe and beyond.

The seventh chapter explores two processes which have been central to the rise of the new right: the demise of welfare spending after the economic crash of 2007–8, and the declining legitimacy of a model of economic development through the perpetual expansion of free trade. When the 2008 economic crisis started, centre-left governments in the US and Britain chose to subsidise the banks without requiring any modification of the relationships which had caused the crisis. This has been a significant problem for the left, which has been blamed by voters for its decision to subsidise the banks at the expense of everyone else. The implementation of austerity in 2008–15 and the failure of the political left to offer any alternative, helped to shape a popular mood which was subversive of the status quo but not revolutionary.[33] The new authoritarianism of the 2016–17 period emerged as an alternative to the previous left-right consensus in favour of cuts. All good things in politics could be achieved: the rich could be protected from taxation, the poor from welfare cuts. All that was needed was the raising of the borders of the world's richest countries and the exclusion of anyone outside them who was hoping to share in their wealth.

The eighth chapter argues that the far right's rejection of fascism may not continue indefinitely. The direction of travel over the past 40 years offers certain disadvantages compared to the older pattern of right-wing thinking. From the perspective of its adherents, fascism is a coherent way of looking at the world, which provides a series of interlocking ideas which justify the use of violence against political opponents and ultimately against the liberal state. New kinds of authoritarianism are emerging, bringing back old ideas in new combinations. Although it remains unlikely that the future will belong to recognisably fascist parties, there is a tendency on the far right to revert back to parts of the fascist programme.

The final chapter ends by insisting that while convergence does not mean that the right wins every battle; it does compel the left to change its approach. A politics which is limited to exposing the right without also bringing better living standards to most voters will fail. The way to defeat the right is for the left to offer more, better wages, cheaper homes, greater benefits, as well as a sustained hostility to the racism and sexism and other ideas of the right. The left needs to go through its own process of reconstitution and renewal. The right has evolved, opening itself up to its outliers. The left needs to takes on some of the anti-capitalist politics of its own radicals but with this anti-systemic politics joined to a sustained hostility to oppression.

CHAPTER ONE

The subordination of the war

For several years the centre right and the far right have been co-operating, forming a new and unprincipled alliance.[1] One theme of this book is that neither Brexit nor Donald Trump are fascist and indeed there is a problem in overusing the term fascism to understand today's politics for the simple reason that fascism is today a less important component of the far right than it was 20 or 40 years ago. Indeed, the popularity of the far right and the decreasing influence of fascism within it are connected. The right's rejection of fascism has contributed to its growing support. Non-fascists and fascists within the far right can be distinguished on the basis that the former have a long-term commitment to electoralism and do not seek to fight their opponents or purge the state. Fascism is a form of politics saturated in violence; in contrast to the non-fascist far right whose criticism of the status quo are more muted and which can be satisfied by less dramatic change. It follows that when distinguishing between fascist and far-right parties, one of the clearest indicators of a fascist party is whether it maintains a private militia to carry out attacks on racial and political opponents and potentially as a means to taking on the state. In the last decade, there have been few mass parties in Europe which have maintained their own street army or held demonstrations in uniforms. The clearest examples are Jobbik in Hungary, Greece's Golden Dawn and the People's Party Our

Slovakia.[2] None has prospered in recent years, not even in the favourable circumstances since 2016.

Jobbik has been trying to reinvent itself as a purely parliamentary movement, using a language of detoxification similar to that of Marine Le Pen's Front National, claiming to reject anti-semitism in favour of Islamophobia and standing down its militia. This has led to splits within Jobbik. A more militant faction broke off to form the Force and Determination party to the right of Jobbik. Yet in the most recent elections Jobbik's vote fell, leading to yet another split between hardliners and moderates.[3]

As for Golden Dawn, this is a party which has insisted on its National Socialism and loyalty to Hitler. It has organised torchlight processions, complete with fascist salutes and a meander flag similar to a swastika. In 2008–10, Golden Dawn established its Athens base through the formation of a citizens' committee, which was obsessively concerned with the supposed Islamisation of the city. In 2011, supporters of the committee carried out a pogrom against Afghans and other migrants. Since 2016, however, Golden Dawn has been struggling following the arrest of its leader Nikolaos Michaloliakos for the murder of the anti-fascist rapper Pavlos Fyssas. The trial began in 2017 and at the time of writing was still ongoing.[4]

Among Our Slovakia's candidates have been Rastislav Rogel, the former singer from the Neo-Nazi band Juden Mord (Death to the Jews). After the party secured 8 per cent of the vote in November 2016, there were mass anti-fascist protests and Our Slovakia's leader Marian Kotleba was charged with using Nazi symbols. In regional elections in November 2017, the party's vote fell sharply.[5]

Even those traditions which seem to struggle the hardest under the weight of their own history can on occasion reject the borrowed slogans, old costumes, and cramped spirits of past generations. Later sections of this book explore the history of the MSI/AN in Italy and the events of the 2017 elections in France to describe the main way the right has been turning away from fascism, i.e. through a sustained turn to electoral politics, which compels even former fascists to treat the liberal state as the sole terrain for politics.

There is also a second, subtler but more significant way in which the fascist-inflected far-right of the 1960s and 1970s has given way to something new. For those on the immediate post-war right who wished to carry out attacks on their left-wing opponents or on blacks or Jews or who had romantic visions of a revolutionary war against the state, the virtue of fascism was that it provided a philosophy of action which could justify the adoption of violence and the defeat of their enemies. This decision was reinforced by reminders of fascism which were all around them. The founder of the American Nazi Party, George Lincoln Rockwell, converted to fascism in 1952–3, during a year spent at the Keflavik Naval Station in Iceland, during which he read and reread *Mein Kampf.* During the same years Rockwell met his wife, Thora, who he was able to take on a honeymoon to Berchtesgaden, Hitler's mountain retreat.[6]

In Italy, fascists maintained an 'underground memory' of the final years of Mussolini's regime, telling themselves that his (Nazi-backed) Republic of Salò had been a radical regime, the authentic successor to Mussolini's pre-1914 socialist ideas. Numerous of the far-right cadres of the 1960s were the sons of unrepentant fascists, defending the legacy of past generations. Claudio Orsi, involved in the bombing of Piazza Fontana in 1969, was the son of the Italian fascist Luigi Orsi and the nephew of Italo Balbo, the Governor of Mussolini's Libya. Roberto Fiore, leader of today's fascist group Forza Nuova, and previously tried for his involvement in bombings at Bologna in 1980, was the son of a fascist who had fought for the Salò Republic.[7]

Everywhere in Europe, the immediate post-war fascist parties had similar links with the past, whether that was the presence in their leadership of veteran fascists, funding from similar sources, or support from the children of interwar fascists.[8]

Today, by contrast, more than 70 years have passed since the end of the war and legends of Hitler or Mussolini or their supporters play a smaller part in the memory of the US and European right than they once did.

The presence of fascism within the far right is shaped by the way in which society as a whole remembers the Second World War. As the latter fades from our collective memory, so its relevance to the far right also diminishes. The war has not disappeared; it is still a presence in popular culture, in films and novels and computer games, and it continues to structure conventional as well as far-right politics. It has been joined in the Western imagination by the legacy of 9/11 and the fear of Islamic terrorism. The mainstream has persuaded millions that Islam is a mortal threat. These dynamics in turn shape the far right. Since 2001, much of the growth of the far right can be seen through the success of street-fighting groups, not connected to any party but to identitarian racism. The tradition of fascism and Nazism has been subordinated. Fascism is still a part of the far right but it has ceded its primacy to other organising models better directed to the crisis of our times.

The war in collective memory

One metaphor which captures something of how we assume memory works is a flashbulb;[9] a bright shining light which endures for a single intense flash before fading to black. The collective memory[10] of the Second World War differs from this model in at least two respects. First, the intensity with which the war has been recalled did not begin at its sharpest only to disappear soon after. If anything, the memory increased in the post-war years, so the war was a more immediate presence in popular consciousness in the 1970s and 1980s than it had been before. Second, what and who we remember has changed. There was not a single flashbulb moment but many different flashes all at once. Some have faded much faster, while others are more visible now than they were in 1945. When most people think about the war today they remember different people and events from those that mattered to previous generations.

In Britain, the war was understood in its aftermath as a heroic struggle in which the country had stood alone against an enemy which had occupied most of Europe. In countries liberated by foreign troops, such as Italy or France, the most important memory was the story of the domestic resistance to fascism. Communists were an important part of this wartime story and remained so at least until 1947–8 and the start of the Cold War. Yet other stories were ignored. Everyone knew that millions of Jews had died, yet no one seemed capable of accepting how they had died or the part played in their murder by tens of thousands of ordinary Germans, Poles and Italians. The chemist Primo Levi's masterpiece *If this is a Man* told the story of his journey to Auschwitz, of the search for bread and the immediate proximity of death; and of Levi's eventual survival of the death camps. In the 1960s and 1970s, Levi's memoir would become a bestseller in many countries, and at the end of the 1990s it was regularly named as one of the great books of the last century. But in 1947 Einaudi, the doyen of Italian publishers, declined to publish Levi's book. *If this is a Man* appeared in a limited edition within a minor, regional publisher, Francesco de Silva. A decade later around half of the book's original 2,500 print run remained unsold.[11]

Elsewhere, indifference gave way to hostility. In August 1947, Britain suffered its first post-war race riots, their victims were British Jews, variously blamed for the murder of two British sergeants by supporters of the Zionist Irgun movement. Slaughtermen in Birkenhead refused to process meat for kosher slaughter. Crowds in Manchester broke the windows of Jewish shops and tore down the canopy on the Cheetham Hill Road synagogue. Supporters of the pre-war British fascist Oswald Mosley held meetings across a dozen London sites, the largest of them in South Hackney with up to three thousand people at a time listening to Mosley's speeches.[12]

One of the obstacles to a complete memory of the Holocaust was that Western troops had liberated the concentration camp at Bergen-Belsen, with television crews recording the emaciated bodies of Hitler's surviving victims, while Soviet soldiers liberated the death camps such as Auschwitz where the deaths had been much greater.[13] In Britain and the United States, the killings were assumed to have been a process of forced labour rather than willed genocide. Meanwhile, in so far as most British people thought about the Holocaust, they regarded the UK as having played a proud role as the eventual liberator of the Jews. There was very little discussion of the role politicians had played earlier in the war as hostile bystanders refusing a home to Jewish refugees fleeing occupied Europe or the part played by the officials of the occupied Channel Islands in collaborating with deportations. Another barrier was that few Jewish people wanted to be reminded of what had happened. A complex mixture of feelings including fear, shame and survivor's guilt combined with the apparent lack of sympathy on the part of the gentile majority. Meanwhile there were others who had their own reasons to forget the war; the 390,000 Italian civil servants who were accused of complicity with fascism and the 1,600 who actually lost their jobs, the victims of Soviet war crimes,[14] the civilian survivors of conventional war.

French historians have written of a 'Vichy Syndrome', to describe the persistent difficulty of acknowledging what happened during the war. Others speak of 'memory lapses' to describe the way in which anti-semitism was erased from Italian memory and the blame for the deaths of Italian Jews was placed squarely on the shoulder of the Nazis (who all Italians had supposedly rejected) rather than the Italians themselves.[15] This process of deliberate forgetting was by no means restricted to Western Europe but was every bit as pervasive in Latvia and Romania with their tens of thousands of volunteers for the Waffen SS, in Austria, with its shallow denazification programme or in Norway, much of whose military had joined Quisling's National Rally.

The later recollection of the Second World War, in which the defining fact of Hitler's terror was his genocide against the

Jews, was shaped not just by the War itself but by subsequent events, including Israel's 1967 and 1973 wars, the hostage-taking at the 1972 Olympics and the deaths of the Israeli athletes. These aftershocks of 1939–45 created the space for the Holocaust to be commemorated.

Between 1970 and 1985, the war was a recurring presence in European and American books, music, films and theatre. It could be seen in Judith Kerr's children's novel, *When Hitler Stole Pink Rabbit* (1971), in Frederick Forsyth's bestseller, *The Odessa File*, about an attempt to relaunch Nazism from Argentina (1972), and in films such as *Cabaret* (1972), *The Night Porter* (1974) and *The Boys from Brazil* (1976).

The legacy of the war was a theme for musicians of the late 1970s, with bands such as Joy Division (later New Order) naming themselves after moments from the history of fascism and playing in a cold, repetitive, industrial style in songs such as They Walked The Line ('All dressed up in uniforms so fine, / they drank and killed to pass the time...'). Numerous punk bands wore swastikas: the Damned, the Sex Pistols,[16] Siouxsie of Siouxsie and the Banshees.[17] Even Mick Jones of the Clash, later a supporter of anti-fascist campaigns, named his first punk band London SS.

The war was an increasing presence in US politics. In 1976, an attempted march through the Jewish district of Skokie by supporters of the National Socialist Party of America led to litigation and months of news coverage; in 1977, the TV mini-series, *Holocaust*, was watched by just under 100 million Americans.[18]

A number of Europe's politicians in the late 1970s or 1980s had been participants in fascist movements or on their periphery. For example, François Mitterrand, the Socialist

President of France, had been in 1934–5, a student supporter of the far right National Volunteers. He worked for the Vichy Regime and became a close friend of René Bousquet the wartime head of the French police who oversaw the deportation of France's Jews. On becoming President, Mitterrand left flowers each year at the tomb of France's collaborationist leader Philippe Pétain. He resumed his friendship with Bousquet, who reciprocated by donating to Mitterrand's election campaigns. Bousquet met Mitterrand at the Presidential Palace, while the Socialist leader sought to justify his and Bousquet's relationship by saying that Bousquet 'saw me as a continuation of his own halted career'.[19]

Kurt Waldheim, President of Austria from 1986 to 1992, had joined the Nazi Party in the aftermath of the Anschluss and fought in the German Army from 1942 to 1945, serving just 20 miles from an extermination camp run by Croatia's Ustaše regime, in which tens of thousands of Jews, Roma and Muslims were killed.

Even as late as the fortieth anniversaries of the war's end, the war remained a recurring story in European news, revived by events such as the 1987 trial of Klaus Barbie, who had deported Jewish children from the town of Izieu to their death, or the 1989 arrest of Paul Touvier, who had responded to accusations of crimes against humanity by hiding in a series of right-wing Catholic monasteries. In 1993, Erich Priebke was interviewed by a television crew in Argentina and accepted his involvement in the Gestapo. Priebke was later extradited to Italy, leading to his trial for the murder of 335 Italians in reprisal for Resistance attacks. In the 1990s, French historians spoke of the Vichy regime as 'the past that refuses to pass,' and wrote of the war years 'which appear curiously more present than ever'.[20]

In retrospect, the 1990s were a hinge. For, even while the dominant narratives about the war remained the same as they had been ten or 20 years earlier; there were growing signs of cynicism and relativism intruding into debates about the past. In Italy, the 1990s saw the final volumes of Renzo de Felice's 6,000-page biography of Mussolini, which sought to place 'progressive' Italian fascism in distinction to its 'reactionary' German counterpart, emphasising the revolutionary content of the former and seeking to exculpate the regime from its responsibility from such crimes as the invasion of Ethiopia. Felice was joined by other writers such as the journalist Claudio Pavone, whose novels emphasised the patriotism of those who fought for Mussolini's regime. In 1997 a magistrate in Rome, Maurizio Pacioni, began a war-crimes investigation of partisans, who had blown up a convoy of German soldiers, accidentally killing an 11-year-old boy. In 2003, then Prime Minister Silvio Berlusconi stated that Mussolini 'wasn't so bad', After all, Berlusconi continued, in an extraordinary inversion of the truth, 'Mussolini never killed anyone.'[21]

In Tony Judt's history of post-1945 Europe, *Postwar*, the legacy of the Second World War was said to have become the experience which had drawn the continent together. One example he gave was the Polish government in 2004, which, as the price of membership of the European Union, acknowledged the part played by its predecessors in facilitating the Nazi Holocaust. The following year, the Romania government did likewise. 'The reason,' Judt wrote, 'crimes like [Serbian mass murders during the Bosnia war] now carry such a political charge – and the reason "Europe" has invested itself with the responsibility to make sure that attention is paid to them and to define "Europeans" as people who *do* pay attention to them – is because they are partial instances ... of *the* crime: the attempt by one group of Europeans to exterminate every member of another group of Europeans, here on European soil.'[22]

Not much more than a decade has passed since 2005 when Judt's book was published, but the direction of travel has changed. In 2012, the Lithuanian government reburied Juozas Ambrazevičius-Brazaitis, who was the head of the country's six-week Provisional Government, declared in June 1941 at the time of the German invasion. (On its dissolution by the Germans, Ambrazevičius-Brazaitis became an opponent of the German occupation.) In 2012, he was given a state funeral, despite his role in 1941 in introducing anti-Jewish regulations, expropriating Jewish property, setting aside state funds to establish a Jewish concentration camp and authorising the formation of a police battalion which was responsible for thousands of Jewish deaths.[23]

At the end of 2017, Poland Law and Justice's government proposed anti-defamation laws making it a criminal offence carrying a maximum of three years imprisonment for anyone to accuse the Polish Nation of complicity in Germany's war crimes.[24] The laws criminalise any serious analysis of moments in Polish history, such as the 1941 Jedwabne pogrom, when a crowd of right-wing Poles killed first 40 of the town's Jewish inhabitants, then forced the remaining 300 into a barn and burned them alive. When media outside Poland reported the authoritarian nature of the new laws, self-declared 'patriots', i.e. far-right street gangs with the patronage of the Law and Justice government, demonstrated outside the offices of President Andrzej Duda with a banner, 'Take Off the Yarmulke – Sign the Law.'[25]

Compared to the 1990s, the war no longer seems to play the same role in our shared memory. The sacrifice and terror of past generations have faded, so much so that when the demand is put to recall the heroic story of 1945 – whether to solve the urgent crisis of global warming, to reinvigorate social democracy, or to stand firm against the right – the call invariably fails. This process has been noticed by the more ebullient of far-right supporters, not least Milo Yiannopoulos, writing during the 2016 elections in the US. 'Millennials,' he wrote, 'aren't old enough to remember the Second World War or the horrors of the Holocaust ... Racism, for them, is a monster under the bed, a story told by their parents to frighten them into being good little children.'[26] Yiannopoulos was exaggerating from a desire to exonerate his allies and to assist their growth but he was not altogether wrong. Compared to the 1970s or 1980s, the war is a diminished presence in European and American life. Fewer people aged under 35 are familiar with its key events, the portion who know what the name 'Auschwitz' represents is shrinking. The images of the war do not fascinate[27] the minds of Americans or Europeans to the same extent as 40 years ago. What is true of the majority of people is especially true of the cadres of the far right, for whom more recent events provide a much simpler justification.

9/11 and the contemporary far right

To the extent that the 1939–45 war has been relegated, it is now joined in our shared memory by the events of September 2001 and the attacks on the Twin Towers. The first day after the attacks, James Atlas of the *New York Times* told readers that 'the end of Western civilization has become a possibility against which the need to fight terrorism is being framed, as Roosevelt framed the need to fight Hitler.'[28] His response was typical of the commentary that followed, both in the way that challenge represented by the hijackers was seen as epochal,[29] and in the analogy with the war.

In Italy former partisan Oriana Fallaci, who was dying of cancer, argued in a piece published within four days of the attacks that 9/11 proved the 'dangers of Islam'. There were 'tens of thousands' of Bin Ladens, she wrote 'in our cities, our streets, our universities'. She accused Algerians and Nigerians of introducing drugs and prostitution to Florence and other Italian cities. The presence of Muslims in Turin, she continued, meant that the town, 'no longer seems to be an Italian city at all. It feels like Algiers, Dacca, Nairobi, Damascus, Beirut.' Fallaci turned her piece into a book, *The Rage and the Pride*. It went through 36 editions in four years, selling over a million copies. After her death in 2006, Fallaci was co-opted by the right; Matteo Salvini has credited her for having awoken ordinary Italians to the threat of Islam.[30]

Fallaci was not the only leftist to blame the attacks on ordinary Muslims and to seek vengeance against them. In Britain, a similar part was played by Christopher Hitchens who described his response to 9/11,

Once I had experienced all the usual gamut of emotions from rage to nausea, I also discovered that another sensation was contending for mastery. On examination and to my surprise and pleasure it turned out to be exhilaration. Here was the most frightful enemy ... I realised that if the battle went on to the last day of my life, I would never get bored in prosecuting it to the utmost.[31]

The novelist Martin Amis, once the Literary Editor of the *New Statesman* and long but loosely associated with the post-1968 British left, told an interviewer:

> There's a definite urge – don't you have it? – to say, 'The Muslim community will have to suffer until it gets its house in order.' What sort of suffering? Not letting them travel. Deportation – further down the road. Curtailing of freedoms. Strip-searching people who look like they're from the Middle East or from Pakistan.[32]

To write of 9/11 is to reflect the common sense of the times which was to speak of the events as an 'alpha point ... Big Bang, Genesis 1:1,'[33] and yet as well as a beginning they were also the culmination of a period of colonial wars and of apologia for western militarism. The justifications for the Iraq and Afghanistan wars were found in essays such as Bernard Lewis's 'The Roots of Muslim Rage,' and Samuel Huntington's 'The Clash of Civilizations?' While both were popularised after 9/11, they had been written during the 1990s.[34] Indeed when one historian of the right Corey Robin began interviewing conservatives in summer 2000 (i.e. just over a year before the attacks), what struck him was his sources' feelings of defeat. William F. Buckley Jr. complained that the young would do better if they were socialists and not conservatives. Irving Kristol reminisced about the loss of an older better US, which had taken up its burden as the world's policeman: 'I think it would be natural for the United States to play a far more dominant role in world affairs. To command and to give orders as to what is to be done. People need that.'[35] The effect of September 11 was to change the tone of right-wing politics, from a register of nostalgia into a new language of confident aggression and assumed public approval.

It was in that context that the words of Atlas and Fallaci had their effect; they were popular because they offered a message for which many people were already yearning. In 1989, the West had won its previous conflict with the Soviet Union, but it did so not as a result of any brave act on the part of politicians or soldiers but because the USSR was defeated in an economic conflict from which it withdrew. September 11 offered the chance for blood, iron and sacrifice and, most important of all, a suitable enemy of monstrous proportions who could be defeated on the battlefield.

One historian Lucy Bond writes of an 'analogical impulse,'[36] which kept the 9/11 attacks at the front of popular memory but at the price of their decontextualisation. Part of this has been the attempt to connect the casualties of September 11 to the events of the Holocaust and to compare the West's new Islamic antagonist to the Nazis. The link to 1939–45 was a theme of the relationship between the British and American leaders, with Tony Blair giving George W. Bush a copy of the 1941 Atlantic Charter and an Epstein bust of Churchill.[37] Yet the fusion of the war and September 11, Bond observes, enabled American politicians on the centre right and far right to claim the moral shield of victimhood even while insisting on the subordination of their new Muslim antagonists. So proposals to build an Islamic cultural centre at Park 51, two blocks away from the site of the destroyed Twin Towers, were delayed by years of right-wing lobbying, with one columnist Charles Krauthammer comparing the proposal to 'a German cultural centre at … Treblinka,' and senior Republican Newt Gingrich calling it 'a Nazi sign next to the Holocaust museum.'[38]

As with 1939–45, the significance of 9/11 lies in its capacity to 'return' again and again, shaping the memory of subsequent events and changing their meaning over time.[39] This process could be seen in France. After 2001, President Chirac did not send troops to support the American war in Iraq. Both the centre right and centre left approved of his decision. For several years afterwards, it seemed that the majority of French voters believed that the country should keep out of US wars. In the 2007 Presidential elections the FN's vote fell from 17 to just 10 per cent. 'Normal' (in other words post-1945) politics asserted themselves, with the centre right and centre left winning around two-thirds of the vote and just under a million voters choosing one variety or another of non-Social Democratic left: Trotskyist, Green or Communist. By 2017, however, France had suffered numerous further terrorist attacks, and common sense dictated that the politicians had been wrong over Afghanistan and Iraq. The political class behaved as if a shared albeit silent decision had been taken and the 2001–7 consensus reversed: it would have been better had the country joined with the US and gone to war on Islam. This sense of retrospective disgust with the positions taken a decade before was reflected in the fates of the groups which had dominated at the time of 9/11 and the wars on Afghanistan and Iraq. The centre-right RPR was replaced, the Socialists went into decline. Four candidates secured more than 10 per cent of the vote in the 2017 election: Emmanuel Macron, Jean-Luc Mélenchon, François Fillon and Marine Le Pen. None had stood ten years earlier. In three out of four cases, their parties (Macron's en Marche, Mélenchon's La France Insoumise and Fillon's The Republicans) had not existed ten years before.

The most basic fact which was known about the 9/11 killers and those responsible for subsequent terror attacks, is that they were Muslim. The religion of the hijackers structures our response to terror. It changes the definition of terrorism so that when, for example, white supremacists kill in similar numbers, their actions cannot be terrorism. They have been treated differently by police, by the courts and by the press. During the aftermath of the 2013 Boston bombing, initial press discussion focussed on whether the arrested person was a 'dark-skinned man' or if CCTV images would show whether the attackers were 'from Yemen or other parts like that'.[40] By contrast, when Anders Breivik was put on trial in Norway in 2011 for the murder of 77 people, mainly young men and women who had been attending a summer camp organised on the island of Utøya by the youth wing of Norway's Labour Party. Because Breivik was white, he was treated as a 'lone wolf' and his trial turned on the question of whether Breivik should be committed to psychiatric care.[41] This was despite the wishes of Breivik himself who insisted on his sanity and on the political motive that underlay his killings. Similarly, the 2017 trial of Dylann Roof, responsible for the Charleston massacre, turned on his mental competence.[42]

The reporting of political violence tells everyone in Britain, the US and France that terrorism is, by definition, an Islamic crime. Yet in the period since 9/11, Islamic terrorism has increased in parallel with right-wing violence. From 12 September 2001 to 31 December 2016, there were 85 deadly attacks in the US by advocates of political violence. Three quarters, with 106 fatalities, were carried out by white supremacists. One quarter, with a death count of 119, were carried out by Islamists.[43]

The 9/11 attacks and their aftermath have justified an extraordinary increase in state violence, expressed in incidents such as the December 2003 raid by British police on the house of Babar Ahmad. It began with the police driving a car into his house as he slept. Fifteen officers then broke into his home, punching him even as he held his hands up to indicate that he would not resist arrest. The officers beat him with their fists and knees and stamped on his bare feet. Doctors recorded 73 separate injuries to Ahmad's body. Six days later, Ahmad was released without charge.[44]

The Islamic nature of terrorism changes what it means to be Muslim, which ceases to be a mere belief. Forms of dress, language and religious rituals have come to signify membership of a racial category. These dynamics can be seen most clearly in the attempts by different European countries to ban the Islamic niqab: France and Belgium in 2011, Holland (in public buildings) and Belgium in 2016, Austria in 2017 and Denmark the year after. At their most basic level, these laws encourage the far right by giving a public seal of approval to the essentialist idea that Europeans and Muslims are culturally incompatible and can live together in peace only if the latter agree to subordinate their wishes and their customs to Western values.[45]

The controversies over the Islamic veil have served to facilitate 15 years of campaigning against Muslims and migrants: the movements in Germany which present all refugee men as potential rapists, the campaigns in Britain of white 'women and children' against rape, which they blamed on Muslim men.[46]

Debates over the veil also serve to fulfil a second function. They contribute to a notion of women's place in society in which half of humanity is incapable of making decisions for itself. On the both sexist and racist logic that Muslim women cannot be trusted to think for themselves and are always the victims of patriarchal men (husbands, fathers), the state is obliged to step in and decide what Muslim women are permitted and are not permitted to wear. This way of thinking fits with a common far-right approach in which women are saved by good men from what would otherwise be a condition of permanent subordination. It is a circuit of male valorisation that begins with men as predators and ends with men as rescuers. In either movement it refuses to see women as the guardians of their own lives.

Centre-left and centre-right leaders have encouraged voters to see post-9/11 politics as a struggle between white and brown people, with the former having a role to play in subordinating the latter, with Prime Minister Cameron telling the Munich Security Conference in 2011 that terrorism was 'a question of identity,' with 'young men ... find[ing] it hard to identify with Britain too, because we have allowed the weakening of our collective identity.' A common purpose, he argued, could be fostered by requiring migrants to speak English and by introducing a compulsory citizen service.[47] In their day-to-day interactions with Muslims, David Cameron insisted, the white British majority needed to be more assertive of their rights. As he put it, 'we must build stronger societies and stronger identities ... we need a lot less of the passive tolerance of recent years and a much more active, muscular liberalism.'[48]

By involving millions of people in structures of repression, the War on Terror has served to racialise a wider set of people than just Muslims, making everyone 'white' or 'black', 'Jewish' or 'Hindu'.[49] It has trained mainstream journalists to see minority groups as united around political projects; and given the nod to essentialist views of white ethnicity, in which immigration, above all Muslim immigration, is a collective suicide in the face of a militant enemy.[50]

The War on Terror has encouraged paranoia in a multitude of forms. The *Guardian* anti-war journalist, George Monbiot has described how in the aftermath of the Iraq war a number of its opponents started sharing 9/11 conspiracy films. Among them is *Loose Change* (2007), a collection of interviews with some of the September 11 firefighters and the flight instructor who had taught the 9/11 pilot, Hani Hanjour. The makers of *Loose Change* claim that their film has been watched by in excess of 100 million people. Denounced by several former admirers for having rejected their conspiracy theories, Monbiot found himself having to defend his scepticism. '[I]t seems to me,' he wrote, 'that the purpose of the "9/11 truth movement" is to be powerless. The omnipotence of the Bush regime is the coward's fantasy, an excuse for inaction used by those who don't have the stomach to engage in real political fights.'[51]

While one kind of conspiracy theorising has been to deny the attacks had ever taken place, other forms of magical thinking have accepted that the attacks were real but insisted that they had been secretly supported by politicians. The most popular forms of conspiratorial thinking about 9/11 in recent years have been the claims either that the US was facing the risk of an Islamic President in Barack Obama or that America was already introducing large numbers of Islamic Sharia laws, at the state or federal level. These ideas were picked up by Donald Trump in 2011 at the time of his first Republican candidacy and have been shared by his appointees.[52]

Historian of anti-Muslim racism, Arun Kundnani, distinguishes between two main responses to 9/11: the 'culturalist' and the 'reformist'. The former (meaning the Orientalist Bernard Lewis and his admirers after 9/11 in the neo-conservative circles around George Bush) have portrayed the West and Islam as in a permanent conflict; the latter (of which the exemplary figure was Britain's Prime Minister Tony Blair between 2001 and 2007) accepts that conflict, but argues that it can be managed if the state isolates the extremist minority within Islam from those who wish to live in peace. While the differences between the two approaches are not small, Kundnani points out the overlap between the two approaches. The reformists have agreed with the culturalists in seeing all young Muslims as potentially the enemies of Britain, the US and France. The reformists also agree with the culturalists in seeing Islamic terrorism as a psychopathy, whether it is triggered by anti-Western resentment, sexual longing or some unique programme of malice contained in the Koran or the Islamic Hadith. Neither group can acknowledge the part played by Western military incursions in encouraging anti-colonial responses, including political Islam.[53]

The mainstream ideas that the West is at war, that its enemies are a racial minority and that this minority requires to be suppressed, have had a far wider audience since 2001 than at any stage before. They have shaped the response of the mainstream to its outliers. After the news broke of the killing carried out on Utøya in summer 2011 by Anders Breivik, press coverage soon moved on to the contents of a manifesto which Breivik had written, which over the course of 1,000 pages insisted that Marxists were secretly trying to promote values of equality, that they had captured the leadership of both the parliamentary right and left, and that Islam was a uniquely evil philosophy which from its inception had instructed its followers to carry out a genocidal war against the Christian West.

A measured response to Breivik's killings might have connected the philosophy expressed in his writing to the murders
he committed and to show how such violence has been
immanent in far-politics. Instead any number of right-wing
politicians applauded Breivik's philosophy, while distancing
themselves from his killings. One of Breivik's key concepts;
that the West was under threat from 'Cultural Marxists' has
been taken up by numerous mainstream writers, including
the Canadian popular psychologist Jordan Peterson. Mario
Borghezio a Northern League MEP declared in a radio interview that Breivik had some 'excellent' ideas when it came to
Islam.[54]

The mainstream response to the War on Terror shares with
the extreme right the ideas that everyone can be defined by the
culture to which they belong, and that people from different
backgrounds can only co-exist with difficulty. It is only a short
journey from the widespread beliefs that the West is at war
with Islam and that the state needs to be more combative to
deal with this threat, to the far-right idea that white people are
being ill served by a timid and pacifist ruling elite.

One relatively simple conclusion to draw from the events
of the Second World War is that fascism was a murderous
ideology that caused the deaths of tens of millions of people,
including Jews, Gypsies, Hitler's enemies on the political left,
as well as all the civilian casualties of war, and that its return
should be avoided at all costs. This was never the only possible
message of the war,[55] but it was a plausible one.

The popular understanding of 9/11 is different. The attacks
have legitimised the supporters of white identity politics. They
have subjected a wider group of visible minorities than just
Muslims to hostile policing and public racism; and obliged a

large number of people who did not previously see themselves in racial terms to adopt racial identities. They have encouraged a paranoid style of politics, more pervasive than the conspiracy theorising of the far right.[56] The attacks have restructured the racial hierarchies of Europe and the US. They have helped to make possible the alliance between the mainstream and the margins which has dragged politics to the right.

CHAPTER TWO

When right-wing parties change

During the 2017 French presidential elections, Douglas Murray, the author of *The Strange Death of Europe,* and a writer who has been enthusiastically reviewed by the provocateur white nationalists of Generation Identity,[1] complained in the *Spectator* magazine about the tendency of Le Pen and Trump's critics to describe them as far right. Murray claimed this term was now being used capriciously, irrespective of whether the groups in question were anti-Islamic, or opposed to the EU, or 'actual fascists and Nazis'. Murray looked back to a time when the term far right had been used as a shorthand for parties of fascist origin. Since then, he argued, the phrase had ceased to have any real meaning. He focused on the tendency of critics to say that because the Front National had been founded by a generation of fascists it therefore was still a fascist party. 'If,' he wrote, 'we allow movement on the political left, surely we must allow it on the political right?'[2] This is a reasonable question which deserves a considered answer.

It is possible to treat Murray's question in isolation from his other positions and accept the logic which underpins it. There are indeed examples of parties moving from one point on the political spectrum to another and there could be no persuasive basis for treating the left and right differently and maintaining that only socialist parties are capable of changing. Where a group had its origins in an attempt to build a mimetic fascist party but has then spent years distancing itself from such politics, there is no compelling reason to say that it should be defined indefinitely by its past.

At least five different sorts of journey might be envisaged. The first would be when a party of fascist origin makes some, albeit limited, efforts to develop in any new direction while retaining the forms of historic fascism (militia, swastikas, the leadership principle, anti-semitism…) and the underlying strategy of a counter-revolutionary war against political and social democracy. Such a party might say that it was different but there would no good reason to accept its claims.

The second would be when a party with a similar past which disavows its support for the fascist legacy but the disavowals are made in bad faith and balanced by signals to its cadre that the party has not changed at all, so that the purported disavowal is a hypocrisy, its real meaning is the opposite of the public message.[3]

A third possible model occurs when a party of fascist origin repudiates its former support for the legacy of Hitler and Mussolini, but there is no coherent alternative behind its rejection of fascism, and the party provides its supporters with arguments derived from the 1930s, with the gap between fascism and post-fascism operating at the level of presentation. Such a party might be trying, to an extent, to evolve away from fascism but for some reason incapable of developing in a new direction.[4]

A fourth pattern occurs when a party of the same origins contains in its leadership elements reflecting more than one of the above strategies and is united only during a period of rapid growth, with any pause bringing to light the conflict between the factions. Such a party might be evolving away from fascism, except that the actual evolution would be limited and could be completed only by a further struggle inside that party, with that conflict having started without being resolved.[5]

Finally, there are parties which emancipate themselves from their fascist origins and become to all intents and purposes another party of the non-fascist right.

It is correct to distinguish between the shallow disavowals of fascism made by any number of post-war fascists, even while they were involved in projects to resuscitate the interwar fascist parties and the more profound journeys away from fascism which at least some prominent supporters of post-war fascism have made since 1990. Accordingly, this chapter gives examples of both continuity and change. The first is represented by the Italian mystic Julius Evola, who is often but wrongly presented as the advocate of a different and non-fascist nationalism. The second is represented by the Movimento Sociale Italiano (MSI), later the Alleanza Nazionale, a party which had been in the 1960s and 1970s merely a collection of nostalgic fascists. The MSI evolved in the 1990s and 2000s into something else, becoming a right-wing electoral party barely distinguishable from Silvio Berlusconi's centre-right Forza Italia.

Movement on the right is indeed a possibility, as the example of the MSI shows. But that does not mean that every former fascist has gone over to the centre ground.

Movement on the left

One part of Murray's argument which should not be controversial is his insistence that there has been political movement on the left. The last 100 years have seen many examples of parties moving from positions outside the political mainstream and rejecting the legitimacy of the state, before standing in elections. Numerous parties have adopted parliamentary politics not as some brief, tactical move but as their consistent approach. One example is the Social Democratic Party of Germany (SPD), which was founded by revolutionary socialists and shaped by years of illegal activity and motivated by Marxist theories about the incompatibility of socialism and the bourgeois state. Frederick Engels was involved in the drafting of the Programme adopted by the SPD at its first Congress at Erfurt in 1891.[6] Over the next 20 years, the SPD was one of the most successful left-wing parties in Europe. For decades, the SPD remained committed to the overthrow of capitalism. In the 'revisionist' controversy of the 1900s, it rejected parliamentary socialism. However, its revolutionism grew ever more tenuous as a result of the decisions taken by its leaders to support the First World War, to stifle the post-1918 workers' council movement, and to make no determined struggle to defend social Germany from the incursions of Chancellors Brüning or von Papen, which opened the way to Hitler. In 1959, at its Congress at Bad Godesberg the SPD renounced any ambitions to reform capitalism to any significant extent and accepted that the German economy would remain privately owned for the indefinite future.[7] The Bad Godesberg programme was consistent with the positions taken by the SPD for decades, at no point since has the party sought to reverse it.

A second example would be the Italian Communist Party (PCI). Shaped, like the SPD before it, by a long period of illegality; the PCI enjoyed enormous popular legitimacy at the end of the Second World War and had the support of over two million members. Communists saw themselves a disciplined minority, committed to transforming capitalism and willing to wait until their ideas had majority support. The PCI was a Marxist party and spoke in a language of revolutionary change. As late as the 1960s, the party statutes insisted that 'The Italian Communist Party is the vanguard organisation of the working class and of all workers which fights ... for socialism.'[8] However, at key moments the party chose to orient in the direction of parliamentary socialism. After 1944, the party agreed to abide by a democratic constitution. There followed a period of 30 years in which the PCI still had the support of over a million members and was by far the largest party in Italy. It secured a consistent 20 to 35 per cent of the vote. It was represented in Italy's regions, culture and media and admired by leftists throughout Europe. Communist reforms, such as public nursery schools in Reggio Emilia or housing projects in Bologna, were widely known and discussed. However, the party could not be permitted to govern at the national level for fear of disturbing Italy's place in the Cold War's Western bloc.[9] There was no single 'moment' when the party rejected the idea of taking power through a revolution; and yet, in reality, long prior to its dissolution in 1991, the PCI had been a parliamentary party and no more revolutionary than Germany's SDP.

Julius Evola and movement on the right

These examples can be kept in mind as comparisons when considering the tendency since 2008 for adherents of the non-fascist far right to cite Evola as an influence. So, for example, in 2014, Steve Bannon addressed a Vatican conference telling his audience that they were 'in an outright war' with political Islam. In the questions that followed, Bannon was challenged to defend his support for the Front National and UKIP, parties which shared Russia's world view. Bannon defended the Russian state, 'at least Putin is standing up for traditional institutions and he's trying to do it in a form of nationalism – and I think that people, particularly in certain countries, want to see the sovereignty for their country.' Putin, Bannon went on, was influenced by Alexander Dugin, 'an adviser who harkens back to Julius Evola'. The following year, when Milo Yiannopoulos was finishing his article, 'An Establishment Conservative's Guide to the Alt-Right,' Bannon accepted the piece for publication on Breitbart, writing, 'I do appreciate any piece that mentions [E]vola.'[10]

Indeed Evola's influence on the contemporary far right is pervasive. Gábor Vona, the leader of Jobbik in Hungary, wrote an introduction for Evola's essays, *A Handbook for Right-Wing Youth*. Evola has also been a long-term influence on different factions within the FN in France. A later chapter describes how in the late 1990s when the Front took control of Vitrolles, the party sought to use this opportunity to test strategies for national government. This included requiring the town's libraries to remove newspapers associated with the left and ordering them to stock copies of Julius Evola's books. Evola has also been a common reference point for all factions of the French far right, the subject of a GRECE summer school,[11] and republished on various occasions by the publications of the Front's youth wings.

At Evola's funeral, the leader of the Movimento Sociale Italiano (MSI), Giorgio Almirante, went so far as to compare him to the Frankfurt School theorists who had inspired the revolutionary left in 1968, calling Evola 'our Marcuse, only better'.[12] Indeed, Evola's articles were reprinted both by the MSI and groups to the MSI's right, the Italian paramilitary factions of the 1950s and 1960s and their successors.

One of the reasons why Julius Evola has been able to influence such a wide set of figures within the post-war right is that his ideas operate through Nietzschean categories, with frequent references to truth, purity, loyalty and so on. Moreover, throughout his life, Evola participated in what he believed were mystical rites and wrote about magic,[13] even in the course of apparently secular books. This Gnosticism, for want of a better word, structures his choice of language so that words such as 'tradition' had for Evola a spiritual as well as a literal meaning. Rather than speak of fascism, Julius Evola eulogised 'the organic state'. Rather than Jews or even Communism, he wrote of 'the Occult'. Because Evola's ideas are coded, abstract and make numerous references to a pre-modern realm of knightly virtues, they have been attractive to people at very different points on the political right.

Another reason for his appeal is that Evola's supporters present him as a non-fascist thinker, an interpretation which rests on the incomplete facts that Evola was at the margins of Mussolini's dictatorship and did not apply for membership of the Fascist Party until 1939. In the post-war years, although he was courted both by Italy's main fascist party, the MSI, and by the terrorist groups outside,[14] he did not join the MSI. Indeed any interest he might have had in clarifying his politics ended with his 1951 arrest for propagating fascist ideas. During his subsequent prosecution, Evola accepted that his ideas were compatible with fascism, but argued they were also compatible with pre-fascist reactionary thought. On that basis, he was acquitted.[15]

Yet Evola's marginality to the fascist regime was not the result of moderation. During the years of Mussolini's regime, Evola argued that fascism should be more radical. He proposed that it should acquire this greater edge by taking on ideas from two sources which were elsewhere treated as antithetical. One was the spirit of reaction going back to the original aristocratic resistance against 1789. This source, Evola termed: 'Tradition ... a single formative force [which] was manifest in both ordinary behaviour and in worship, in law in myth, in the arts as in political life – in short in every domain of existence.'[16] The other was Nazi Germany, which in Evola's mind was a better, more coherent and more traditional society than fascist Italy. Evola defended Hitlerism in his 1934 book *Revolt against the Modern World*,[17] and from then until his death. Evola's belief that Italian fascism needed to be reformed in order to become more German attached him to various patronage structures within the fascist regime and abroad. He wrote for *Il Regime Fascista*, a pro-Nazi newspaper controlled by Roberto Farinacci,[18] and travelled to fascist Austria and to Nazi Germany where he was treated as an ideological loyalist not of Mussolini but of National Socialism.

This support was reciprocated. In 1937, Evola published an Italian edition of the *Protocols of the Elders of Zion*. Evola was well aware that the document, with its claims of a worldwide Jewish conspiracy, was a Tsarist forgery. But it was the patriotic duty of all nationalists, he wrote, to tell themselves that the *Protocols* were true: 'Above all, in these decisive hours of western history, they cannot be ignored or dismissed without seriously undermining the front of those fighting in the name of the spirit, of tradition, of true civilisation.' The Jews, Evola went on, lived under a communal duty 'to destroy every surviving trace of true order and superior civilisation.' Behind every enemy the West faced, a Jew could be found,

> One Jew is Freud, whose theory is understood to reduce the interior life to instincts and unconscious forces. Another is Einstein, who has brought 'relativism' into vogue ... Schoenberg and Mahler, leading exponents of the music of decadence ... It is the race, it is an instinct at work here.[19]

In its first decade, Italian fascism employed racial categories repeatedly but loosely, with Mussolini denouncing Jews in speeches and calling himself an Aryan and stating that fascism represented the interests of the white race. Yet the language of the regime was casual and without the grim focus of a Streicher or a Hitler. This began to change from 1935 and the war with Ethiopia. As the latter dragged on, the Italian regime both used much more systematic violence (castrating or decapitating captured African soldiers, destroying civilian districts, using poison gas against insurgent villages), and became more consistent in its use of racist language. In 1938, Mussolini gave the 'Germanist' wing of fascism his approval to draft the racial policies of the Italian regime. Under their influence, Mussolini began to present himself and the Italian people as 'pure Aryans of the Mediterranean type'. The same year, Italian government introduced anti-semitic legislation modelled on German race laws. As a result of the new politics, Evola played an increasing role in the regime as a writer, popularising its racial thinking. Between 1940 and 1941, Evola wrote for various journals calling for a synthesis of Italian and German fascism, including

Defense of the Race, whose other writers included Giorgio Almirante, later the leader of the MSI and the man who delivered the eulogy at Evola's graveside. Evola spent the last years of the war in Vienna, conspiring to set up a successor to the Italian fascist party.[20]

After 1945, Evola's ideas, or their presentation, changed. It was no longer open to him to argue for a National Socialist victory. He settled in Vienna and from exile he rejected the two main Italian parties, the Christian Democrats and the Communists, arguing that they were two faces of a decadent materialism. His ideas were still fascist, save that classical fascism was intermingled to a greater extent than before with the older notion of a conservative revolt against the Enlightenment.[21]

Through these various twists and turns, Evola remained an anti-semite. Even his admirers do not deny that he was a lifelong racist, they argue however that his racism operated at the level of culture ('spirit') not biology. Evola's friend and translator H. T. Hakl insists that Evola had no difficulty with actual Jews but with the behaviour stereotypically associated with them of which, Evola was privately aware, very few actual Jews were guilty.[22] Yet it takes a heroic effort to sustain this benign interpretation in the face of Evola's writings, for example his *Synthesis of the Doctrine of Race* (1941), which argued that civilisation had been created by a Hyperborean people, genetic Aryans who had settled the whole world and whose racial descendants were the Germans. Subsequent racial inbreeding had reduced the German stock, as had contact with 'primitives,' in other words black people and below them the Jews, the 'precious instrument for the secret front of global subversion.'[23]

Anti-semitism recurs in Evola's later writings. By the 1950s, the events of the Holocaust were known to Evola and the world. Moreover, following his own prosecution he had every reason to limit himself to guarded remarks. Yet in his 1953 book, *Men among the Ruins*, Evola continued to assert that 'the forces of global subversives,' were waging 'an occult war' on Europe. These opponents, Evola explained were 'Jews ... secret agents of world subversion'. He described those who disbelieved in the *Protocols* as 'rabid,' and insisted that the *Protocols* were an accurate description of Jewish behaviour, even if they had in fact been forged by anti-Semites.[24]

This defence of the Protocols, alongside the many favourable references to Nazism in his work, suggests that it is wrong to see Evola as escaping from fascism. For 'tradition' did not mean just the values of pre-1789 Europe, but their modern defenders, in other words the German National Socialist regime and in particular the large numbers of non-German citizens who by the end of the Second World War had volunteered in their tens of thousands to serve in the Waffen SS and had participated in large numbers in the Holocaust.[25] Evola referred to the SS as, 'the wonderful sight of the principle of a supernational European Army and the legionary spirit of volunteers from many nations who ... fought on the Eastern front against the Soviets.'[26] These men, Evola argued, had been the high point of modern European life.

Evola was part of a generation of post-war fascists who wanted to rebuild the far right. Within this group, there were a range of opinions from those who wished to moderate fascism to those who wished to keep the core of the ideas while simply presenting it as something new. In contrast to either of those factions, Evola wished to radicalise fascism, make it more German and less Italian. His project was not to reject fascism or even to repackage it, but to eulogise its most violent elements. His plan was not to redefine fascism but to harden it and reject any possible reform.

The MSI: rejecting the war against the state

In contrast to Evola, whose response to the post-war world was to argue much the same politics as before, it is also possible to find examples of far right parties undertaking a journey towards moderation. The paradigm case is the Italian Social Movement (MSI), which despite having originated as a mimetic fascist party, was capable of developing from the early 1990s onwards in a new direction.

The MSI emerged from the Italian Social Republic founded by Mussolini with German support in 1943. The party's first three leaders all served under Mussolini: Giorgio Almirante as chief of staff in the Salò Republic's Ministry of Popular Culture, Augusto De Marsanich as a member of the Fascist Grand Council and Arturo Michelini as Secretary of the National Fascist Party in Rome. Meanwhile the MSI's Honorary President, Rodolfo Graziani, had been involved in numerous massacres during Italy's colonial wars and in the Second World War; and was sentenced after the war's end to a 19-year jail term for his participation in the fascist regime.[27] For much of its history, MSI was at its heart a fascist party. Its leaders were loyal to Mussolini's memory and described themselves as fascists, with Almirante telling the party's 1982 congress; 'Let everyone know, if they search for fascism, that fascism is here.' It participated in elections but also in violent street politics and refused to subordinate the street to parliament. The dual politics of the MSI were termed *il doppiopetto e il manganello,* 'the double-breasted suit and the bludgeon'.[28]

From its start, there were different factions within the MSI,[29] and there were pressures to prioritise either a street or an electoral strategy. The party's success lay, in part, from deferring this choice as long as it could. During the 1950s, the party's then leader Arturo Michelini saw a route for the MSI to enter government as the junior partner in a pro-NATO coalition. The party sought to cultivate first the Italian monarchists and later the Christian Democrats (DC), using MSI votes to keep the DC in power in Rome. The 1958 elections left the Parliament evenly balanced between left and right and from March 1960 Fernando Tambroni was Prime Minister of a minority DC government with MSI backing. At the end of June, the MSI was due to hold its congress at Genoa, a city with a long anti-fascist tradition. Anti-fascist protesters against the congress were attacked by the police using armoured cars, horses and riot squads. They attempted to clear the left from the streets but were resisted forcefully and by the end of the day a ceasefire was declared only at the instigation of a committee of former partisans who had taken effective control of the city. The MSI had no choice but to cancel their conference. In the days that followed, reprisals against the left included the killing of three anti-fascists in Sicily and five in Reggio Emilia. A number of Catholic intellectuals wrote an open letter to *La Stampa*, demanding that the coalition be brought to an end. A week later Amintore Fanfani replaced Tambroni and the alliance between the DC and MSI was over.

Between 1960 and 1992, the MSI maintained the consistent support of between one and a half and three million Italian voters, never securing less than 4.5 per cent of the national vote or more than 9 per cent. This support was large enough so that the party could feel that it was entitled to be a major force in Italian politics and yet, such had been the crisis in 1960 and such was the fear on the centre right of further protests, that there was no prospect of the MSI ever being in government.[30]

These dynamics help to explain the ongoing relationship between the MSI and political terrorism, and why (for example) it was considered appropriate for the MSI's leader Almirante to address the funeral of Evola, even though the latter was also the patron of the smaller terrorist groups. The terrorists were useful to the MSI, brought the latter influence, and gave them an authority as the only politicians capable of restraining them. The MSI was not a normal political party, it was excluded from government. If it was associated with irresponsible acts, such as political violence, there was no mechanism by which it could be sanctioned. That said, the ordinary rules of politics were never disregarded entirely; while the leaders of the MSI knew and patronised the terrorist groups, they did keep some distance from them.

This dual orientation could be seen in the career of another MSI leader, Pino Rauti. Through the 1950s he was a patron of paramilitary groups on the edges of the MSI including the Fasci d'Azione Revoluzionaraia. In 1957, Rauti left the MSI (in rejection of the policy of making overtures to the centre right) and was instead a member of a rival group Ordine Nuovo (ON), which organised numerous physical attacks on Communists and the left. In 1969, Rauti re-joined the MSI. Rather than face a lengthy period in the wilderness as a punishment for his excessive radicalism, he was co-opted onto the party's Central Committee.[31] Over the next six years, the police recorded over 4,000 acts of political violence, more than three quarters of them carried out by members of the MSI or the smaller far-right groups. Rauti himself was investigated in 1972 as a participant in a fascist bombing at Piazza Fontana in Milan in December 1969, which killed 17 people, although the charges against him were dropped.[32] Rauti's ultimate significance to the MSI is not his involvement in terrorism but his position in the leadership of the party immediately before it renounced violence. His legacy operated as a negative image, a symbol of the past which the MSI needed to shed. Between 1990 and 1991, Pino Rauti was the general secretary of the MSI. A vote of less than 4 per cent for the party at local elections in 1990 was seen as a disaster requiring new leadership after which he was replaced by a younger leader.

Pino Rauti's successor as general secretary, Ginafranco Fini, presented himself as a moderate. Under Fini, the party renounced its fascist past. 'Fascism is now irreversibly consigned to history,' Fini told one interviewer, 'like all Italians, we are not neo-fascists but post-fascists.' Fini's move was an attempt to make the party electable in favourable circumstances where the historic party of the Italian centre right, the Christian Democrats, had collapsed in face of corruption scandals, and where the left was debilitated by a crisis of self-belief following the end of the USSR. If the right was capable of uniting, then there was a real chance of forming the next government. In 1994, the party joined Silvio Berlusconi's government. The following year at its Congress at Fiuggi, the MSI resolved to change its name to Alleanza Nazionale (AN) (the National Alliance). The individual who best expressed the MSI's continuity with the 1930s and 1940s, Mussolini's granddaughter Alessandra, was expelled from the party.

Unlike the SPD or the French Communist Party (PCF) in earlier periods, this was a rapid lurch towards new positions; little had been done to prepare for it. The MSI/AN had not spent 20 years arguing for parliamentary politics; its sudden disavowal of fascism contradicted the party's long-established behaviour. One 1996 survey of party members founded that 62 per cent believed that fascism had been on balance a 'good regime' and 7 per cent that it was 'the best regime ever conceived'. The Fiuggi conference came at the start, not at the end, of a period of moderation. However, it was sustained. The AN was a part of three government coalitions, from 1994 to 1995, from 2001 to 2006 and from 2008 to 2011. Ginafranco Fini was at different times Vice President, Italy's representative in the renegotiation of the EU Treaty and minister of Foreign Affairs. Save for the two exceptions of Fini's involvement as Deputy Prime Minister during clashes with anti-capitalist protesters at Genoa in 2001[33] and his part in the 2002 Bossi-Fini anti-immigration law, the AN left few traces on Berlusconi's regime.

For a time, the public positions of the Alleanza were at odds with the party's internal politics. It sought to maintain a youth culture which looked back to the street years of the 1960s. The language was of self-sacrifice, of war against 'parasites,' with references to Julius Evola, torchlight processions and attempts to rename streets after the fascist martyrs of previous generations. Yet in office its leaders went along with Berlusconi's government. The gap grew ever wider between the party's role in parliament and its internal culture. A generation of young fascists were 'torn between worshipping their elders and hating them'. Over several elections the Alleanza lost votes to Berlusconi's party with which it briefly merged before splitting off again.[34] Fini himself ended up in a new party, Future and Liberty, which lost its remaining seats in 2014. The MSI's closest counterpart in present-day Italy is the Brothers of Italy. With 4.4 per cent of the vote in the most recent Italian elections, it is no more than the third or fourth most successful player on the crowded scenes of Italy's far right.

The relative normality of life under Berlusconi, despite the presence of the AN in government, shows that Douglas Murray is to some extent right. Fascist parties can evolve to the point where they cease to be recognisably fascist.

Yet not all Euro-fascist, let alone all far-right parties have been following the same path since 1995. The first to break with the MSI/AN were their allies in France. In response to the Fiuggi conference, Jean-Marie Le Pen made it clear that he had no plans to change his party's name. Indeed, this disdain was reciprocated when in 1998 Fini broke off all relations with the Front, saying his party was heading in a different direction.[35] The Fiuggi Congress has served since 1995 as a negative example to right-wingers, a cautionary tale about what happens when a path is followed too far and a warning to be invoked at any suggestion of opportunism by the MSI's successors.[36]

Since 2014, the AN has been replaced on the right by a new set of fascists in groups such as Forza Nouva, Casa Pound and La Destra, which revive the MSI's old willingness to defend Mussolini and its historic commitment to street violence.[37]

Meanwhile Italian politics have been shaped by new kinds of right-wing politics: including the League (previously the Northern League) which takes over Berlusconi's anti-Communism and his claim that any government is illegitimate which does not have the support of the business owners of Italy's rich, industrialised, north. The success of the League dates back to a crisis in 2012–13. The founder of the Northern League Umberto Bossi had suffered a stroke in 2004 and his party was stuck at around 4 per cent in the polls. Bossi was investigated for corruption, his party having appropriated some €40m of public money, hundreds of thousands of which had been spent on housing and educating Bossi's family. In the crisis that followed Matteo Salvini became the League's Federal Secretary. In quick succession, he reinvented the organisation, discarding its previous attacks on Southern Italian farmers, and exchanging them for attacks on immigrants. Salvini also replaced a message of regional separatism with one of Italian nationalism: promising to support the Italian football team in the 2014 World Cup, sharing platforms in Rome with the post-AN fascist parties and accusing migrants of being criminals and rapists.[38] Part of the League's success is down to the recent character of its adoption of Italian nationalist politics and the way it has joined them on to its previous beliefs in regional autonomy. While the message of the 2017–18 era League was much like that of the Forza Italia or the AN of 20 years ago, the party also feels heterogeneous and fluid. It is this mobility which enables it to grow, in contrast to the likes of Forza Nouva, or La Destra which seem caught in an ideological moment which is decades old.

The League has allied with Beppe Grillo's Five Star Movement (M5S), which combines an idealisation of online democracy reminiscent of such left-wing outsider parties as Podemos in Spain or France Insoumise with a belief system in which the individual is utterly isolated in relation to the state, itself long captured by a caste of corrupt businessmen and their political lackeys. Grillo's party has supplanted Italy's

Democratic Party as the main recipient of working-class and blue-collar Italian votes. Its hostility to the state is however akin to right-wing libertarianism, so that it supports reduced taxation and the replacement of welfare spending with a (modest) universal income and opposes trade unions and other collective movements.[39]

The politics that enable the League and M5S to co-operate is a shared opposition to migrants. Virginia Raggi, the M5S candidate for mayoral elections in Rome has stood on a platform of removing Gypsy encampments, while Grillo instructed his supporters in 2013 to obstruct measures to decriminalise unlawful immigration, saying, 'How many illegals are we able to receive if one Italian in eight does not have money to eat?' The following year, he argued that migrants from North Africa brought Ebola and TB.[40] By winter 2017–18, the League and the MSI were in an unspoken but effective electoral coalition and since 2018 they have been in government. They threatened a vast extension of the police and the courts and the militarisation of the Italian state in relation to its unwanted migrant minority. Half a million people, they promised, would be deported.

Journeys away from fascism, towards violence

The introduction to this book argued that the relationship between different components of the right is changing compared to 40 years ago. One way to conceive of the difference is to imagine right-wing politics as a scale divided into three imbricated categories. As you move away from the centre, the first bloc is conservatism, the second is the far right and then within the far right there is a final and partially overlapping portion of the scale held by ideological fascists. In the mid-1970s, by far the greatest parts of the scale (at least in Europe and the US) was taken by conservatives. There was then a far right milieu, however it was small compared to the mainstream right. Within it, almost the only coherent bloc was the fascists.

Since then, the fascist part of the scale has shrunk. The MSI is not the only group to have disavowed fascism: the Front National in France and its imitators outside (notably the BNP in Britain) have also committed themselves to electoral politics. Even such supporters of the American far-right as Jared Taylor and Richard Spencer learned in 2016 to present themselves as conservatives, gatekeepers of the mid-right merely defending their own positions from a neo-Nazi swamp beyond.[41]

One way to visualise this process would be to imagine a line above the right-wing scale with a small arrow pointing from the margins towards the mainstream, to reflect this rejection of fascism. At the same time, the non-fascist far right has grown. It now contains not just former fascists but also groups of anti-Muslim street protesters who emerged outside fascism and have very little if any continuity in terms of ideas or personnel with the post-war fascist parties. The growth in Islamophobia post-9/11 has created a space for a mass electoral politics which is capable of sustaining itself between conservatism and fascism. Such parties as the AfD are a new phenomenon. Their existence and growth changes the balance between the centre right and the far right, enlarging the latter at the expense of the former. In addition, parts of mainstream parties have moved from mainstream to more radical positions, working in alliance with individuals or parties who would in previous times have been considered extreme. Their journey can be compared to that of the former fascists, except that they are moving in the opposite direction and there are more of them. There needs to be a second and larger arrow, in other words, pointing from the centre ground towards the far right, and taking many more people with it.

There is a relationship, moreover, between these two journeys. One of the main reasons that the far right seems a more attractive proposition to its new centre-right allies is because it has been purged to some extent of its historical obsessives. It is possible to attend a Donald Trump rally without feeling that every person you meet will be an obsessive like Richard Spencer. The relative normalisation of the far right and its partial rejection of fascism has enabled the non-fascist right to grow.

The reconstitution of the far right provides a particular challenge to the far left, which in previous decades was able to take on and defeat mimetic fascist parties. In recent years, those tactics have been less effective. The Italian far left has a very long anti-fascist history, including mass mobilisations in 1947 following the murder of pro-Communist demonstrators in Sicily and even larger demonstrations the year afterwards after the attempted murder of communist leader Palmiro Togliatti. There were the mobilisations in 1960 against Tambroni's MSI-backed government, marches of tens of thousands of people through the 1960s and 1970s against fascist terrorism, and more recent protests such as Genoa in 2001, part of which was a mobilisation against the presence of former fascists in the AN-Berlusconi-Northern League alliance. That tradition is, however, notably harder to invoke against a new right which emerges on a different model, is expressly anti-political, and disavows any ties to fascism.

These processes moreover are far from restricted to Italy or even Western Europe. They provide the context to the international convergence of the centre right and far right, a process expressed to some extent in the victory of Brexit and then (even more clearly) in the election of Donald Trump.

CHAPTER THREE

Brexit and the prospect
of convergence

The subject of this book is alliance between elements of the right which were previously considered incompatible. This chapter examines the 2016 referendum on Britain's membership of the European Union as a case study of the convergence between the mainstream and the far right. Brexit, it is argued, was always intended to change domestic policy. The reason that Leave supporters campaigned for the UK to leave the EU was because they wanted to make Britain a lower-tax economy in which the rich and business were liberated from unwelcome social legislation and environmental regulation. To achieve this goal a generation of ardent Thatcherites, the likes of Alan Sked, Nigel Farage, Arron Banks and ultimately Douglas Carswell, believed that they were obliged to reject the Conservative Party. From this perspective, the problem with the Tories was that most MPs saw the issue pragmatically, and approached questions such as budget rebates or new EU Regulations on an issue-by-issue basis. For the keepers of the Thatcherite flame, this approach was wrong in principle and disloyal to the memory of the party's greatest post-war leader. Brexit was their mechanism for replacing a pragmatic response with an ideological one.

The demand for a British departure from the European Union crystallised into organisation among a generation who abandoned the Conservatives and chose instead to inhabit the small-group circles of the radical right.

Yet Brexit did not remain indefinitely an issue restricted to the margins of right-wing politics. During the referendum itself, a clear majority of Conservative voters chose the Leave camp. Indeed, in the run up to the referendum, there were many signs that the base of the Conservative party was abandoning its leaders: the 900,000 votes won by UKIP in the 2010 general election, the 4.3 million votes won by UKIP in European elections in 2014, the 3.9 million votes won by UKIP in the 2015 general election. Believing that the best chance of leading the Conservative Party came from courting these disgruntled Tories, such politicians as Boris Johnson and Michael Gove backed Leave in the 2016 election and chose to run the campaign as an alliance of the centre right and of the anti-European fringe. The vote to leave the European Union could not have succeeded, in other words, without moderates and radicals on the right having chosen to work together despite their other disagreements.

There is a second sense in which Brexit was a strategy for convergence. Given the role played by the right in pressing for Britain to leave the EU, it is no surprise to see that most voting in the referendum was on party lines. Almost every single UKIP voter (99 per cent) supported Leave. So did the majority (58 per cent) of Conservatives; while an even larger share of Labour voters (63 per cent) supported Remain.[1] Yet although by far the largest number of Leave voters were Conservative and UKIP voters mobilised by familiar right-wing motives, they alone would not have been sufficient to secure a majority for Leave. The majority was won by offering a small but significant group of working class and non-Conservative voters a vision of Brexit as a way of protecting the welfare state but at the price of its racialisation.

Brexit won over a particular cohort of Labour voters; not the centrists who had admired Tony Blair, but a generation who depend on benefits (above all, on pensions) and were enthused by promises to protect welfare by racialising it.

Moreover, the politics of Brexit have continued beyond the 2016 vote. Because the referendum was interpreted by almost every politician as a proxy vote on immigration, so the Brexit result has required the Conservative government to make life ever harder for migrants. After the Brexit vote, a policy of creating a 'hostile environment' for immigrants was extended to even legal migrants with a right to be in the UK (EU citizens) as well as those who had been living in the country for five or six decades (the Windrush generation). The alliance at the heart of Brexit, the combination of right, far-right and some voters newly won to the right, has not frozen British politics just where it was but taken it in a new and malign direction.

The roots of Brexit

Despite the link between party affiliation and voting in the most recent referendum, there is nothing innate to the European Union which requires its opponents to be either left or right-wing.[2] A two-choice referendum by its nature simplifies and diminishes political choice. Over 30 million people voted in the referendum, many choosing their side with difficulty from a mixture of motives. It was possible to be a fiscal conservative and to support the EU's budget rules; or to be a Bennite or an anti-capitalist and to see the European Union as the state and therefore the enemy.

Right-wing opposition to the European Union is a product of the Thatcher government of the 1980s. In the preceding decades it was the centre right who campaigned for the UK to join. Harold Macmillan's Conservatives made the first attempt to join the EU's predecessor the Common Market in 1963 and the Conservatives were also in power in 1973 when the UK became a full member. The European Communities Act 1972, the legislation which makes the UK subject to EU law was passed by Ted Heath's Conservative government. Among the MPs who voted for the UK to join the EU were such future Thatcherites as Norman Fowler, Keith Joseph, Norman Lamont, Nicholas Ridley, Norman Tebbit and even Margaret Thatcher herself. After becoming Conservative leader, Thatcher campaigned for the UK to remain in the EU in the 1975 referendum. In 1977, she said that the Conservatives were 'the European Party in the British Parliament'.[3]

The first skirmish between the Conservatives and Europe came in winter 1979–80 over the extent of the UK's contributions to the EU. Around 70 per cent of EU spending went on the Common Agricultural Policy which subsidised farming and from which the urbanised UK economy gained less than others. Margaret Thatcher negotiated an £800 million rebate in the UK's contributions. The broadcaster Kenneth Harris's biography of Mrs Thatcher recalls the turmoil in the Foreign Office caused by the Conservative leader's 'dictatorial' negotiating style. Yet he goes on to applaud her success in securing the rebate, portraying it as the first sign of the victories that were to follow against General Galtieri and the miners, 'This was when the world in general and Europe in particular, became aware of the quality of the new British leader.'[4]

As the decade wore on, Margaret Thatcher became more hostile to the European Union, persuading herself that its leaders were the equivalent of the moderate Conservatives (the 'wets') who were unwilling to fight for a victory for capital over labour.[5] This hostility was still compatible with membership. Thatcher approved the creation of the single market and argued for the expansion of the European Union eastwards. She became increasingly hostile though to EU social policies.

In September 1988, the President of the European Commission Jacques Delors addressed the annual Congress of the TUC at Bournemouth, setting out the Commission's proposals for a social dialogue between employers and unions, whose agreements Delors argued should form the basis of future Directives of the European Council. Delors promised that future European Treaties would include, 'The establishment of a platform of guaranteed workers' rights, containing general principles, such as every worker's right to be covered by a collective agreement and more specific measures concerning, for example, the status of temporary work.' The delegates to Congress, conscious of the hostile domestic climate since the defeat of the miners' strike, were so delighted that they sang *Frère Jacques*.[6]

Margaret Thatcher's response to Delors was her Bruges Speech, during which she likened the EU to Russian Communism and contrasted the triumph of the values of free enterprise in the UK with their apparent failure in Europe:

It is ironic that just when those countries, such as the Soviet Union, which have tried to run everything from the centre, are learning that success depends on dispersing power and decisions away from the centre, some in the Community seem to want to move in the opposite direction. We have not successfully rolled back the frontiers of the state in Britain, only to see them re-imposed at a European level with a European super-state exercising a new dominance from Brussels.[7]

This was the birth of British Euro-scepticism. Without the Bruges Speech, there would have been no UKIP, no referendum and no Brexit.[8] It was also a fateful moment in the Thatcher government; the idea that the EU was Britain's new Soviet enemy seemed so far out of kilter with reality that it encouraged Thatcher's inner party critics. Opposition to Thatcher over the EU became the issue through which it was possible to raise all their other objections to her government and to her personally.

In the weeks following the Bruges speech, a 20-year-old free-marketeer and future publicist for General Pinochet,[9] Patrick Robertson, launched the Bruges Group, a think tank demanding British departure from the EU.[10]

Since UKIP was born from the Bruges Group, it is worth describing that alliance in some detail. The Bruges Group's first President was Lord Harris of High Cross, an advocate of the privatisation of libraries, the devastation of the welfare state, and the removal of any restriction on the tobacco companies' freedom to trade. For Harris and his co-thinkers, the problem with the EU was not the single market but that Europe had adopted at the time a whole raft of social policies. Among his particular criticisms, Harris listed the 48-hour week, equal treatment of part-time and full-time workers and equal pay between men and women.[11] What all these policies had in common was that they tended to increase the bargaining power of labour at the expense of capital. Indeed, they were having this effect just at the very same time that Thatcher was successfully reducing the UK's social wage. By 1990, the Bruges Group had ceased to be a mere think tank and was becoming a party in embryo, with the support of up to 100 MPs marshalled by Bill Cash and John Redwood and a six-figure budget donated by the multi-millionaire Jimmy Goldsmith, later of the Referendum Party. It also had a series of emulators across Europe, including in France, where a Committee for a Europe of the Nations affiliated to the Bruges Group. The Secretary General of that Committee, Yvon Blot, was a Front National MEP.[12]

The final two years of the Thatcher government were dominated by the split in her Cabinet. The leader's supporters saw themselves in a permanent albeit managed conflict with Europe, while another faction in her cabinet led by successive Chancellors of the Exchequer (first Nigel Lawson and then Geoffrey Howe) wanted to reduce the conflict with Europe in order to protect Britain's trading relationships with France and Germany. After years of argument, Europe combined with the unpopular Poll Tax to cause Thatcher's resignation,[13] and for many years afterwards nostalgic Thatcherites saw the pro-Europeans as having 'knifed' their chosen leader in the back. The Conservative right's belief that they had been betrayed over Europe justified any number of apostasies, from the willingness of the Tory 'bastards' to rebel against John Major, to the schisms which caused the defeats of the next three Conservative leaders, William Hague, Iain Duncan Smith and Michael Howard. In retirement, Thatcher encouraged these divisions, accepting the chair of the Bruges Group and writing in a book *Statecraft*, 'Europe is ... a classic utopian project, a monument to the vanity of intellectuals, a programme whose inevitable destiny is failure.'[14]

UKIP's predecessor, the Anti-Federalist League was launched in 1991, by Alan Sked, who had until then been a member of the Bruges Group. UKIP's first recruits were political amateurs, almost all of them former Conservatives who had recently left the party. Sked was excluded from the Bruges Group in 1991, after the Iraq war, for issuing a press release which attempted to harness the group's sense of betrayal following Thatcher's removal as Prime Minister to a criticism of John Major for failing to continue the Iraq War.[15] On being sacked from the Bruges Group, Sked took a copy of its membership list and wrote to all of the Group's supporters announcing a new party. Around 150 people joined. The Anti-Federalist League's first election was in Bath in 1992. It secured 117 votes; and its main public meeting was attended by just six people. A piece in Glasgow's *Daily Record* listed the League as one of several 'kamikaze' parties (along with the yogic-flying Natural Law Party), doomed to remain forever on the margins of British political life.[16]

The name United Kingdom Independence Party was adopted in 1993. Four years later, UKIP's election manifesto promised a bonfire of regulations. The return of the billions that the UK was squandering on the European Union would go on deficit and tax reduction. The party opposed any policies of job creation for the unemployed, 'not a pursuit that the government should attempt to follow'. Rules to protect employees from rogue employers or the environment from pollution were among UKIP's targets: 'Regulations destroy jobs and the UKIP is determined to reduce the regulatory burden on industry and on small businesses in particular.' UKIP would reintroduce flogging in schools, called for 'serious pruning of the welfare budget,' and privatisation, starting with the pensions of public employees.[17]

During this period, UKIP was a right-wing party, with a programme of economic liberalism which overlapped with mainstream Conservatism. UKIP's millionaire backer Arron Banks describes his pride at having once been the youngest Conservative council candidate anywhere in the country (an accolade confirmed by a letter from his heroine, Margaret Thatcher). Nigel Farage describes in his biography the exhilaration he felt at Thatcher's victory in 1979, 'It was as if the pebble-dashed back wall onto which our windows had for years looked out had been demolished to give us glimpses at least of rolling hills and a bright sea.' In a similar vein, the UKIP leader told the *Sun* in 2013 that he would have remained a Conservative all his life, if the party had not betrayed its greatest ever leader.[18]

Indeed the impression that UKIP was an external faction of Conservatives is heightened if they are viewed alongside the Tories who allied with UKIP in campaigning for Brexit. Daniel Hannan is a Conservative MEP for Southeast England. In 2012 he organised the meetings that would result in the formation of the Vote Leave campaign and was rumoured to be thinking of joining UKIP at the same time as Douglas Carswell.[19] Hannan is just two years younger than Patrick Robertson and like Robertson formed a Leave think tank while a student, the Oxford Campaign for an Independent Britain. The politics of Hannan's and Robertson's organisations were almost indistinguishable. The Oxford CIB warned of the risk posed by Euro-federalists to 'the identity of Britain,' and demanded that

Britain be allowed to become again 'an independent nation.' It organised drinking sessions where its supporters could toast the demise of Jacques Delors or commemorate the anniversary of Thatcher's resignation. The speakers invited by Hannan's Campaign for an Independent Britain between 1991 and 1992 included Alan Sked and Ray Honeyford, the Bradford headmaster who had argued that the successful education of white English children was made impossible by 'a growing number of Asians,' who he claimed wanted nothing more than 'to produce Asian ghettoes'. Ray Honeyford also denounced what he called 'an influential group of black intellectuals of aggressive disposition, who know little of the British traditions of understatement, civilised discourse and respect for reason.' The task for the right was to take up the cause of 'indigenous children'. Other speakers invited by Hannan included Bruges Group veterans, Bill Cash, Lord Harris of High Cross and Patrick Robertson.[20]

To this day Daniel Hannan, like Robertson, cites General Pinochet's Chile as a model, admiring its privatised pension system. He is also, like Sked and Farage, a champion of a different, privatised Britain with that vision of the United Kingdom at the start and at the end of his politics and the seeming fixation with the European Union a mere means to that end. Daniel Hannan has praised Enoch Powell and called for the privatisation of the NHS and for welfare cuts. He argues that taxes should be reduced; as should be the benefits given to the poor: 'Taxes should be lower, simpler and flatter. Welfare should be simplified and localised.'[21] It is hard to see how any of these views would have been incompatible with membership of UKIP. The point at which Daniel Hannan and Nigel Farage's politics diverged, and the two men were never close,[22] was that Hannan believed that with sufficient time it was possible to win the Conservative Party to the politics of Brexit. By contrast, Farage refused to forget the Conservatives' treatment of Thatcher and insisted that the Tories would always stay in Europe no matter what happened. The launch of UKIP therefore had the effect of maintaining Thatcher's legacy both inside the Conservatives and out.

Yet if the goals of UKIP have overlapped at times with those of the Conservatives, at other times the party has felt more like its rivals on the far right. In spring 1997, UKIP's Director of Research Mark Deavin was revealed by *Searchlight* magazine to be a member of the BNP. UKIP's leader Alan Sked promptly expelled him. Deavin however received support from other members of the UKIP leadership, including the party's most successful election candidate Nigel Farage, who was seen by Deavin as the leader of the party's 'nationalist' wing. Sked also expelled Farage. When it became clear that the membership would not tolerate Farage's removal, Sked himself resigned, complaining that many of UKIP's members 'are racist and have been infected by the far right'.[23] After Sked's departure, Farage was photographed meeting Mark Deavin at St Katharine Docks in Wapping. Also at the meeting was Tony Lecomber, who in 1986 had attempted to bomb the South London headquarters of Vanessa Redgrave's Workers Revolutionary Party, for which he received a three-year jail sentence. Farage was able to replace Sked as leader only because of the Deavin affair. To this day, he denies that the purpose of the meeting was to negotiate with Deavin or the British National Party (BNP) but simply to obtain 'information about Sked,' to be used in his ongoing battle to take over the leadership of UKIP. 'Deavin,' he insists, was 'conciliatory but had no new intelligence to convey.'[24]

In 2004, UKIP was boosted by the recruitment of Robert Kilroy-Silk, a TV presenter who had been dismissed by the BBC after writing a newspaper column denouncing Arabs as limb-amputators and claiming falsely that after 9/11 Muslims had 'danced in the hot, dusty streets to celebrate the murders'. After learning of his dismissal, it was UKIP who approached Kilroy-Silk. He was invited to join the party and encouraged to stand for UKIP in the European elections of 2005.[25] On being elected and trying but failing to become UKIP's leader, Kilroy-Silk launched a further party, Veritas, which later folded into the English Democrats, another far-right sect.

In 2007, David Abbott, a member of UKIP's NEC was found to have dined with Nick Griffin of the BNP and to have given donations to the American Friends of the BNP. In 2008, UKIP's Buster Mottram, a former professional tennis player who had once reached the fourth round at Wimbledon and was a former member of the National Front, addressed UKIP's NEC. He claimed to be bringing a message from the BNP's Nick Griffin and proposed an alliance between the two parties. UKIP's NEC agreed to hear the offer but declined it. In 2008, WikiLeaks placed online a copy of the BNP membership list; there were defectors from UKIP in Balham, Crawley, Eastborne, Essex, Leicester, Pembrokeshire and Stafford. Although the Conservatives had 20 times more members than UKIP in the late 1990s, there were as many defectors on the list from UKIP as there were from the Conservatives.[26]

In 2009, then leader of UKIP, Baron Pearson invited the leader of the Dutch Party for Freedom, Geert Wilders, to

Britain to show an Islamophobic film; although the Home Office ultimately refused permission for Wilders to enter.

Between 2010 and 2016, the Deputy Leader of UKIP was Paul Nuttall, a former history student with an enthusiasm for the Holocaust denier David Irving.[27] Nuttall was not just Deputy Leader; in this period UKIP adopted a 'Northern strategy' of seeking to win over working-class voters in Labour's industrial heartlands. The approach suffered from a credibility defect; the majority of the party's leaders were businessmen from London who struggled to present themselves as authentic champions of the Northern working class. Nuttall, who had been born in Bootle on Merseyside, was pushed forward as the expression of this new approach. While Deputy Leader, Nuttall described the media as 'mind-benders' (a phrase seemingly cribbed from a pamphlet written by the BNP's Nick Griffin). He attacked the press as 'Cultural Marxists' (a term popularised by the far right terrorist Anders Breivik).[28]

UK Independence: a far-right demand

From the mid-2000s onwards, UKIP courted the BNP's anti-immigrant vote. This began with the 2004 recruitment of Kilroy-Silk but became more strident after 2010 and continued until the 2016 referendum. In 2014, the political scientists Matthew Goodwin and Robert Ford argued that as a result of its shift to anti-immigrant politics, UKIP could best be characterised as a far-right party. 'Far from a catch-all party or one focussed on winning over disgruntled Conservatives, they have tailored a Eurosceptic, anti-immigrant appeal for disadvantaged, working-class voters who feel under threat from the changes that surround them and alienated from a seemingly unresponsive and disengaged established political class.'[29] UKIP's leaders have repeatedly employed racist language. During the 2015 general election campaign, for example, Nigel Farage claimed that 60 per cent of all new cases of HIV in Britain affected non-British nationals, saying that 'You can come to Britain from anywhere in the world and get diagnosed with HIV and get the retroviral drugs that cost up to £25,000 per year.' During the 2016 referendum on the European Union, Farage sought to draw links between migration and Europe, claiming that voting Brexit was the only way to stop foreigners carrying out sexual attacks against British women.[30]

While the early Thatcherite supporters of Brexit rarely called themselves far right, on occasion, they used similar terms. In one pamphlet Lord Harris the Chairman of the Bruges Group and the intellectual grandfather of today's Eurosceptics, described himself as a 'radical reactionary'. In this phrase, 'reactionary' stands for right wing and 'radical' marks Harris out from the perceived moderates of the mainstream right. Harris used the phrase as the title of one of his pamphlets, writing that he was: 'Conservative about the principles of a free society but radical about the measures necessary to ensure its dynamic operation and continuing evolution.'[31]

This book distinguishes the mainstream right from its outliers. The centre right follows a method of conservatism, respects the institutions of the liberal state and takes its lead from the dominant opinions at any moment among business and the rich. The far right argues for the restoration of a world that has been lost and is willing to reject the choices of the capitalist class. The idea that the far right are nostalgists fits Nigel Farage perfectly, a man whose slogan for UKIP's 2015 conference as, 'We want our country back,'[32] a slogan with the emphasis very much on the final syllable.

The success of UKIP illustrates once again the need for a category 'far right,' which is different from and broader than 'fascist'. Unlike its predecessors on the British right, the party was not inspired or set up by former fascists. UKIP lacks the emphasis on personal leadership of a typical post-fascist party, the emphasis on the street over parliament and any ambition of purging the liberal state. UKIP was born from the Conservatives and when UKIP turned towards anti-immigrant politics it was following the logic of its own anti-Europeanism. If you were to tell most members of UKIP they were fascists they would not be horrified or excited, just bemused.

Behind the British far right's fixation with the EU lies a series of political calculations. Far right groups in other countries have not seen independence as the same defining task. After all, European elections have seen any number of far right candidates elected and most have made peace with the European institutions.[33] Some of the reason for this hostility relates to the character of the EU. It is an agreement between states at different levels of prosperity, which gives their citizens an equal right to travel. The Union was negotiated as part of a post-1945 settlement, at a time when even right-wing politicians accepted a degree of equality and where there was a pressing need to import labour to staff a booming economy. By contrast, NAFTA, the free trade agreement between the US, Canada and Mexico, does not allow free movement; neither does the Pacific TPP.[34] These treaties were negotiated at a different stage in the history of capitalism, after 1979–1980 and the neoliberal turn.

Free movement within the European Union is a mechanism which is intended to level up the incomes of those living in poorer countries until different regions of the EU enjoy comparable living standards. It is complemented by other policies such as investment in agriculture and infrastructure and the targeting of subsidies towards underdeveloped regions which have a similar effect.

Free movement for EU citizens is by no means an unambiguous boon; just as the borders within the EU states have been lowered, the borders at the edges of the continent have raised. Since 2000, tens of thousands of migrants from North Africa have died attempting to cross the Mediterranean to Europe.[35] Yet, even though free movement within the EU is an inadequate means towards equalisation, it is incompatible with the world the far right is trying to make in which white and black are intended to be kept far apart, and with the latter living everywhere in poverty.

The referendum vote

In the referendum a large amount of voting was on party lines. As noted above, almost every UKIP voter supported Leave, as did a majority of Conservatives. Despite rumours to the effect that Jeremy Corbyn was a secret Brexiteer, an even larger share of Labour voters supported Remain. There were also clear demographic preferences: six out of ten voters aged over 65 voted for Brexit while Remain won among all age groups under 49. In all these respects, the vote was a left-right split, little different from the general elections in 2015 or 2017. That does not mean that Brexit was nothing more than a left-right vote. Some of the ways in which it broke with the patterns of normal British politics can be seen by looking at the six seats with the largest leave majorities. The top three, Boston and Skegness,

South Basildon and East Thurrock and Castle Point, were small towns surrounded by countryside. Boston and Skegness is a constituency in rural Lincolnshire, the others are in east Essex. All three were Conservative seats, with Boston and Castle Point having voted Conservative for decades. However the next three largest Leave majorities were in Kingston upon Hull East, Stoke on Trent North and Doncaster North, all of them Labour areas associated with single industries, in Hull fishing, in Stoke pottery, in Doncaster coal mining.[36]

It would be wrong to exaggerate the extent of working-class Leave voting. Remain had a majority in London and in other large cities: in Manchester, Leeds and Bristol. It won in areas defined by their left-wing politics, such as Liverpool, Glasgow and West Belfast. Most black and ethnic minority voters chose Remain.[37]

A key weakness of the Remain campaign was that it was led by Conservatives and had very little to offer most voters. The core message of the Remain campaign was that Brexit would be bad for the economy. 'Tacitly,' Jeremy Corbyn's biographer Richard Seymour writes, the Remain campaign 'seemed to rely on the idea that most people admire and respect capitalists, their success granting them a kind of celebrity status ... [as if] we all had and felt a stake in their gains.'[38]

Neither Hull, Stoke nor Doncaster were booming, nor had they been for decades. From constituencies such as these, a message came back to the politicians; voters would not vote in sufficient numbers for someone else's prosperity. Moreover, as the campaign wore on, the debate was structured more and more around immigration. 'Three themes dominated the list of issues in which the leavers had the advantage: border controls and the immigration system ... and the ability to control our own laws.' The most effective of the Leave campaigners were those who claimed that by excluding migrants, white voters' incomes would rise. Leave.EU's millionaire funder, Arron Banks, told one interviewer that 'less immigration would also mean less competition for jobs and higher wages,' insisting that if the availability of labour was reduced, then as a matter of logic, its price in wages must increase.[39]

The most striking image of the campaign was Leave.EU's 'Breaking Point' poster, which showed a queue of Syrian Arab refugees threatening to enter Europe and (impliedly) the UK. 'The UK has failed us all,' the poster said. 'We must break free of the EU and take back control of our borders.' The queue of arrivals was intended to echo an older poster: Labour isn't Working, which the Conservatives had used in 1979 to undermine Jim Callaghan's then Labour government with an unspoken (but real) promise that the Tories would not allow unemployment to remain at its then scandalous rate of over a million. The central image of both posters was a queue; in 1979 of the unemployed, in 2016 of migrants. The Muslims coming into Europe would take the place of 'our' jobless workers. The promise set out in the older poster was not kept; the unemployed doubled under Thatcher. But in an epoch of fake news a deceit does not matter, an argument is evaluated not by its core truth or otherwise, but according to the bravado with which it is argued. What Breaking Point shared with its original was not merely a deep cynicism but a very specific political argument, that the right alone could be trusted to protect poorer voters. This was the theme of the right almost everywhere in 2016–17; that, as a rule, affluent societies are allowed to have social welfare or immigration: they cannot have both.

Not every Leave campaigner employed this logic, nor did every worker accept it. Most unions advocated Remain and a bare majority of those in employment voted against Brexit.[40] Leave was ahead, however, among people who did not work and depended on welfare benefits, above all, among pensioners.

The referendum was a contest between competing visions for the social wage. Remain was a coalition of those who wanted to maintain social spending (the majority of Labour voters) and those who wished to cut it, albeit at a relatively slow pace (David Cameron and George Osborne). Vacillating between both sides but finding no independent position of their own were the young and the most left-wing of voters. Leave was an alliance of those who wanted to cut the social wage more quickly (UKIP voters and three-fifths of the Conservatives), with those who believed that the social wage could be protected albeit only by restricting access to social housing, the NHS, etc., to British nationals and excluding everyone else.

The decision of those who voted for Brexit as a strategy to defend working-class living standards was not without precedent. The historian of Britain's multi-racial working class, Satnam Virdee, argues that the state and British capital have long sought to win workers to the politics of national belonging. 'Between the 1850s and 1940s, the British elites ideologically incorporated ever larger components of the working class into the imagined nation ... [workers] too began to imbibe a British national identity constructed in opposition to ... Irish Catholics, Jews, those of Caribbean and Asian descent.' Social welfare also has a history of racial distribution: whether that was the discomfort of parts of the British ruling-class at the number of workers who could not be conscripted for the Boer War army because they simply were not well enough to serve or the Fabian arguments for welfare as a means to protect the nation's racial stock.[41] These dynamics diminished between the 1940s and 1970s, during a period of high taxation, as the coercive and discriminatory mechanisms of the Poor Laws were replaced by a new ethic of universal inclusion. However, they were re-established first in 1988 with regulations requiring social security officers to check applicants' immigration status. Laws were tightened again under Tony Blair's New Labour government, which dispersed asylum seekers away from London, housed many in buildings which were unfit for human occupation and gave them vouchers rather than cash benefits. When vouchers were declared unlawful, Labour agreed to pay asylum seekers benefits, albeit at a lesser rate than British claimants.[42]

The reasoning of a small but significant proportion of Leave voters was that by keeping migrants from the European Union out of Britain, there would be fewer people living in decent housing, or enjoying healthcare or welfare benefits. It followed that everyone who still had access to these resources would have more of them. While this message seemed to be compatible with left-wing values of mutual support and the use of state resources to protect the poor, it proposed to maintain services at the costs of their racialisation and the exclusion of migrants from equal treatment. As the aftermath of the referendum was to show, politicians took the message of Brexit to be not merely that future migrants were to be excluded (although that would have been bad enough) but that the dynamics of exclusion should be projected backwards, to encompass those who had come to Britain legally and people who had been here for decades.

May takes on the saboteurs

In the aftermath of the referendum, Prime Minister David Cameron had no choice but to resign and was replaced by Theresa May. After several months spent trying to establish a consensus within her own party over the terms of Britain's departure, an exercise which appears to have done little more than convince her of the difficulties of keeping her party united, May announced a further general election. It was fought on the slogan, 'Brexit means Brexit.' Behind her campaign was an idea of how to govern, in which Brexit was seen not as a burden but as an opportunity, a chance to remake the Conservative Party and alter the balance of British politics for a generation. The centre right took up politics which had until recently belonged to UKIP.

The Conservative pitch towards far-right voters had been gathering slowly for several years. In 2011, David Cameron claimed that Muslims failed to absorb British values and that anti-racist legislation had cowed whites and prevented them from challenging the true racists (in other words Muslims). Cameron declared, 'When a white person holds objectionable views – racist views for instance, we rightly condemn them. But when equally unacceptable views or practices come from someone who isn't white, we've been too cautious – frankly even fearful – to stand up to them.' On the day of his speech members of the English Defence League (EDL) were marching through Luton. Both the centre right and the far right were demanding that Muslims privilege their British identity over their international association with other Muslims.[43]

In 2012, and in response to the rise of UKIP, then Home Secretary Theresa May told the *Daily Telegraph* her aim 'was to create here in Britain a really hostile environment for illegal migration'. The following year she approved the hiring of advertising vans which toured black and minority ethnic areas of Britain with the message: 'Here illegally? Go home or face arrest.' Legislation was also used to make the UK an unwelcoming environment for potential new arrivals. The Immigration Act 2014 made it a criminal offence for a landlord to let a room to a tenant who turned out not to have a right to remain in the UK. A further Immigration Act 2016 made it a criminal offence for an employer to employ a worker who lacked the right to reside.[44]

The clearest sign of the direction in which British politics were heading, even prior to Brexit, was the introduction of NHS fees for foreigners. These were set at two bands: for tourists who were in the UK lawfully, an initial £200 per year from April 2015; while for those who the Home Office said were in the UK unlawfully (a far wider group than those who in fact lacked immigration status) charges were meant to copy what the NHS would demand if it was a private health care provider, for instance £54,000 for the treatment of prostate cancer.[45] These various measures drastically intensified border enforcement, while also expanding its scope and personnel. The term border fails to do justice to today's reality, it makes it seem as if a potential migrant to Britain or Europe has only to cross at a single place (by a plane, say, from Washington or Lagos to London) after which they have arrived and can stay in a new country. Whereas policy now dictated that as many social interactions as possible should be bordered. More and more people involved in non-managerial roles within the welfare state found themselves obliged as part of their duties to double up as part-time immigration officers: doctors and nurses, university and college lecturers, council housing officers, workers at the Drivers and Vehicle Licensing Agency processing applications for driving licenses, even registrars in charge of weddings.[46] In all these ways, the governing Conservatives were positioning themselves as the champion of those who wanted welfare services to be restricted along racial lines.

The convergence of centre right and far right did not begin during the referendum; it did however accelerate afterwards. As leading Conservatives shifted towards Brexit, so they adopted the rest of UKIP's programme. The nature of the result could be seen in publicity sent out by Vote Leave in May 2016 which insisted (untruthfully) that the European Union had already approved Turkey's application for full membership of the EU, a decision which would enable some 76 million brown-skinned people to settle in Britain. The direction that migrants would follow if Britain was foolish enough to remain in the European Union was illustrated by a giant red arrow pointing towards England, reminding older audiences of the approaching arrows with which the TV show Dad's Army had once visualised a Nazi invasion of Britain.[47] The message of the Conservatives' Vote Leave campaign were the same, in substance, as those of UKIP's Leave.EU. British voters could take back control – of social policy, of NHS funding, of welfare provision – by extending the UK's borders.

Brexit was treated by politicians as a referendum on immigration and the vote used to justify a series of attempts at tightening policies in order to punish those who were in the UK lawfully but had been born overseas. After the Brexit referendum, the Home Office adopted a new policy, 'European Economic Area (EEA) administrative removal,' to justify the deportation of around five thousand European rough-sleepers before the High Court declared the policy unlawful. The Department for Education required schools to collect the nationality of children and by the end of 2016, school records were being passed to the Home Office at the rate of 1500 a month.[48]

A covert decision was also taken to derecognise the immigration status of many people from the black Caribbean who were threatened with deportation or having to pay huge charges for NHS fees after living in the UK for more than 50 years. After months of press stories reporting the ill-treatment of this Windrush Generation and faced with the prospect of having to justify this policy to her fellow leaders at a Caribbean summit, May briefly retreated, accepting in principle that the Windrush Generation were British citizens but justifying the authoritarian treatment of them on the grounds that (for example) some had committed crimes in the UK. In the *Guardian*, Home Secretary Sajid Javid could be heard promising to 'do right' by the Windrush generation. Meanwhile the tabloids were given the opposite message: 'I don't want them back,' the Home Secretary was quoted as saying.[49]

Theresa May's speech to the 2016 Conservative conference used the phrase 'working class' seven times; it promised a 'quiet revolution' which would benefit skilled workers, doctors, the unemployed – everyone except for immigrants. The new Prime Minister insisted that no one could travel to Britain without their presence making someone here poorer, 'To someone who finds themselves out of work or on lower wages because of low-skilled immigration, life simply doesn't seem fair.' It was already her party's policy that citizenship was a conditional gift: it was to be offered to some migrants, so long as they obeyed the laws and their social superiors, and could be taken back at any time. Now, May went further, questioning the values of those who wrongly saw themselves as European or internationalists, rather than British:

> If you believe you're a citizen of the world, you're a citizen of nowhere. You don't understand what the very word 'citizenship' means.[50]

Meanwhile, the wider political culture also grew more intolerant with the tabloid press, encouraged by the referendum victory, denouncing even those who made the modest-sounding proposal that before leaving the EU Brexit should be subject to at least some sort of approval from Parliament (the Brexiteers' preferred alternative was to have the entire process determined by the Prime Minister). Gina Miller funded a Judicial Review of the refusal to allow a Parliamentary vote, and the High Court and the Supreme Court both decided that as a matter of principle, she was right; Parliament and not the executive should have the task of repealing the European Communities Act. The High Court decision was met with dismay from Britain's tycoon press, with the *Daily Mail* putting on its front page a picture of the three judges in their wigs, with the headline 'Enemies of the People.' One of the judges, Terence Etherton, was described as an 'openly-gay ex-Olympic fencer,' working a message of homophobia into the story's malevolent nationalism.[51]

The Conservatives' 2017 manifesto spoke to the same audience: 'It is our objective to reduce immigration to sustainable levels, by which we mean annual net migration in the tens of thousands ... We will increase the earnings thresholds for people wishing to sponsor migrants for family visas ... Leaving the European Union means, for the first time in decades, that we will be able to control immigration from the European Union too.' It also proposed to triple the NHS fees for legal migrants.[52]

Between Brexit and the 2017 election, under the guidance of Theresa May's Eurosceptic Chief of Staff, Nick Timothy and her director and speechwriter Chris Wilkins, an attempt was made to reorient the party. The biggest swing demographic in British politics, the Conservatives, decided we're 'Working-Class Strugglers.' In other words, older voters living in white-dominated industrial areas and owning their own home who agreed with the right over immigration and Brexit and who, after having voted in the past for UKIP, were now going over to the Conservatives.[53]

In her election announcement speech, May insisted that Brexit had brought 'a record numbers of jobs and economic growth that has exceeded all expectations,' but this prosperity was endangered by a nascent coalition of Labour, the SNP and anti-Brexit peers. 'At this moment of enormous national significance, there should be unity here in Westminster but instead there is division,' May complained. 'The country is coming together but Westminster is not … They underestimate our determination to get the job done and I am not prepared to let them endanger the security of millions of working people across the country.' The coded authoritarianism of the speech, with its suggestion of concealed enemies, hidden dangers and an opposition failing in its overriding duty of patriotism, was brought out in numerous favourable press headlines, not least the *Daily Mail*'s front page, 'Crush the Saboteurs.'[54]

That there was a demographic for May's campaign was brought home, at the start of the 2017 election by focus groups and by polls predicting a 20-point victory for the Conservatives.[55] At set-piece occasions, such as a BBC Question Time special in York, Corbyn was challenged over his willingness to meet with the Palestinian group Hamas, his supposed links to Irish Republicans and above all his unwillingness to pledge that he would use Britain's nuclear weapons at the first opportunity. His hostile questioners were seemingly without exception older white men; the very demographic on which the Conservative election gamble was based.

Brexit was and remains a serious attempt to move British politics to the right. Yet in summer 2017, this attempt stumbled when put to the population at a general election. It is not that the Conservatives did badly. In that vote, UKIP's vote fell as the Tories had predicted, from 13 to 2 per cent. Just under half of those former UKIP voters (45 per cent) went over to the Conservatives. A much smaller proportion (11 per cent) switched to Labour.[56] There were in consequence a string of Conservative victories in industrial English seats in which UKIP had flourished, including Derbyshire North East, Mansfield, Middlesbrough South, East Cleveland, Stoke-on-Trent South and Walsall North. The most visible of these was Mansfield, a seat won by the Tories for the first time in their history and located symbolically between the Yorkshire coalfields (the heart of the strike in 1984–5) and the Nottingham coalfields (the base of the return to work movement). The 12.35 million votes won by the Conservatives in England were more than the party had won in any election since 1992.

Precisely because Brexit was intended to change Britain, and because many voters saw clearly the threat it represented to them personally, it polarised the electorate. If the Conservatives did better than in 2012 in northern seats, this was matched by Labour victories in Battersea, Brighton Kempton, Canterbury, Ipswich, Reading East. These seats showed a different side of working-class life, one shaped by and comfortable with social change. For every voter attracted to May's vision of a racialised social Brexit, another was horrified by the same message.

From a purely mathematical approach, the attraction of convergence must have seemed obvious to the Conservatives. In the 2015 election, they had won 37 per cent of the vote and UKIP a further 13 per cent. Combine the two and the right would be unassailable. Yet politics is about more than mere arithmetic. In moving towards policy positions which had been UKIP's, the Conservatives had to reposition themselves as a different sort of party, more suspicious and authoritarian. Britain's right-leaning press saw and emphasised the difference. Millions of voters saw the direction in which the country seemed to be heading and did all they could to resist.

The problem with the Conservative gamble over Brexit and indeed with the way that Theresa May has governed since the election, is that their party has focussed on managing its own divisions over Europe over everything else. The government has prioritised unity even over working out its own bargaining goals.[57]

One of the few wry comments attributed to Theresa May is the phrase she used on becoming Prime Minister, to dismiss George Osborne, the Chancellor of the Exchequer and a leading figure in David Cameron's previous tax-cutting but socially liberal leadership. She is said to have told Osborne that he needed to 'get to know the party better'. May's gift as a politician had been to survive under previous Conservative leaders, resolutely failing to antagonise either wing of her party.

As Prime Minister, the calculations of the shifting balance of opinion among backbenchers has been the overriding concern of May's government and she has concluded that there are more MPs that will threaten to destroy the government should it be seen to appease the EU than there are who will break ranks if no deal can be reached.

The result has been to shift power incrementally within the Conservative Party towards its backbenchers and to those of them who stand furthest to the right. By the end of 2017, the bookies' favourite to replace May was Jacob Rees-Mogg. Prior to Brexit, Rees-Mogg had been among the least well known of the Conservative backbenchers, a man with so little reputation to lose that in 2013 he accepted an invitation to be the guest of honour at a meeting of the Traditional Britain Group, a gathering largely composed of former members of the BNP. In 2015, he called for a Conservative-UKIP electoral pact. Over subsequent years, he has met Steve Bannon and given lengthy interviews to Breitbart. Yet Jacob Rees-Mogg is not merely a Brexiteer with unpleasant public associations, he is also a consistent misogynist. The father of six children, he has boasted that he has never changed a nappy in his life. He has used his increasing profile to argue against abortion, saying that it should be refused in all circumstances including rape and incest.[58] The longer that this period of deference to the far-right lasts, the more we will see of such politicians, and the further they will go in pushing back everyone's else rights, not just those of immigrants and their descendants but of anyone who opposes their 1950s-style vision of Britain.

Brexit requires the Conservatives to negotiate fresh trade agreements with the EU and with the rest of the world. One of the myths associated with Brexit was that it would enable an alternative free trade zone with Australia, Canada and New Zealand, with Boris Johnson accusing the 1973 (Conservative) government of having 'betrayed' the Commonwealth by joining the EU.[59] The logical next step was to say that if citizens of the United Kingdom lost the right to move freely across Europe, they should have the benefit instead of a 'bilateral free labour mobility zone' between the UK and former white colonies such as Australia.[60] Nothing was offered, however, to the Commonwealth countries of south Asia, Africa or the Caribbean, just as many of whose citizens had family connections to the United Kingdom.

Awkwardly for Theresa May, the discussion of white Commonwealth preference could not take place without citizens of other countries noticing, a process brought home in winter 2017, when India's Prime Minister, Narendra Modi, made clear the price for any trade agreement with India: more visas for Indian nationals. In that moment, the promises of Brexit (imperial free trade *and* reduced migration) found themselves in conflict.[61]

Yet the difficulties that even a sympathetic government has had in trying to enact the fantasy of British independence, without the industrial or military power which once maintained her empire, has not brought about a new period of buyer's remorse. Rather the right has found a new energy by insisting that Brexit has never been given a fair chance. Former Foreign Secretary Boris Johnson originated this narrative, complaining that in the negotiations, Theresa May's Conservatives had been 'sending our vanguard into battle with the white flags fluttering above them'. That message was enthusiastically taken up by others better capable of speaking the language of the streets, with the *Daily Express* printing front-page stories warning 'Ignore the Will of the People at Your Peril' and Nigel Farage telling LBC that the hopes of Brexit were being betrayed.[62] The champions of British independence will fail, but they will not accept responsibility for their defeat. Instead, they will blame it on the leaders on their own side, justifying further cycles of national malaise and fantasies of rebirth.

Brexit, meanwhile, has taken on a meaning that is wider than events in Britain or the European Union. It has been seen internationally as a step away from free movement and from the politics of free trade. Long before the 2017 general election, Britain's departure from the EU had ceased to be a matter of purely domestic politics. The boost which Brexit has given to the international far right could be seen in the 2016 and 2017 elections in the United States and France.

CHAPTER FOUR

Remaking the G.O.P.

Five months after Britain's vote to leave the European Union, Donald Trump was elected President of the United States. In the days before the referendum, the pro-Trump website Breitbart published numerous updates on the British vote, reproducing Nigel Farage's articles for the British tabloids. On the news of the Leave victory, Donald Trump tweeted, 'Many people are equating Brexit and what is going on in Great Britain, with what is happening in the U.S. People want their country back!' Three days later he added, 'I called Brexit (Hillary was wrong), watch November.' Over the subsequent weeks, Trump insisted that he represented 'Brexit plus, plus, plus.' Within a week of appointing Steve Bannon as his campaign manager, Donald Trump invited Nigel Farage to join him in addressing a meeting in Jackson, Mississippi. Trump told his supporters, 'I was very supportive of their right to do it and to take control of their own future, like we're going to be voting for on November 8th. They voted to reclaim control over immigration, over their economy, over their government.' After the rally, Trump tweeted, 'They will soon be calling me Mr. Brexit.'[1]

In trying to make sense of Trump's rise and the success of the other right-wing authoritarians to whom he can be compared,[2] a language needs to be found which is capable of accurately describing the politics Trump represents. Two common ways of characterising the new right are as a 'populist' revolt against the establishment or as a proto-'fascism'. The first is one of the main terms used to describe Trump in the US press, the other has been a common approach among prominent Democrats and in the social movement. This chapter argues that these labels disguise the character of Trump's administration and should be rejected. Instead, he represents a convergence of Republican politics with those of the non-fascist far right. The same politics can be seen in his campaign for the White House and in his government.

What 'populism' illustrates and what it conceals

When people describe Trump as a populist they often mean to compare his politics to those of previous right-wing politicians such as Andrew Jackson, a general and slave plantation owner who founded the Democratic Party on its initial programme of the defence of slavery and whose campaign against the re-chartering of the Second Bank of the United States attacked financial monopoly.[3] Other populists to whom Trump is often compared include the Ku Klux Klan of the 1920s with its three million members;[4] or the 1968 campaigns of George Wallace, the Governor of Alabama, who had vowed during his 1963 inauguration address to uphold 'segregation now, segregation tomorrow, segregation forever'. Wallace stood for the Presidency as an Independent, receiving the endorsement of the Klan, of the white supremacist Citizens' Council and the John Birch Society. By destabilising the alliance between supporters of civil rights and Southern Democrats, Wallace opened up the way for the successful Republican 'Southern strategy' of Presidents Nixon and Reagan.[5]

The comparisons have not been foisted on the Trump campaign from without but reflect the way its protagonists have seen themselves. After the 2016 Presidential election, Trump's advisors gave him biographies of Andrew Jackson and supplied him with quotes from Jackson. These historical predecessors, in common with Trump, presented themselves as outsider movements of the dispossessed. Further, the appeal of such right-wing populism has long been racialised; Jackson, the Klan and Wallace all thrived on white fears of racial equality. In common with these populists, Trump does not just employ a rhetorical device of counterposing the people (who are pure) against the elite (who are corrupt), but goes further in the sense that, because the people are always by definition Trump supporters, he cannot comprehend the fact of opposition to him. Populism is always a paranoid way of doing politics, which pathologises its critics. Trump shares that hatred of being challenged.[6]

If it was just a matter of comparing Trump to these racial populists, the term might have some explanatory power. But any number of other traditions have also been called populist. Even if the term is limited to examples from the United States, the first self-declared populists in American history were the People's Party of the 1890s: reformers who fought for agricultural and urban labour and were influenced by Henry George and the women's suffrage campaign. These populists included some who were unwilling to change the racial hierarchies in the South. The movement also contained, in North Carolina, anti-racists who formed an alliance with anti-slavery parties. Populism of this sort lasted just a decade and its legacy is contested. It can just as well be seen as 'the first of the great American leftist movements', or as a more ambiguous form of politics, whose simplified and de-classed language of social change was capable of adoption by the right.[7] Its ideological descendants are the likes of Bruce Springsteen and Michael Moore rather than Donald Trump.

When writers call Trump a populist, they are often defining him according to his rejection of the Washington consensus on free trade. Such critics typically suggest that his closest ideological counterpart must be a left 'populist' such as Bernie Sanders, who is supposed to have given a cover to Trump's approach. This approach can be traced back to Hillary Clinton's Presidential campaign, which sought to neutralise its critics on the left, presenting them as misogynists ('Bernie bros') and closet Trump supporters.[8] This approach fails to understand how Trump won. Trump is the inheritor of all the bile that has accumulated in the United States' two-party system, with its intense party loyalism. Trump was elected by Republican voters. Despite the mainstream Republican Never Trump campaign – 90 per cent of registered Republicans who voted, voted for him. In his first year, the major piece of legislation which Trump pushed through Congress was a budget which reduced corporation tax from 35 to 20 per cent, the income tax of company owners from 40 to 25 per cent and took large swathes of the richest of Americans out of the inheritance tax system.[9] Trump is not outside normal politics. He was elected and has governed from the right.

The term populism has been used to describe anti-capitalist protests (such as Occupy Wall Street),[10] military rulers promoting developmental dictatorships (Hugo Chávez in Venezuela),[11] insurgent politicians of the far left who have chosen a 'Populist' as opposed to a 'Marxist' rhetoric (Podemos in Spain),[12] politicians seeking to shift rightwards a centre-right party (Sebastian Kurz in Austria);[13] anti-immigrant electoral parties (the Lega Nord in Italy),[14] and parties with fascist roots (the FN in France). These phenomena are so broad, the ties connecting them are so varied and imprecise, that they cannot meaningfully be encompassed within a single term.[15]

Why Trump is not a fascist

Similar caution also needs to be exercised in the face of the notion that Trump is a potential 'tyrant'[16] or that he points, in some other way, towards fascism.[17] The popularity of this idea could be seen in the success, in the midst of Trump's victory, of novels such as Margaret Attwood's *The Handmaid's Tale,* Herman Melville's *The Confidence-Man,* George Orwell's *1984,* Philip Roth's *The Plot Against America or* Sinclair Lewis's *It Can't Happen Here.* Lewis's novel portrays a President Buzz Windrip who attacks Mexicans and is helped by a Bannon-esque 'brain,' the 'editor of the most widely-circulated paper in all that part of the country,' Lee Sarason, who topples Windrip and becomes President following a coup of his own.[18] During the 2017 campaign, the idea that Trump was an autocrat underpinned Hillary Clinton's description of half of his supporters as 'a basket of deplorables ... racist, sexist, homophobic, xenophobic, Islamophobic, you name it.' After the election, other senior Democrats insisted on Trump's similarity to Mussolini, including Obama's former Vice President Joe Biden and Madeleine Albright, whose *Fascism: A Warning* described the interwar years as 'a wound from the past'. Allowing Trump into the White House, she insisted, was 'like ripping off the bandage and picking at the skin'.[19]

The British left-wing historians Neil Faulkner and Sam Dathi describe Trump as a 'creeping fascist.' In their model, the fascism of the past was a tool to destroy a rising socialist movement, its counterpart today arises out of the confidence of the right and the numerous defeats of the left. The US Marxist John Bellamy Foster has termed the Trump administration 'neo-fascist,' suggesting that its politics echo the elitism of the inter-war years. In the same piece of writing, however, Foster retreats from the analogy, saying that these are 'leanings', rather than outcomes and acknowledging that Trump lacks a key asset of the inter-war fascists, namely an organised militia of supporters willing to use violence against his opponents.[20]

One problem in making analogies with fascism is that it is the most loaded of terms, associated with different kinds of experience: with a political party characterised by top down leadership and a one-party state, with the suffering of millions of people, and with broader notions of intolerance. This is why those who moderate online discussions invented 'Godwin's law,' the maxim which provides that the longer an online discussion continues the greater the likelihood that one or another of the participants will compare someone to Hitler. The point of the rule is to warn people against hyperbole. Far too often, a comparison with fascism turns out to mean little more than 'I really, really, don't like X,' whatever X turns out to be.

Another difficulty, even with more accurate definitions of fascism, is that they presume that the horrors of the future are going to manifest the same forms as those of the past. The years since Hitler's suicide have seen capitalism transformed; democracy become normalised, first the establishment of welfare states and since 1979–80 the neoliberal politics of privatisation and tax breaks for the rich.

Many of the characteristics which are said to define fascism, for example, that it is a middle-class protest movement,[21] map awkwardly onto the present date. Part of Trump's base, as we shall see, has been a generation of underemployed male internet warriors around the website Breitbart. These young men ('Neets': not in Education, Employment or Training), are college-educated and compete for a shrinking number of professional jobs, often while depending on their parents to cover their student debts. The comparison with the social layers which populated interwar fascism is unconvincing. In Italy, Gramsci described how the Italian state was maintained at a local level by military bureaucrats chosen from a caste of wealthy landowners who had every good reason to fear for their privileges in the event of a Communist revolution;[22] while, in Germany, students, teachers and junior civil servants were also committed to maintaining their status difference from the mass factory working class. In both countries, the fascists found their first recruits among such layers, rather than industrial workers, who were immunised by a sub-culture of workers' clubs and socialist unions and newspapers. Everywhere in Europe, university students were a main social base of fascism.[23]

Eighty years later, the American state does not depend on the support of a caste of aristocrats. Nor could the left claim to have the same sustained link to the working class as it enjoyed prior to fascism. When groups such as students and teachers have appeared in large numbers in high-profile clashes such as at Charlottesville, they have been the base of the anti-Trump movement not of the right. The alt-right has attacked the universities, not because it expects to win new recruits there but in the same spirit that Italian fascism once attacked the socialists in their trade union halls – to intimidate its most resolute enemies in the spaces where they should feel strongest.

David Neiwert argues that there is a 'significant resemblance between Trump's ascendance and that of previous fascist figures,' accusing Trump of using an 'eliminationist' rhetoric in relation to migrants from Mexico. Neiwert cites Trump's first campaign speech, where Trump declared, 'When Mexico sends its people, they're not sending their best ... They're bringing drugs. They're bringing crime. They're rapists.'[24] Yet this was not the first instance of a Presidential candidate appealing to racist voters in a recent American election. In 1980, Ronald Reagan began his presidential campaign in Neshoba, Mississippi, a town where three civil rights workers had been murdered in 1964; Reagan spoke in defence of 'state's rights,' in other words the mechanisms by which white ascendancy had been maintained in the US South by poll taxes and other laws preventing black citizens from voting. In 1988, George H. W. Bush ran for Presidency claiming that his opponent Michael Dukakis had allowed a black murderer Willie Horton out of prison, enabling Horton to rape a white woman. In 1992, Bill Clinton returned from campaigning in order to oversee the execution of a lobotomised murderer Ricky Ray Rector who was black. Both the main parties have a long record of treating black people, Mexicans and other racial outsiders as criminals and rapists.[25] The 2016 presidential campaign was continuous with these precedents. Trump's racism is not a break with the racism of ordinary US politics; to understand it, there is no need to invoke the ghosts of 80 years ago.

In 2016, Donald Trump differed from his rivals in the consistency with which he argued for the extension of the wall excluding Mexicans from entering the United States. But the logic of the proposal needs to be set in the context of both of the main parties' hostility to migrants. There was, even before he stood, a 700-mile border wall between the US and Mexico.[26] The purpose of extending the wall was to act as a symbolic warning to those who were allowed in, requiring them to accept their permanent subordination, compared to white workers.

Trump's plans to extend the border wall[27] were, in other words, little different in spirit from the laws brought in under Britain's Conservative government, which have introduced fees for migrants' healthcare, converted hundreds of thousands of public sector workers into part-time immigration police, and offered illegal migrants ultimately the same choice as in the US between leaving the country and losing their children.[28] They show a close resemblance also to the idea of 'national preference,' as proposed by the FN in France, which proposes to limit social benefits to white citizens and to make life unpleasant for Muslims who are to have an inferior choice of jobs, housing and so on. These are plans for subordination, not elimination.

Moreover, the core of the fascist project is not racism as such, but the goal of destroying the existing state and replacing it with a new one, without political or social democracy, and to defeat forever any possibility of capitalism giving rise to a more equal social order. This is a project which requires very high levels of political violence, to discipline its political and racial opponents. Within six months of coming to power in Germany, Hitler had banned both Communists and Socialists and taken the German unions under state control. Tens of thousands of his opponents were imprisoned. Under Mussolini the same processes took place more slowly but nonetheless were complete within three years of the fascists joining the government. By contrast, Trump has not jailed his opponents, and below the top level of senior political appointees (which, in every US administration, unlike Britain or Europe, are in the control of the incoming President) there has been no attempt to purge the state. Trump's threats of violence against his opponents, while novel and shocking, remain rhetorical.

To insist that Trump is no fascist is not to prettify his record. It is simply to insist on using language accurately. He is not the final evil that this generation of voters will face and it is important to be consistent in characterising both Trump and those who will follow him. The space discovered by Trump was not fascist, nor even proto-fascist. He was and is a Republican politician working with forces to his right, in particular with a far-right audience that he first courted in 2011, in promoting the conspiracy theory that Barack Obama was a Kenyan-born Muslim.

Trump, the Birther

Trump's decision in summer 2015 to run for the Presidency was the third time he had stood. The first came in winter 1999–2000, when he ran for nomination to be the Reform Party candidate for President. Trump's entrance into the campaign coincided with that of former Republican Pat Buchanan and they competed against each other in two primaries. What is striking, in retrospect, is the vehemence with which Trump denounced Buchanan, previously Reagan's Director of Communications, and a former candidate (1992 and 1996) for the Republican nomination to the Presidency. Buchanan's 1999 book, *A Republic, Not an Empire*, sought to rescue the reputation of Charles Lindbergh and other campaigners who had opposed the US entrance into the Second World War. Pat Buchanan blamed the war on Britain, France and the US, calling Britain's decision to go to war with Hitler 'the greatest blunder of the century'.[29] Trump condemned Buchanan, calling him 'a Hitler lover ... an anti-Semite. He doesn't like the blacks, he doesn't like the gays. It's just incredible that anybody could embrace this guy and maybe he'll get four or five per cent of the vote and it'll be a really staunch-right wacko vote.' After quitting the Reform race, Trump attacked 'the fringe element that wanted to repeal the federal income tax, [or] believed that the country was being run by ... a Swiss-Zionist conspiracy to control America.'[30]

Donald Trump's second run at the Presidency began in March 2011, when he appeared on *Good Morning America*, saying that he did not believe that President Obama was an American citizen. He was later interviewed on ABC's *The View* where Trump claimed that Obama was Kenyan. 'There's something on his birth certificate that he doesn't like,' Trump said. 'Maybe it says he's a Muslim.'[31] If the story had been true, it would have been incendiary. Under the American constitution, only natural-born citizens of the United States are eligible to stand for the Presidency. If Obama was not American, then his right-wing opponents would have the option of removing him from office through impeachment proceedings, and without having to challenge him in a second election which Obama might win. Over the next weeks, Trump maintained the allegation on NBC and elsewhere. On 30 March 2011, he claimed that Obama 'doesn't have a birth certificate or if he does, there's something on that certificate that's very bad for him.' On 7 April, he described Obama as a foreigner and 'one of the greatest cons in the history of politics'.[32] The story dominated the American news for weeks, before finally being shown to be without foundation at the end of April 2011 when Hawaii released a copy of the President's long-form birth certificate.

Until Trump's intervention, the 'birther' movement was a subset of the far right. Other prominent birthers included Joe Arpaio the Arizona sheriff who was later sentenced to six months imprisonment after repeatedly breaching a federal court order requiring him to cease a long-term campaign of harassment against Hispanic youth in his district; Andy Martin, who had run for the Florida Congress in 1986 with a campaign Committee titled, 'the Anthony R. Martin-Trigona Congressional Campaign to Exterminate Jew Power in America'; and Orly Taitz, whose other campaigns had included protests against US voting machines which she said were controlled by the Venezuelan military and against Congress which she maintained had built six labour camps for dissidents such as herself.[33]

Donald Trump's move was not just a pitch to those tens of millions of white Americans who disliked the idea of a black President. Nor was it just an attempt to exaggerate the President's racial otherness, by making him both black and a Muslim, at a time when Muslims were the country's most reviled racial minority. It was also a decision to build a Presidential campaign on the support of the hundreds of thousands of voters for whom the world was run by shadowy conspiracies.

What happened between Trump's attack on Buchanan in 2000 and Trump's own adoption of birther theories in 2011, causing Trump to woo voters who he had previously described as 'wacko' was the rise of the Tea Party, which in November 2010 won a series of victories in Congressional elections.[34] Its success persuaded Trump that the next Republican nominee would come from the party's far right.

The Tea Party began as a movement of those trying to resist Barack Obama's victory in the 2008 election, motivated in part by a belief in the sacred position of the Presidency in American life, and driven also by a range of intense feelings to the effect that Barack Obama was an illegitimate President, either because he was a secret Socialist or Communist, or because of his race.[35] The Tea Party movement was also funded by various plutocrats for whom it was a ramp of Republican voters, who could be mobilised to demand lighter labour or environmental regulation and decreased taxes. The Tea Party drew on conspiracy theories, for example that the Federal Reserve Bank was engaged in a treasonous war on American patriots.

The Tea Party refused to concede defeats on the terrain of culture or religion even once it had become clear a majority of Americans would never share its opposition to abortion or to gay marriage. In contrast to previous Republicans, the Tea Party was more than willing to risk economic instability, as during the argument over the debt ceiling which led to the 2013 federal shutdown.[36]

Over time, the Tea Party's central message was no longer about Obama himself but about what the sociologist Arlie Russell Hochschild calls 'line-cutters':

> You are patiently standing in a long line leading up a hill, as in a pilgrimage. You are situated in the middle of this line, along with others who are also white, older, Christian and predominantly male, some with college degrees, some not.

Just over the brow of the hill is the American Dream.

Look! You see people cutting in the line ahead of you. You're following the rules. They aren't. As they cut in, it feels like you are being moved back.[37]

Hochschild wrote this narrative with the hope that those she was describing would find it an accurate account of their own world view and some of the most powerful parts of her book *Strangers in Their Own Land* record Tea Party supporters' engagement with it. In order not to labour the point, she kept their prejudice implied. But the mindset which she was describing was a racist perspective: those who viewed the line-cutters were white and those they criticised were black or Hispanic.

Donald Trump's 2011 candidacy met little resistance from senior Republicans. Rather than criticise Trump for wooing the far right, senior Republicans welcomed him. Reince Priebus, then chairman of the Republican National Committee, was asked what he made of 'the birther debate'. 'I think all these guys are credible,' he answered. 'Obviously, people are going to have different opinions. And you know you're going to have a lot of different candidates … having a diversity of opinion is fine.'[38] Later, Mitt Romney allowed himself to be photographed receiving Trump's endorsement for his nomination campaign. Speaking from a gold-painted Trump lectern, Romney praised Trump for 'an extraordinary ability to understand how our economy works and to create jobs' and for being 'one of the few who has stood up to say China is cheating' in international trade. Afterwards, Trump boasted to journalists about Romney's weakness and relative poverty, boasting, 'I have a Gucci store that's worth more than

Romney.'[39] On the occasions in 2016 when Romney declared his opposition to Trump's candidacy, journalists took pleasure in reminding their readers of his meeting with Trump and the pair's previous alliance.

Breitbart and convergence

In the run-up to 2016, Trump's main way of keeping himself in consideration as a future Republican candidate was to give interviews to right-wing websites. The most important of these was Breitbart News, which had been launched in 2009 by Andrew Breitbart, a former staffer at the *Drudge Report* and *Huffington Post*. Breitbart's 2011 memoir, *Righteous Indignation*, includes amongst other things a compendious account of the machinations of the 'cultural Marxist' left, in which Andrew Breitbart includes Marx, Gramsci, Lukács, the members of the Frankfurt school and their ideological descendants: the majority of directors and actors in modern-day Hollywood. *Righteous Indignation* ends with the Tea Party's success in the 2010 elections, a victory which Breitbart claimed was his sole work, and a prediction that the Tea Party was about to score some unexplained but lasting political victory.[40]

Trump himself was not mentioned in Breitbart's book, and there is little evidence of a relationship between him and Andrew Breitbart prior to the latter's death in March 2012. In winter 2013–14, Breitbart's new Chief Executive, Steve Bannon, was looking to open up offices in London, California and Jerusalem and seeking to recruit additional staff.[41] Not long afterwards, media websites began to speak of a relationship between Breitbart and Trump, with industry insiders referring to the website in February 2014 as 'Trump's PR firm,' after Breitbart was used to run hit pieces against a journalist McKay Coppins who had criticised Trump. Bannon's new funds enabled Breitbart to grow. Between February and August 2014, it rose from the 49th best-read news website in the US, to 27th in the US internet news rankings, with 3 per cent of American web users finding their news there.[42]

Crucial to Breitbart's growth was the part played by one of its journalists Milo Yiannopoulos, hired by Breitbart as a tech editor with the 2014 funds. This was a more significant appointment than it perhaps sounds. Steve Bannon, Breitbart's executive chair, had, in 2005, worked for the video company behind the game *World of Warcraft* and in 2006 persuaded Goldman Sachs to buy that game, leaving Bannon with a lasting fascination in the way that millions of smart, affluent young men dedicate their lives to gaming.[43] In due course Yiannopoulos was involved in two stories which would make Breitbart infamous. The first was Gamergate, the second was an attempt two years later to sanitise the far right before a mainstream audience.

Gamergate began in August 2014, when Eron Gjoni, a former boyfriend of the game designer Zoë Quinn published a 9,000 word piece online blaming Quinn for the breakdown of their relationship, accusing her of having cheated on him and saying that her game *Depression Quest* had succeeded only because she had slept with a journalist, Nathan Grayson who had positively reviewed it. Within days, other gamers were posting about Gjoni's allegations on sites including 4chan and reddit and tweeting about it at the rate of up to 50,000 tweets per day, with almost all of the tweets being sent from new and anonymous accounts.[44] Their anonymity made it impossible to trace the multiple threats of rape or murder that were being directed against Quinn.

Even while the Gamergaters contacted Quinn's father, school friends and former employers, attempted to investigate her and Grayson's financial circumstances and threatened her; they also insisted that theirs was a moral crusade whose sole business was to purge the industry of its moralistic excesses. The Gamergaters' key assertion was that Quinn had been using sexual favours to secure favourable reviews of her work. But Grayson had never reviewed any of her games.[45]

The campaign soon moved on to other women working in the games industry, including Brianna Wu, who received death threats with the name of her partner and threats that the Gamergaters knew her home address.[46]

The one major news outlet to take the side of the Gamergaters was Breitbart. Its tech editor Yiannopoulos described Quinn as 'unpleasant and manipulative'. He criticised her for approaching the sites which hosted threats of violence against her and asking for the threats to be taken down, accusing her of 'leverag[ing] friendships' to censor legitimate comment. He repeated the Gamergaters' central accusation which even Yiannopoulos, a man not unacquainted with Google's search facility, must have known to be false: that Grayson had reviewed Quinn and been 'rewarded with sexual favours for promoting substandard work'. He minimised the death threats Quinn, Wu and others had received, saying they were 'injudicious responses from bewildered men'. He said the women were 'pathetic' for complaining, writing that 'an army of sociopathic feminist programmers and campaigners, abetted by achingly politically correct American tech bloggers, are terrorising the entire community – lying, bullying and manipulating their way around the internet for profit and attention.'[47]

Yiannopoulos' message, that the people who had baited Quinn were being silenced, was a success with its intended audience of bored and disaffected middle-class men. Yiannopoulos appealed to a student demographic.[48] In an America characterised by massive personal indebtedness, a shrinking public sector and diminished employment opportunities for everyone save for the rich and their children,[49] there are any number of disappointed people who can vacillate between blaming themselves for the crisis and blaming blacks, feminists or liberals. It is an audience which has some similarity to that of social justice organising, with the result that the battles between left and right can feel at times like a quarrel between members of the same family. Gamergate began with a relationship breakdown; Eron Gjoni even claimed that Zoë Quinn's activism had been part of her attraction to him.[50] But the post-2008 crisis plays out in different ways for men and women. As the number of middle-class jobs in the public sector have shrunk and their pay and status has fallen, they have become identified as women's work. These are low-reward but stable futures. In the new dispensation, middle-class men can aim for better-paid private sector jobs (but the failure rate is high) or reconcile themselves to working in the women-dominated public sector (which offends their masculinity) or settle for parental dependence, debt and long-term unemployment. This sense of male discontent helps to explain why of all the social factors which indicate whether white men are likely to identify with supremacist views, the one which bears the strongest correlation is not income, age, religion, or party identification but divorce. Yiannopoulos played up to these dynamics, for example by setting up an educational charity (the 'Privilege Fund') to support the university careers of white men.[51]

Central to Yiannopoulos's appeal was his seeming non-conformity. His was a capture the flag exercise, fronted by a gay man who might have been expected to side with the metropolitan wing of America's cultural wars but was declaring instead his support for Breitbart, 'Daddy' Trump and their allies to the right. The new cultural far right which he embodied did not share the values of the older generation and has been hostile to their caution, their Christianity and their conservatism.[52]

Yiannopoulos's support for Gamergate won a larger online audience for Breitbart. Between August 2014 and June 2015, that is, during the height of the Gamergate controversy and prior to the launch of Trump's election campaign, Breitbart's share of the American news audience increased from 3 to 6 per cent. By itself, this milieu could not have been large enough to win any candidate the election. It was, however, large enough to make Breitbart appear relevant and new.[53]

In spring 2016, Bannon commissioned a further article from Milo Yiannopoulos, 'An Establishment Conservative's Guide to the Alt-Right.' For the piece, Yiannopoulos contacted the neo-reactionary Curtis Yarvin and quoted Andrew Auernheimer ('Weev') of the *Daily Stormer*. Multiple drafts were sent for comments to Devin Saucier, a self-declared White Nationalist, who runs the American Renaissance website. At around the same time, Yiannopoulos was filmed singing America the Beautiful to an audience of white race supremacists including the alt-right's Richard Spencer while these fans waved Nazi salutes back at him.[54]

Trump and America First

If Trump had offered voters nothing more than verbal attacks against Mexicans and Muslims, threats to use torture against terror suspects and promises to stand firm against abortion, his novelty would have been limited. On many of these policies, his position was indistinguishable from other Republican candidates. Trump's selling point was that he combined these demands with a message that the success of Wall Street, Goldman Sachs and free trade had left millions of Americans poorer:

> Globalization has made the financial elite who donate to politicians very wealthy. But it has left millions of our workers with nothing but poverty and heartache. When subsidized foreign steel is dumped into our markets, threatening our factories, the politicians do nothing. For years, they watched on the sidelines as our jobs vanished and our communities were plunged into depression-level unemployment. Many of these areas have still never recovered.[55]

This was not the politics of the Bush administrations; nor of the likes of Mitt Romney or Ted Cruz. It sounded much closer to the sorts of 'Buy America' politics with which employers have since the 1970s and 1980s sought to engage such previously militant unions as the United Auto Workers or the International Ladies' Garment Workers' Union. It was a message which resonated with some groups of workers including in America's car factories, whose union reps reported a sharp rise in racist incidents in 2016–17, and among industrial unions including the United Steelworkers.[56]

The idea behind 'America First,' as Trump explained it, was that the American nation was in retreat. The police were under attack (assaults on police officers have in fact fallen by two thirds in the last 40 years)[57] and US cities are prey to terrorism. The borders of the US allowed rapists to cross without hindrance. Underlying all these problems was a crisis of American capitalism. Restoring the hegemony that America had enjoyed in the 1950s would require trade wars with other countries. By voting for him, workers would guarantee an improvement to their living standards.

Trump's success in the electoral college was enabled by victories in Wisconsin, Michigan and Pennsylvania, three states that had not voted Republican in any Presidential election since at least 1992. In each of these states, union density was declining, including by 6.9 per cent in Wisconsin from 2008 to 2016, faster than any other state in the US.[58] The reason union membership was falling faster in Wisconsin than elsewhere else was that in 2011 Scott Walker, the Republican governor and local representative of Charles and David Koch, two 'libertarian' oil billionaires who have donated over $700 million to fund Republican and right-of-Republican causes,[59] introduced laws removing public sector unions' ability to bargain over pensions and health care and removing automatic check-off of union subscriptions. Walker's attack was opposed by demonstrations of up to 100,000 people and an occupation of the Wisconsin State Capitol. Democrats won an argument, however, that Walker could best be defeated by a recall election. A fresh vote for state governor followed in 2012, with the Democrats managing to nominate a candidate Tom Barrett who would not even promise to repeal Walker's legislation. Barrett lost the election and it was in that context, of a long, slow, but continuous assault on labour, that Trump won Wisconsin; against an ill-led defeated and demoralised opposition.[60]

In a single episode, Wisconsin summarises a whole period of asymmetric polarisation.[61] In other words, the wealthiest Americans and the Republicans have been moving to the right on both economic and cultural issues. The Democrats have moved to the left on some cultural issues but for several decades (and save for the Sanders insurgency) have vacated the terrain of economics to the right. The result is an unequal fight which the Republicans have most often won; and in which politics has been pulled onto their preferred terrain. Even when Democratic candidates have won elections, they have not reversed US politics' long drift to the right.

In speaking of America First, Trump managed to convey a greater interest in workers than either Hillary Clinton or his Republican rivals. The effects of this process are hard to monitor, however, because of the methodological poverty of political research in the US, which barely attempts to measure class except through proxy data. Journalists noted that from the start of his candidacy, Trump polled well among voters who had left school without attending college. By the time of the election, Trump had a strong lead among voters who reported that their finances had deteriorated under Obama, four-fifths of whom went on to vote for Trump.[62]

The message of the liberal press, after Trump's victory was that millions of working-class voters in districts such as Wisconsin or Michigan had switched to Trump, winning the election in his favour. The truth was less dramatic. Trump did better than Clinton among voters without a college degree; yet in the United States, as in Britain and the rest of Europe, the number of 18–21-year-olds attending college has risen over the past four decades. The sheer fact of a degree represents much less of a workplace advantage than it once did. A large number of low-paid occupations which did not previously require a degree now do. When college-educated workers in their mid-20s are compared to their predecessors of 40 years ago, the workers of today have a lower likelihood of owning their own home, increased debts, worse pension rights and a lower standard of living. Progress in the workplace is determined more than anything else by the advantages which rich parents are able to pass on to their children. Compared to that, educational achievement is a minor factor. Most supervisors and most managers do not have a degree.[63] Trump's lead among voters who left education earlier, it follows, is a marker of two processes working in combination, age and class, rather than the simple proxy for class which it is often assumed to be.

The median income of Trump supporters was higher than the median income of Clinton voters. Trump outperformed Clinton among voters earning over \$100,000 per year, but lost to her among voters earning less than \$50,000 per year.[64] Compared to the previous Republic candidate, Mitt Romney, in 2012, Trump won just 335,000 extra votes among voters earning \$50,000 per year in Iowa, Michigan, Ohio, Pennsylvania or Wisconsin. This was not the millions-strong army of poor and working-class white voters on which the liberal press has fixated.

The greater shift was on the other side. Among poorer voters in these four states and compared to Obama in 2012, Clinton lost 1.7 million supporters who did not vote. These states were subject to sustained disenfranchisement campaigns. The number of polling stations was reduced, voting hours were cut and voter-identity laws were introduced, to reduce black voting.[65] Yet these processes are not sufficient to account for the extent to which the Democrats lost support in industrial districts.

In theory, Clinton's campaign offered workers more than Trump's: an increase to $15/hr of the minimum wage (although this figure was to be reached only 'over time'), the restoration of collective bargaining rights for unions (how far they would be restored was never specified) and of some welfare benefits (although not to the level they had been prior to 1993 when Bill Clinton was elected). But politics is more than a comparison of programmes; it is also about which groups a candidate is seen to prioritise and about the memories that a candidate brings with them.

At a time when Obamacare was suffering, with major insurers pulling out, Clinton refused to endorse any more radical package than the status quo, in particular opposing single payer healthcare. The Democratic candidate also opposed proposals to restore the Glass-Steagall Act, which had once separated investment banks from commercial banks and would have limited to some extent the chances of a return of the 2008 crisis. She suffered from the legacy of her husband's first administration and the role that she personally had played in 1996 in persuading the Democrats to adopt cuts to social welfare, which capped the period for which anyone could receive benefits to a lifetime maximum of five years and restricted the benefit entitlement of even legal migrants to the US.[66] Long ago, Clinton had persuaded millions of working class voters that she offered nothing to them.[67] It was this seeming indifference, combined with Trump's hostility to globalisation which dissuaded enough former Democrats from voting and in that way secured the Presidency for him.

The GOP loses control (again)

During 2016 numerous leading Republicans attempted to isolate Trump, in the hope that a more moderate right-wing candidate might emerge. Three conservative magazines, the *Weekly Standard, National Review* and *Commentary,* opposed Trump. A campaign (Delegates Unbound) was launched, to persuade Republicans at their National Convention that, however they had been mandated, they could still vote against Trump for the nomination. Such high-profile Republicans as Senators John McCain and Ben Sasse refused to endorse him. The previous Republican candidate Mitt Romney warned against Trump's bankruptcies, his 'personal qualities, the bullying, the greed, the showing off, the misogyny, the absurd third-grade theatrics.' Former President George W. Bush told friends he would not vote at all; while George H. W. Bush appears to have voted for Clinton. The Republican political action committees Our Principles and Club for Growth spent $20 million on anti-Trump Republicans.[68]

The campaign against Trump failed to motivate Republican voters, who saw their leadership as having failed over the past decade to implement causes the dearest to conservatives, not least the abolition of President Obama's health care policies, which had been, in their eyes, the key task facing the Congress after 2008. For several years, polls had found that Republican voters were to the left of their leaders on economics, with around three-fifths of the former demanding increased spending on social security. This led them to vote for the sole candidate offering both entitlements for US nationals and immigration control. Explanations for the failure of the Republican anti-Trump campaign have tended to focus on Trump's profile, his platform on the David Letterman and Howard Stern shows and as the star of *The Apprentice,* the way the media reported his every utterance, providing him with free publicity, and the desire of his supporters and many Americans for change. Eight months before the election, a prominent Democrat Michael Cooper predicted Donald Trump's victory, writing in *US News* that, Trump's supporters 'realize he's a joke. They do not care. They know he's authoritarian, nationalist, almost un-American and they love him anyway, because he disrupts a broken political process and beats establishment candidates who've long ignored their interests.'[69]

Yet if Trump is perceived as a 'change' candidate, it was not obvious in advance that such a figure would emerge from within the Republican Party rather than through, say, the Reform Party. Part of the context is that the obstacles to viable third parties are higher in the US than anywhere in Europe. The most important obstacle is money. In American elections, the prospects of the candidate who spends the most are unusually high. In Congressional contests in 2016, 96 per cent of contests for seats in the House of Representatives were won by the candidate with the largest budget, as did 94 per cent of campaigns for the Senate. For that reason, both parties raised funds at a rate unimaginable in most other countries. A little over $6 billion was spent in 2016 by Congressional or Presidential candidates, at an average of a little more than $10 million per seat. By way of contrast, this is over 100 times more than the average amount spent per candidate in the UK's 2017 general election.[70]

Elections in the United States also take place on a first past the post system, with no proportional element and this penalises third-party candidates. In addition, to be on the ballot in California in 2016, a candidate needed the support of over 170,000 names on a petition, 120,000 in Florida, just under 100,000 in North Carolina and Texas, and so on. To stand in every state in 2016, a candidate needed just under a million signatures; a viable task for an existing organisation, almost impossible for an outsider party. Most US states require parties to gather signatures at a rate equivalent to 1 per cent of those who voted in the previous Presidential election but by all international standards this is an exceptional requirement. Illinois sets the bar even higher, requiring support equivalent to 3 per cent of voters.[71] Since George Wallace in 1968, no third party candidate has secured enough votes to be entitled to even a single vote from the electoral college that chooses the President.

While the American political system makes successful third party candidates rare, the two main parties are also much more permeable by candidates from outside (provided, of course, that they are millionaires). Indeed in 2016 it became clear that the Republican Party was even more open to such a move than the Democrats.

In the 2016 elections there were 'change' candidates on both sides: Bernie Sanders and Donald Trump. The former secured the support of 13 million voters, attacked Wall Street and despite raising almost no campaign contributions from business, won 46 per cent of the delegates from primary elections and caucuses. Yet, of the two gatekeeping apparatuses, the Democrats' proved more successful. Hillary Clinton was able to draw on her husband's two successful contests for the Presidency as well as her own previous attempt in 2008; a supportive think tank (the Centre for American Progress) and an international campaign (the Clinton Foundation). She was supported by unions, women's and LGBT campaigns, and dozens of newspapers. She had the support of the Democratic National Committee, the Democrats' leadership between elections, which would have supported her on ideological grounds, even if it were not for the DNC's financial dependency on funds given to it by her campaign. She also received the support from the Democrat's 400 unelected 'super-delegates,' senior Democrats who agreed to vote for Clinton irrespective of Sanders support in their own states and whose willingness to vote for her was leaked to the press, seemingly to demoralise Sanders supporters and force him to concede.[72]

The story of the elections was the much greater success of the Clinton camp in keeping hold of the Democratic Party than of Romney or the Bushes on the other side. 'Incredible though it may seem,' one *Jacobin* commentator observed, the US's political system is 'better girded against a soft left than a hard right'.[73]

By the end of 2017, the Republican Party at a local level was far to the right of where it had been ten or 20 years before. Between 2011 and 2016 Republicans in Congress voted down over 100 proposals for federal gun control, while their counterparts in state legislatures passed similar numbers of laws actually liberalising access to guns.[74] Even before the announcement of Trump's candidacy in 2015, ten state legislatures had passed laws banning 'Sharia law'. What was being criminalised was the use by US Muslims of any Islamic concepts, for example where parents sought to negotiate where children would live following a marriage breakdown.

Because of the long Republican move rightwards, when Donald Trump challenged for the nomination he was not alone in arguing for policies somewhere between conservatism and the far right. During the campaign Ben Carson argued that Islam had to be opposed in all circumstances. He insisted that Muslims and the US were in a 'civilizational jihad'. Chris Christie said that the waterboarding of Muslim detainees was not torture and that, as President, he would use it. Jeb Bush also refused to rule waterboarding out. Marco Rubio sought to position himself as more anti-Muslim than Trump, so that when the latter argued that the state should spy on mosques, Rubio responded that surveillance should be extended to cafes, diners and internet sites.[75] Ben Carson stated that he believed neither in evolution, nor climate change. Marco Rubio insisted that abortion should be unlawful even in cases of rape or incest. Meanwhile Ted Cruz claimed that the United Nations was engaged in a war to impose global Communism through environmental standards, 'Agenda 21'.[76]

Jobs for the boys

Having won the Republican nomination in summer 2016, Trump focused on his Democratic rivals, 'Crazy Bernie' and 'Crooked Hillary', declaring the latter a 'criminal' and insisting that she 'has to go to jail'. Supported by such online vendors of far-right merchandise as Alex Jones of InfoWars (on whose show Donald Trump had been a guest in late 2015), Trump led his supporters in chanting, 'Lock her up.'[77] Trump encouraged violence against protesters: telling supporters in Iowa, 'If you see somebody getting ready to throw a tomato, knock the crap out of them would ya?'; in Nevada, 'I love the old days. You know what they used to do to guys like that when they were in a place like this? They'd be carried out on a stretcher, folks;' and in Michigan, 'We had four guys, they jumped on him, they were swinging and swinging. The next day we got killed in the press – that we were too rough. Give me a break.'[78]

Trump's promises of violence against Clinton had a misogynistic element, which became even clearer at the start of October 2016, when tapes were released in which he was heard boasting to Billy Bush of sexual violence against women, 'When you're a star they let you do it … Grab them by the pussy. You can do anything'.[79]

The idea that a country, that a democratic state, could be led by a president who boasts of his participation in sexual violence against women is so unpleasant, and the remarks were so awful, that it seemed almost inevitable that Trump would go on to lose. The problem with this assumption is that it underestimated the capacity, in a moment of convergence between the right and the far right, for Republican voters to accept sexist and misogynist excuses for his behaviour.

Richard Spencer rallied to Trump's defence, insisting that men were by definition incapable of sexual violence. Women, he insisted, always consented. 'At some part of every woman's soul,' he said, 'they want to be taken by a strong man.' Alex Jones of Info Wars concurred, saying that 'A woman climbing on top of you is not sexual assault; that's what mammals do.' For Breitbart's Milo Yiannopoulos, Trump's involvement in sexual harassment was precisely a reason to support him, 'He'd rather grab a pussy than be one.'[80]

Few of the far right's Republican allies were willing to go quite so far in arguing that women always, because they are women, agree to be attacked. The more typical approach was to try to pass off the comments as banter. Corey Lewandowski said that his former boss had been talking in the way that 'people talk around their dining room table'. Another Fox journalist Bill O'Reilly said the Republican's comments had been nothing more than 'crude guy talk'. Stacy Washington blamed the remarks on what she said were the crimes of liberal media, hip-hop and Hollywood, insisting that these institutions, not Trump, were responsible for coarsening American manners.[81]

A number of Republicans called on Trump to quit the race, including Senators John McCain and John Thune and Republican National Committee chair Reince Priebus. His poll ratings were so low that defeat seemed inevitable. Behind the scenes, however, Trump was buoyed by a wave of financial support with last-minute donations from the super rich coming in much faster even than at the same stage in Mitt Romney's unsuccessful race for the Presidency in 2012.[82]

The final period of campaigning also saw a reshaping of Trump's campaign team. In August 2016, on the advice of the hedge fund billionaire Rebekah Mercer,[83] Trump dismissed his campaign chair Paul Manafort and replaced him with Steve Bannon. A '*de facto* merger between Breitbart and the Trump Campaign represents a landmark achievement for the Alt-Right,' Hillary Clinton complained, 'a fringe element has effectively taken over the Republican Party.'[84]

This move explains the authority which Steve Bannon enjoyed at the start of Trump's administration. He was, as far as millions of voters were concerned, a dangerous plotter whose website Breitbart had published any number of paranoid and racist articles from Gamergate onwards. From the perspective of Donald Trump, however, Bannon was the link to the Breitbart audience which had converted him from a real estate and TV celebrity into a political leader. It was Bannon who led the Trump campaign from its crisis in August to victory three months later.

Within a week of Trump's election as President, the majority of Trump's Republican critics had made their peace with his administration. Lindsey Graham who had described Trump as a 'race-baiting bigot' prior to the vote announced afterwards that Trump in fact wanted 'to bring us together' and there were similar post-election concessions by Ted Cruz, Ben Sasse and Mitt Romney.[85] Since then, parts of the Trump administration have pushed him to govern like a conventional Republican politician, in line with the Reagan-Bush programme of tax cuts for the rich, free trade and spending increases for the military. During the election, Trump had denounced the financiers of Goldman Sachs. After his victory, they were given key posts in the administration: Steve Mnuchin as Secretary of the Treasury, Gary Cohn as head of Trump's Economic Council. Trump had promised to repudiate the North Atlantic Free Trade Agreement immediately. Instead, he left the pact in place. He had promised to withdraw troops from Afghanistan; when in power, he left them where they were. Rather than dealing with the rich, Trump appointed to his Cabinet billionaires Betsy DeVos (inheritor of the Amway company, a company which makes its millions by a pyramid scheme in which self-employed vendors are required to buy vast quantities of nutrients before selling them on, often to family or friends) and Wilbur Ross (a specialist in acquiring insolvent manufacturing and steel companies and selling their land and other assets at a discount). Trump's administration was the wealthiest in US history.[86]

Supporters of the far right were given positions in his government: Steve Bannon as White House Chief Strategist,

Sebastian Gorka, the former Breitbart associate who had championed the anti-semitic Hungarian Guard, as Deputy Assistant to the President,[87] and Stephen Miller as National Policy Director. They were able to influence policies adopted in the first weeks of the administration, including the ban on visas of any kind for visitors from seven countries with Muslim populations and the decision to remove from the White House website any reference to global warming.

One way to understand Trump's administration, at least in its first eight months, is to imagine Trump within a triangle. At one vertex was Trump's family, in particular his daughter Ivanka Trump and her husband Jared Kushner. At a second point was Trump's chief of staff Reince Priebus, the link to the Republican party. At the third was Steve Bannon. Trump moved between these groups, preventing each from obtaining an ascendancy. The advantage held by Bannon was his ideological conviction. He had a vision of Trump's Presidency which accorded with Trump's own sense that the election represented a popular insurgency.[88]

The influence of Steve Bannon could be seen and heard in Donald Trump's inauguration speech, which described America as in a state of 'carnage': and painted a bleak picture of 'mothers and children trapped in poverty in our inner cities; rusted-out factories scattered like tombstones across the landscape of our nation; an education system, flush with cash, which leaves our young and beautiful students deprived of knowledge.' The United States would be reborn under Trump's government through 'a great national effort to rebuild our country,' with the inauguration being 'the day the people became the rulers of this nation again.'[89]

The numbers attending Trump's inauguration were less than for Obama's 2009 and 2013 celebrations. In the days that followed, with the President exaggerating the attendance numbers and his Press Secretary Sean Spicer insisting that the ceremony has seen 'the largest audience to ever witness an inauguration,' another spokeswoman for the regime Kellyanne Conway defended Spicer saying that he had given 'alternative facts'. This phrase seemed to encompass a whole period of mendacious campaigning, going back to 2011. Time and again, Trump had lied. He should have been punished for his deceit; instead he was now the President.

On 27 January 2017, the new administration introduced an executive order banning immigration to the US from Syria, Libya, Iran, Iraq, Sudan, Yemen and Somalia. To defend the move, Trump's representatives spoke of terror attacks at 'Bowling Green' and at 'Atlanta,' which were said to have been Muslim-inspired. No such attacks had ever taken place, they belonged to the regime's imagination. The ban led to protests at numerous airports and sustained public opposition.[90]

In July 2017, Donald Trump addressed supporters of Poland's Law and Justice government in Warsaw. He positioned himself as their American friend, endorsing the party's message that the survival of Poland and the West were under threat from the rise of Islam. 'A strong Poland,' Trump said, 'is a blessing to the nations of Europe … A strong Europe is a blessing to the West and to the world … The fundamental question of our time is whether the West has the will to survive.'[91]

Trump's allies take to the streets

The risk that convergence could enable the far right to take to the streets is illustrated by events at Charlottesville on 11 and 12 August 2017. For 18 months the city had been discussing a proposal originating with a campaign by a school student Zyahna Bryant, for the city to remove the statue of Confederate General Robert E. Lee from the Lee Park. In March 2016, that campaign was adopted by the City's Vice Mayor Wes Bellamy. Opposition to the plans centred around one supporter of the far right, Jason Kessler, a former psychology student and one-time supporter of Occupy Wall Street, who had worked as a dishwasher, handyman and gym technician and failed in other attempted careers including as a poet and novelist.[92] Through 2017, the right organised three main protests against the removal of the Lee statue. The first took place in May 2017 and was led by Kessler together with Richard Spencer, the right-wing militant with a 'fashy'-haircut[93] who had first coined the phrase 'alt right,' and whose response to Trump's election victory had been to bring an audience of around 100 followers of different far right groups to Washington DC where he delivered a speech culminating in the words, 'Hail Trump.'[94] Spencer rejected the label white supremacist but did so in an opportunistic fashion, standing in the separate but still fascist-inflected tradition of Alain de Benoist[95] and the French New Right.

The first 2017 protest in defence of the Lee statue also drew the support of other fascist groups, the Traditionalist Workers Party, Identity Europa and American Vanguard. There was a second march in July 2017 called by the Ku Klux Klan and a third event in August billed as 'Unite the Right' which was intended to mobilise the supporters of both the Klan and the followers of Kessler and Spencer.

On the evening of Friday 11 August, Kessler and Spencer were able to gather a crowd of 300 supporters, many in khaki pants and white polo shorts and chanting far-right slogans,

'Blood and soil' and 'Jews will not replace us.'[96] They confronted
a group of 30 anti-fascists who were protecting the University's
statue of Thomas Jefferson. Spencer's supporters attacked the
students, spraying them with mace and throwing their torches
at them; local police took no action. This was followed by a
further mobilisation on the Sunday, which was dispersed by
the police, but not before Klan and Spencer's supporters had
carried out numerous attacks against anti-fascists.

The clashes between the two sides culminated in an attack by
James Fields Jr., a supporter of the fascist American Vanguard
group. Fields drove his grey Dodge Challenger car into the
crowd. A widely-reproduced photograph shows the bodies of
his victims, including a young black man Marcus Martin in red
trainers flung into the air, and a white man with his tattooed
back turned and his feet spinning high above his head. Fields'
final victim was a 32-year-old bartender, anti-fascist and trade
union organiser, Heather Heyer. She died as Fields drove his
car into her.[97]

The press coverage of Charlottesville focused on the relationship between President Trump and his far right supporters.
Trump's initial response, on the evening of 12 August was to
'condemn in the strongest possible terms this egregious display
of hatred, bigotry and violence on many sides, on many sides'.[98]
In the days that followed, journalists asked Trump why he was
incapable of condemning the fascists in particular, given that
footage from Charlottesville confirmed that they had been
there in greater numbers, had been armed to a greater extent
than their opponents and had initiated the violence. On 15
August, Trump again maintained that the right-wing protests
were legitimate, 'Not all of those people were neo-Nazis,
believe me. Not all of those people were white supremacists

by any stretch.' He criticised the attempt to remove General Lee's statue, saying that the left wanted to 'change history'. He said there were 'very fine people on both sides' and blamed the fighting on anti-fascists:

> What about the alt-left that came charging at, as you say, at the alt right? ... You had a group that on one side that was bad. You had a group on the other side that was also very violent ... I'll say it right now. You had a group on the other side that came charging in without a permit and they were very, very, violent.[99]

In the aftermath of Charlottesville, Trump came under criticism from within Congress, with both Democrats and Republicans condemning the president. Multiple resignations followed from the President's American Manufacturing Council, National Infrastructure Advisory Council and the President's Committee on the Arts and Humanities, causing Trump to announce that these bodies were now disbanded. He dismissed two members of his administration, Steve Bannon and Sebastian Gorka. The removal of Bannon deprived the far right of its main link to the regime.[100]

Trumpism without Bannon

While the relationship between Trump and the far right was weakened by the removal of Bannon, this did not bring an end to Trump's desire to govern in a different way from his predecessors. Trump continued to present himself as the friend of the Charlottesville right, telling one meeting of his supporters in Arizona on 22 August 2017, 'Does anybody want George

Washington's statue [taken down]? No. They're trying to take away our culture, they're trying to take away our history.'[101]

By the end of 2017, Trump needed a new policy to show his supporters that he was delivering for them. He settled on trade, where Trump remained committed to a strategy of tariffs and competition with the US's previous allies of China and the European Union. He threatened tariffs against the US's competitors, giving his administration a coherence which it had lacked in the months since Bannon's removal.

Over the following months, the street right showed its weakness in comparison to its electoral allies. Richard Spencer's speeches faced consistent opposition from anti-fascists and his audience shrunk. Matthew Heimbach of the Traditionalist Worker Party was arrested for assaulting his wife. The Daily Stormer had its hosting facilities revoked. Milo Yiannopoulos was in disgrace, dismissed from his job with Breitbart over a scandal involving his apparent justification of paedophilia, with a parting message from Robert Mercer regretting having ever appointed him.[102] Anti-semitic propagandist Tim Gionet (Baked Alaska) had his twitter account shut down. When, a year after Charlottesville, Jason Kessler sought to organise a second Unite the Right, this time in Washington, fewer than 30 white racists attended and were outnumbered by several thousand opponents.[103] The Charlottesville right was criticised from its own side, for having miscalculated the depth of its support, and for taking to the streets at a time when the majority of Americans were against them. As one right-wing blogger put it, 'it was delusional to ignore the possibility that a rally advertised using the symbol of the *Luftwaffe* and the Confederate flag, which featured several hundred people chanting "blood and soil" and "Jews will not replace us" while waving tiki torches, might meet some resistance from the locals."[104]

Yet the important point, as so often in recent years, is not to mistake the setbacks of these more marginal figures for the defeat of the electoral far right. What mattered most was Trump's continuing strength at the head of the Republican Party, the willingness of most conservatives to support Trump himself, and the weakness of Trump's Republican critics. The failure of the remaining anti-Trump conservatives to isolate the President is well illustrated by the fate of Jeff Flake, the Senator for Arizona. A neoliberal and an advocate of cuts to welfare, Flake published in August 2017 a book *Conscience of a Conservative*, criticising Trump for his mendacity. Flake is a Mormon and his book compares the persecution that Mormons suffered for decades to Trump's attacks on Mexicans and Muslims. 'That kind of talk,' he wrote, 'is a dagger in the heart of Mormons. It is a dagger in my heart.'[105] It might be thought that a Senator was well placed to enact such anti-Trump politics, taking every opportunity to vote against the President. Yet Trump has ignored Congress so far as he can, seeking to stamp his mark on the country through Presidential orders, removing environmental protections, cutting federal money for sanctuary cities and introducing his travel ban, all without requiring Congressional approval. Such bills as Trump has brought to Congress were ones which his Republican opponents found ways to support: reducing regulations on banks, or providing funds for the military. In the first year of Trump's administration, Flake voted for Trump positions 85 per cent of the time. By the end of Trump's first year in office, the split between the President and Republicans in Congress had not healed but the result was a stagnation with which Trump appeared comfortable.[106]

Meanwhile, a series of alt-right candidates were standing for election as Republican candidates. They included Russell Walker, the GOP nominee in North Carolina, whose website insists that Jews are descendants of Satan. Arthur Jones, formerly of the National Socialist White People's Party was selected as Republican candidate in Illinois. His campaign website insisted that the death of six million Jews in the Holocaust was 'the biggest, blackest lie in history'. In Virginia, Corey Stewart, an advocate of Southern secession from the United States, won the Republican nomination as well as Trump's personal support.[107]

American politics has been moving to the right for decades. In 1960, the Republican Party accepted the necessity of 'free collective bargaining' between workers and employers. By the end of 2017, 28 American states had laws limiting union's bargaining rights and their ability to take dues from their members. Among the states to have adopted this legislation after 2016 were Kentucky, Missouri and West Virginia. Under Eisenhower, the top rate of tax had been 91 per cent. Today it is less than 40 per cent.[108] The failure to tax wealth or inheritance leads to decaying schools, hospitals and universities. Democracy itself is diminished by a two party system in which both of the main parties are the advocates of the rich, leaving the conditions for Trump to emerge and for his message to seem like some sort of change.

When future Republicans come to replay in their minds the 2016 election, Trump will always be changed from what he actually was (an outsider candidate riding his luck at key moments) into what he has become: the man who was destined to become President, and who chose wisely at every moment. For this reason Trump is becoming 'the new normal,'[109] the template that other Republicans will need to copy if they are serious about following him to the Presidency.

Since 2016, the right has been radicalised. Forms of behaviour which were once associated with isolated figures on the margins of politics have acquired the sanction of Presidential approval. Threats of violence against opponents, promises to jail those who dissent, a disinterest in whether an argument is true or not so long as it advances a cause, all have been legitimised. There is no reason to think that the radicalisation of US politics has reached its natural end. Instead, hard-line right-wing politics have now been entrenched. 'Trump-ism,' Tucker Carlson predicts, 'some soft form of nationalism, will become what the Republican party stands for ... it's what the majority of Republican voters want.'[110] If, in future, Republicans continue to believe that their best hopes is in an alliance between conservatism and the far right then others will follow the same road, further and more furiously even than Trump himself.

CHAPTER FIVE

Breaking the centre: the Front National and its rivals

Donald Trump was far from alone in claiming that Brexit vindicated his politics. A similar move was made by the Front National's Marine Le Pen, who tweeted after the referendum vote that the result was a 'Victory for freedom,' and 'the most important event our continent has known since the fall of the Berlin Wall.' Through winter 2016–17 Le Pen positioned herself as the French advocate of Brexit, saying that France needed its own referendum.[1] In a New Year message to French voters, Marine Le Pen declared that 'Brexit and the election of Donald Trump' represented 'a return of peoples' global aspiration for independence.' In an interview in February 2017, she insisted that the Front National was part of a larger trend: 'The entire world, it's true for Brexit, it's true for Mr. Trump, is becoming conscious of what we've been saying for years.' If she was elected, Marine Le Pen promised, she would hold within months a French referendum to leave the Eurozone. Seven-tenths of her programme, she insisted, could not be achieved unless France left the European Union.[2]

The French Presidential election, like the American Presidential election six months earlier, saw convergence between the mainstream and far right. While, in America, convergence took the form of a centre-right party using people and ideas from outside as a way of heading in a more radical direction, the pattern in France was different. Here, both centre right and centre left have faced for three decades the threat of an insurgent party to their right. Part of the response has been to seek to keep the Front National out of the National Assembly and the Presidency, by borrowing its politics while telling voters that the Front itself remained unacceptable. This process could be seen as a form of gatekeeping, albeit one that has worked by stealth; since the FN's opponents have been unwilling to state directly why Front's voters were wrong. Their failure to articulate a clear alternative to the Front has led to them conceding the argument that the Front is right about Muslims and that an authoritarian Presidency is needed. Such hostility to the far right came under unprecedented pressure in the 2017 election, when Marine Le Pen came second in the first round, beating two centre-right candidates. At this point, new approaches came to the fore.

One part of the centre right began to argue that gatekeeping was no longer necessary, that the Front had sufficiently moderated its positions and the mainstream could make peace with it. That approach was expressed in the decision of Nicolas Dupont-Aignan, a centre-right candidate for the Presidency, to endorse Marine Le Pen for the second round. The other new approach was to follow the previous anti-FN strategy but to do so in an even more top-down way than before. The eventual winner, Emmanuel Macron, promised to govern through a permanent state of emergency, subordinating Parliament to an autocratic Presidency. Rather than address the problems of growing inequality and political passivity, Macron exulted in them, encouraging the popular disenchantment on which the right thrives. While at first sight his success was a more favourable outcome than events in the US or Britain, the danger is that anti-democratic and authoritarian politics have been normalised. The victory of the right was not prevented, but simply postponed.

A detoxification process which has still not ended

Founded to contest the 1973 elections, the FN has been one of the main parties in French politics since 1983, when its candidate Jean-Pierre Stirbois won 16.7 per cent of the vote in the first round of local elections at Dreux, a small industrial town outside Paris with a large rural hinterland and high unemployment. The mainstream right in the RPR supported a joint RPR-FN list for Dreux, enabling the FN to have three deputies elected to the local council.[3] Encouraged by widespread coverage on television and in the newspapers, in 1984 the Front won 11 per cent of the vote in European elections. There followed a period of slow and uneven growth until 2002 when Jean-Marie Le Pen, the party's leader, came second in the country's Presidential election, securing 16.9 per cent of the vote in the first round. After 2002, progress slowed again but the party grew again from 2011 after Jean-Marie Le Pen's replacement as leader by his daughter Marine. In Presidential elections in 2012, she won 17.9 per cent of the vote. In 2017, this share increased to 21.3 per cent, enabling the Front to reach the second round of the Presidential elections where (with the field narrowed to just her and Macron) she increased her party's vote again to 33.9 per cent, the largest proportion of the vote that the Front had won in any national election.

A contrast needs to be drawn between 2002 and 2017. In the first of these Presidential elections, Jean-Marie Le Pen's success in reaching the second round was met by protests, with 400,000 people marching in Paris on May Day and 600,000 more marching in other cities. In 2002, the FN's vote grew by just 1 per cent between the two rounds, with the defeated Socialists, Greens, Communists and Trotskyists all urging their voters to transfer their votes to the Gaullist Jacques Chirac, under the slogan of 'better the crook than the fascist'. By contrast, protests against the Front in 2017 involved just a few thousand people and ended in clashes with the CRS riot police who were then praised by Le Pen,[4] and the non-Front candidates were divided in their proposals for the second round, with the parties of the far left in conflict over whether they should call for abstentions or a Macron vote. It is not just that the Front received its highest vote, it also succeeded in demoralising its opponents.

The Front's recent success is often ascribed to a policy of *dédiabolisation* (detoxification), which is said to have been adopted in 2011 after the replacement of Jean-Marie Le Pen by his daughter Marine. This is the most common explanation of the Front's rise in the news media and has its counterpart in political science with the argument that in many countries the largest number of people willing to vote for an anti-immigrant party is around a third of the population. The reason the contemporary far right does not reach its ceiling more often, Nigel Copsey has argued, is because of the right's reputation for extremism. No far-right party can maximise its vote without a 'reputational shield' – a way of fending off accusations of racism and extremism.[5]

The toxicity of the Front is often associated with its founder Jean-Marie Le Pen. From 1954 to 1956, he was a supporter of Pierre Poujade's protest movement against taxation, which won

12 per cent of the vote on a platform of support for peasants and small businesses. Le Pen was elected to Parliament as a Poujade supporter. He fought in the Algerian War in 1957 and was subject to a police investigation following allegations of torture (although under amnesty laws passed in 1964 and 1967, he has been protected from prosecution).[6] On his return to France, Le Pen became one of the main spokesmen of the settlers' campaign against Algerian independence; a campaign which insisted on its loyalty to France while supporting terrorist tactics in Algeria and France, in which two thousand people were killed. He has been convicted by French courts on six occasions for challenging a crime against humanity, that is, by describing the Holocaust as a mere 'detail' of history.[7] The fact of Marine Le Pen's gender persuaded any number of commentators that her party had changed, a narrative reflected in gushing press references to her 'high-heeled boots, silk shirts and strict blazers'. Marine Le Pen expelled her father from the Front and removed his title of honorary President.[8] She has been more guarded in her use of anti-semitic comments, while on occasion appealing to French Jews on the basis that she and they have a common enemy in political Islam. She has also associated herself with figures who come from a different political background, such as Florian Philippot, her leading advisor between 2009 and 2017, a gay former civil servant and graduate of the École Nationale d'Administration (France's equivalent of the Oxford PPE degree).[9]

Indeed, this process of detoxification was acknowledged by others on the right. The two main centre-right candidates in 2017 were François Fillon of the Republicans and Nicolas Dupont-Aignan of Debout la France. Fillon was the more significant figure. After he was chosen by his party in November

2016, polls showed him to be one of the frontrunners, before he was engulfed in allegations of fraud. Yet Dupont-Aignan was also rooted in the centre right. Over the previous 20 years, he had held elected positions as mayor of Yerres and then as a member of the National Assembly for Essonne, for the centre-right UMP party. Dupont-Aignan justified his decision to endorse Marine Le Pen in the second round of the elections by saying that the Front had changed and that Marine was nothing like her father. Dupont-Aignan characterised the fears of the Front as 'folklore and delirium ... phantasmic'.[10]

Yet, even as the Front was repositioning itself as just another electoral party, the links to the past continued to reassert themselves. Marine Le Pen's election campaign was subsidised by a six million Euro loan from her father's business Cotelec. Moreover, through the campaign, Marine Le Pen signalled to the FN's core voters that the party had not changed. In April, for example, she told the LCI television channel that France should not apologise for events at the Vel d'Hiv cycling stadium in 1942, when 13,000 Jews had been rounded up before being killed in the Holocaust. According to the FN leader, French politicians had 'taught our children that they have all the reasons to criticise [the country] and to only see, perhaps, the darkest aspects of our history. So I want them to be proud of being French again.'[11]

To make sense of today's Front National and therefore of its rivals on its right, it is necessary to recall that the FN emerged from a far-right milieu, part of which was fascist. It began through a process of partial and managed detoxification, which was never intended to be complete and which continues to this day.

A key text was Dominique Venner's pamphlet *Pour une critique positive*, written in 1963 by a former French soldier who had taken part in various activities of the French far right, including a 1956 attack on headquarters of the French Communist Party (PCF) and had been a member of the group Jeune Nation (JN), which was banned in 1958 for involvement in terrorist acts. Jeune Nation merged with a successor group, the Organisation de l'Armée Secrète, which too was banned and Venner was prosecuted and jailed. Writing from prison, Venner attempted to reorient the far right away from clandestine activities towards possible growth during what was most likely to be a long period in which the ideas of nationalism were doomed to remain marginal. To grow again, Venner argued, fascism would need to 'educate its supporters'. The far right, he complained, lived in a permanent atmosphere of dreams, with its supporters reading spy novels, memoirs from participants in the war years or the secret services. He insisted that nationalists needed to maintain their vision of the complete reconstruction of society, but argued that this required a lengthy period of preparation. A fascist seizure of power, he insisted, would face numerous obstacles, including that fact that the inhabitants of Europe were much richer than they had ever been and disinclined to accept military rule. What the far right needed, Venner argued, was 'a hierarchical body of cadres' working in the tradition of National Socialism. These cadres should see their role as persuasive. Venner urged his supporters to join farmers' federations and students' unions, recruit teachers and engineers. The far right faced a long battle of battles, he argued, a conflict 'without glory or panache'.[12]

Dominque Venner's pamphlet was taken up by others on the right, including François Duprat, the Toulouse organiser of Jeune Nation, and later a member of the fascist party Ordre Nouveau. It was Duprat who persuaded Ordre Nouveau to set up the Front National in 1972, after which he was in effect the FN's deputy leader under Le Pen until Duprat's death in 1978. He praised Venner for the influence he had had on the French right in the 1950s and 1960s, likening his pamphlet to Lenin's *What is to be Done?* Venner also inspired the formation of GRECE (the Group of Research and Study for European Civilisation), another influence on the FN.[13]

The idea of a Front National was proposed by Duprat at the June 1972 congress of Ordre Nouveau. 'The final goal of the organisation remains the capture of power by revolutionary action,' Duprat argued, 'however this moment has not yet come'. Drawing on Hitler's National Socialists, as well as the recent success of the Italian MSI,[14] Duprat insisted that it was possible to be both electoral and revolutionary. The turn towards electoralism was based on a gamble that the political situation was not going to remain as unfavourable to the right forever; in five national elections from 1967 to 1978, no far right candidate won more than 1 per cent of the vote.

The formation of the Front National was itself a detoxification measure, aimed at uniting the non-fascist right behind Ordre Nouveau. Various well-known figures on the right were invited to join, notably Jean-Marie Le Pen, who was a member of Ordre Nouveau, but was associated in the public mind with 'patriotic' far-right politics rather than with fascism. Above all Le Pen was known for the 1965 campaign for the Presidency by Jean-Louis Tixier-Vignancour, which Le Pen had organised, and whose central demand had been the maintenance of Algeria as a French colony.

That said, detoxification was never supposed to go too far. Initial recruits to the Front included Victor Barthélemy, who became the FN's Administrative Secretary and was a former General Secretary of Jacques Doriot's fascist Parti Populaire Français. Barthélemy had recruited a French unit of the Wehrmacht and later worked for the PPF in Mussolini's Salò Republic. The formation of the FN was not intended to be more than a temporary moderation; Dominque Venner continued to call for the murder of racial enemies while Duprat published Holocaust Denial literature including British fascist Richard Verrall's *Did Six Million Really Die?*[15]

A second stage in the detoxification process was the adoption by the FN of ideas borrowed from a far right literary network GRECE (the Group of Research and Study for European Civilisation), founded by Alain de Benoist, who had under the pseudonym Fabrice Laroche been a member of the editorial board of Dominique Venner's magazine *Europe-Action*. De Benoist had been for years a white supremacist. One of the stories he tells in his memoir is of an occasion when he was in a restaurant and a nun asked if he would give to charities operating in the Third World, to which he replied that she 'look[ed] after monkeys'. De Benoist's writings in the mid-1960s are in no way separable from these politics: praising Nietzsche, declaring his adherence to militant nationalism, warning of the self-destruction of Europe unless immigration ended.[16] Yet in the 1970s de Benoist changed his approach and began to insist that all races were equal and that at the global level diversity should be supported. This was not a move towards moderation but towards obfuscation. For by 'diversity' De Benoist meant something different from the term's normal use; that in each nation there should be complete nationality and racial homogeneity. Diversity meant, in other words, a series of multiple regional and national apartheid states. By 1994, there were six supporters of GRECE on the Front National's politburo and numerous GRECE followers wrote for its publications.[17] From GRECE, the Front derived the idea that the right should ignore race and speak of 'culture'. GRECE's ideas became FN theory. In this way, a policy of removing migrants could be presented as a kindness. 'I love North Africans,' Le Pen said, 'but their place is in the Maghreb.'[18]

Jean-Marie Le Pen's role within the FN was to popularise ideas developed by others and to win publicity for the group. At times, his method was a right-wing contrarianism, saying something unspeakable so that the FN would be attacked and he could accuse his opponents of hypocrisy. All he was saying out loud, he argued, is what ordinary people were thinking in secret. One example of this approach came in 1984, between the breakthrough at Dreux and the European election results, when Le Pen told a broadcaster that France was not a brothel for six million immigrants.[19]

At other times, Jean-Marie Le Pen defended Vichy or fascism in Germany. In these cases, his role appears to have been to remind FN supporters that their party was not interested in just being popular, it was loyal to the fascist tradition. These comments, including his promise in 1983 to 'bring together the fasces of our national forces so that the voice of France is heard,' his 1988 reference to the Socialists' (Jewish) minister of the public service Michel Durafour as '*Durafour-crématoire*,' or Le Pen's frequent use of the term 'six million' in multiple contexts seemingly unrelated to the Holocaust, make most sense if they are seen not as the needling of his opponents but instead the continuation of an old idea of the Front going back to the days of Venner and Duprat. They were an insistence that the FN was still a party of revolutionary nationalists.

They were intended to radicalise the supporters of the Front, training them in a fascist world-view and converting them from voters into cadres.[20]

For Jim Wolfreys, the pattern is a series of steps towards moderation which are interspersed with episodes of re-radicalisation. In this perspective, detoxification can continue for decades without shifting the Front from its fascist starting point. On that analysis, Jean-Marie Le Pen's role within the Front has been to re-engage the party's fascist cadre and to prevent the Front from becoming just another mainstream party. Indeed radicalisation has not been left just to him. It had its counterpart in the 1990s when a series of town halls were captured by the Front and used as testing-grounds for government. In Vitrolles, the director of the local cinema was dismissed for putting on films sympathetic to the victims of AIDS. Mainstream papers such as *Libération* were removed from libraries and replaced with the FN's *Identité* and *Krisis*. The shelves were restocked with far-right propagandists such as the French collaborationist Robert Brasillach and the Italian fascist Julius Evola.[21]

The word *dédiabolisation* was first used at an FN summer school in 1989, by figures around Bruno Mégret, who emerged at the end of the decade as a rival to Jean-Marie Le Pen within the FN.[22] Mégret had left the Gaullist RPR to join the Front National in 1982 and became Le Pen's Deputy. His role within the organisation was as a bridge to centre-right voters, telling an interviewer from *Le Monde* in May 1998, 'Many of the Gaullist values in 1940 at the time of the RPR and after 1962 are perennial values which, today, are embodied by the FN: the independence of France, the greatness of our country, the refusal of a regime dominated by political parties.'[23] Mégret's criticism of Le Pen was that by positioning the Front as a party which was in continuity with Vichy and the German occupation rather than the Resistance, he was preventing a coalition with Gaullists, the party's most direct route to power.

The rivalry between Jean-Marie Le Pen and Bruno Mégret grew ever more bitter. While a Front congress in 1998 gave Mégret a temporary ascendancy, Le Pen refused to resign and the following year expelled his rival from the party. Had Mégret succeeded, no doubt there would have been some attempt at reconciliation with the centre right; Le Pen's victory delayed that possibility by decades.

Meanwhile, the context to the Front's activity has changed. The Front has grown as a result of terrorist attacks in France and the response of French politicians to them. In 1995, the Armed Islamic Group (GIA) carried out bombings of the Paris Métro and RER in an attempt to undermine French support for the Algeria military government. Eight people were killed. In 2004, the Indonesian Embassy in Paris was attacked. In 2012, Mohammed Merah walked into a Jewish day school in Toulouse and shot the rabbi Jonathan Sandler and three children, two of whom were Sandler's own children aged just six and three.[24] In January 2015, ISIS supporters Saïd and Chérif Kouachi attacked the *Charlie Hebdo* magazine killing eight journalists and four other people. Two days later, Amedy Coulibaly carried out further attacks in a kosher supermarket, killing four Jewish hostages. Then, in November 2015, multiple shooting and suicide attacks, including on an Eagles of Death Metal concert in Paris resulted in a combined death toll of 130 people.

In the first years after 9/11, as elsewhere in Europe, newer groups on the right seemed better able than the Front to profit from what was a growing mood of anti-Muslim racism. The most important of these new groups was Bloc Identitaire (BI), set up by Fabrice Robert and Guillaume Luyt, self-declared 'National Bolsheviks' influenced by De Benoist's New Right. In 2002, Robert's previous party, Unité Radicale, was dissolved after one of its members, Maxime Brunerie, attempted to murder the French President Jacques Chirac. Bloc Identitaire was more interested in creating a social movement and in high profile stunts to generate press interest, than in replicating the Front's electoral success. Together with its youth wing, Génération Identitaire, Bloc Identitaire put on 'charity soup kitchens' for the homeless with pork on the menu and wine so as to exclude Muslims. They occupied mosques and the offices of the Socialist Party. They also found allies among some former leftists, principally Riposte Laïque, a coalition of secular feminists (Annie Sugier of the Socialist Party, Anne Zelensky of the Women's Rights' League, Christine Tasin) and former Trotskyists (Pierre Cassen, previously of the Ligue Communiste Revolutionnaire) who have organised joint campaigns with the Bloc and publicised its events.[25]

Invited by journalists to explain her journey from left to right Christine Tasin says that the decisive moment, in her words 'the slap', came in 1989 when schoolgirls at Creil chose to attend their school in Islamic scarfs, and were excluded, and Socialist ministers were divided over the school's response, with some supporting the students and others insisting that headscarves were an insult to France and had to be banned. Tasin supported the latter view. She has been convicted for inciting violence against Muslims. In the run up to the 2017 elections, the Riposte Laïque website ran favourable articles on Le Pen and criticised others on the far right who failed to endorse her.[26]

The success of Marine Le Pen has come in part from moderating the FN's approach towards groups which were seen by her father as the Front's implacable enemies, including some of France's Jews,[27] while at the same time adopting a more hostile message in relation to her party's main enemies, Arabs and Muslims.

As with Brexit and Trump, part of Le Pen's success has been her ability to win support among working-class voters, a group previously associated with the left. In the mid-2000s, the Front dropped its previous support for the politics of austerity, and in 2017 its main proposal was to leave the Euro. This measure, it promised, would reduce inequality and restore full employment. The FN said that it would introduce tariffs to support French business, privilege industry over finance, and use spending by the central bank to increase growth levels. The Front portrayed as pro-worker, and this signalling was accepted by the Front's critics on the centre-left and right.

Some 26 per cent of employees voted for Le Pen in the first round of the 2017 Presidential elections, more than for any other candidate. She under-performed among the young (who voted for Jean-Luc Mélenchon) and the old (who voted for the Republicans) but was ahead among voters aged between 35 and 60. Among voters who had left school at 16, one in three voted for her in the first round.[28]

It is in the context of the Front's re-radicalisation over Islam and over social issues that the events of 2016–17 have to be seen, including: Jean-Marie Le Pen's funding of his daughter's 2017 election campaign, her refusal to apologise for events at Vel d'Hiv, the ongoing dispute between father and daughter as to whether the 2017 election campaign should be seen as a success and Marine Le Pen's proposals after the election to change the name of her party to the Rassemblement National.[29]

The Front was already too close to the centre for some of its supporters. In May 2013, Dominique Venner, the man whose writing 50 years before had inspired the FN's formation, shot himself in public. The building where he killed himself was the Notre Dame Cathedral. Before shooting himself, Venner posted a suicide note on his website complaining that the right was losing, that the government's legalisation of gay marriage represented a defeat for Catholic France. Venner further claimed that the population of Europe was coming under Islamic control and would soon be placed under sharia law. The conversion of France into a totalitarian Islamic state, he warned, was now inevitable: 'It will not be enough to organise polite street demonstrations to prevent it ... We are entering a time when words must be authenticated by deeds.' The man who had warned the right against an obsession with acts of violence found himself reverting to the politics he had once rejected. On the news of his death, Marine Le Pen took to twitter offering her respects to Venner whose last, political gesture had been (she said) an attempt to wake the French people. Yet the more straightforward interpretation of his gesture was that rather than acting out of sympathy with the Front, in the shadow of looming elections, he was rejecting the party's strategy of postponing to the indefinite future its politics of revolutionary nationalism. Not even the electoral success of Marine Le Pen could deliver the triumph he needed.[30]

The Front National had long ceased to take part in elections just in order to popularise an underlying philosophy of

National Socialism. Even when it came to race, the Front's politics had moderated; instead of proposing repatriation it spoke of 'national preference'. In other words, it argues that employment, social services, housing and pensions should be reserved for French citizens who would live alongside others and be given a permanent structural advantage over them.[31]

Yet the Front still presented itself as an outsider party, insisting that its opponents belong to a 'dictatorship of the banks'. To a much greater extent than other parties, it portrayed France as in a state of crisis, with the family in decline and the cities at war. The Front retained a small security apparatus overlapping with the smaller neo-Nazi groups. The party remained apart from purely electoral politics. It had the support of a number of leading members who has previously been the cadre of fascist parties (albeit alongside figures from other right traditions). Detoxification was not complete; nor did the Front show any signs of wanting it to end.[32]

The flattering of the FN electorate

The second half of this chapter is concerned not with the Front but with the moves that have been made by the mainstream to woo its voters. The phenomenon begins at Dreux in 1983, with the willingness of the centre-right Rally for the Republic (RPR) to reach an electoral pact with the FN. The two parties collaborated in the initial elections and then in a re-run, from which three Front councillors were elected. Jacques Chirac blamed his party's decision to work with the Front on the governing Socialists, 'those who have made an alliance with the Communists are definitely disqualified to give lessons in the matters of human rights and the rules of democracy.'

Claude Labbé of the RPR agreed, 'Le Pen exists, it is one of today's political realities.'[33]

There followed a significant increase in press coverage of the Front which lasted until the Front's success in the 1984 European elections. Far from challenging FN myths around immigration in 1983–4, the centre right copied the FN, with the centre-right mayor of Toulon complaining that immigration had made France 'the dustbin of Europe,' and *Le Figaro* carrying 18 articles during the 1983 elections, blaming crime on immigration. The head of the RPR, Jacques Chirac, made a number of anti-immigration speeches between summer and autumn 1984, appealing to Front voters. In October, he said, 'If there were fewer immigrants, there would be less unemployment.' In November, he contrasted the falling French birth rate with rapid immigration. A particular low point was reached when Chirac responded to the racist murders of three children aged under twelve by blaming the dead: 'France no longer has the means to support a crowd of foreigners who abuse her hospitality.'[34]

The same pattern could be seen in elections in 1988, with Charles Pasqua of the Gaullists saying that the Front and the mainstream right shared values, an approach echoed by Jacques Chirac who said that the membership of the Front 'has the same preoccupations and the same values as the majority.'[35] Two years later a young supporter of the RPR, Nicolas Sarkozy, worked with the Front on a seminar to work out how benefits could be restricted to French nationals. In another speech in June 1991, Chirac spoke of the noise and smell brought by immigrants and said that he sympathised with the humiliation felt by French workers when they saw immigrants living in families with 'three or four wives and about 20 kids and who earn 50,000 francs in state benefits without ever working.' Local pacts between the FN and centre-right parties were a feature of the 1980s and 1990s. They continued into the 2000s, securing the election of mainstream politicians, such as Charles Million, Charles Baur, Jean-Pierre Soisson and Jacques Blanc with Front support.[36]

At times, the centre left has called for a 'Republican Front' against the FN. Within the Socialist Party there was, however, no consensus in favour of treating the Front as a pariah. In 1983, Socialist President Mitterrand responded to a letter from Jean-Marie Le Pen complaining about the lack of coverage of his party, by forwarding the request to the Minister of Communications. This resulted in an invitation for Le Pen to appear on the evening news. Mitterrand's associates argued that the growth of the far right would be a disaster for his centre-right opponents. Similar thinking appears to have influenced Mitterrand's decision to introducing proportional representation for elections to the National Assembly in 1986, to widespread criticism that the move would boost the FN's representation in Parliament, which indeed it did.[37]

Again and again, the left has joined in the argument that immigration must end, or supported the Front in criticising Muslims. In 1984, Laurent Fabius, a former Socialist Prime Minister said that, 'Le Pen poses good questions but gives the wrong answers to them.' During the 1989 controversy over veiling at Creil, ministers in the Socialist government, including Jean-Pierre Chevènement, the Communist Party's paper, L'Humanité, and Che Guevara's former admirer, Régis Debray, all demanded laws criminalising the wearing of Islamic headscarves in schools. In 1991, the Socialist Prime Minister Édith Cresson boasted that she would out-muscle Le Pen by sponsoring charter flights to repatriate immigrants. This move was followed by an election campaign in which the Socialists campaigned hard against the Front. Yet, her message was made incoherent by the Socialists' promises to cut immigration. In 1993, the Socialists lost control of the National Assembly, which was captured by the centre right. Meanwhile, the Front increased its vote to 12.6 per cent.[38]

In 2006, schoolteacher Robert Redeker published a piece in the conservative paper *Le Figaro*, arguing that Islam was opposed to 'generosity, open-mindedness, tolerance, gentleness, freedom of women and morals.' He compared Islam to the other monotheistic traditions, insisting (with considerable indifference to the actual words of the Old Testament) that Judaism and Christianity had always promoted peace over war.[39] Redeker described the Koran as a book of 'unheard-of violence'. Mohamed was said to have been a murderer of Jews and 'a master of hatred'. Robert Redeker was a product of the French left, a member of the editorial board of *Les Temps modernes*, a journal founded by Jean-Paul Sartre. His arguments were then taken up by a group of intellectuals long seen as on the left, but whose politics were now dominated by 9/11. This group included Alain Finkielkraut, previously a supporter of Daniel Cohn-Bendit and May '68, Élisabeth Badinter, an advocate of women's 'nature' against 'feminist ideology,' and the former Maoist André Glucksmann.[40]

For these writers and for much of the French left, the starting point in thinking about Islam is not the position of most French Muslims in the working-class or the obstacles to those Muslims in terms of higher unemployment, police harassment and social ostracism. The key consideration is rather *laïcité* (secularism), a term of multiple even contradictory meanings.

At times secularism is the specific and neutral-seeming belief that the institutions of the state, including primary and secondary schools, should not contain religious symbols. In another incarnation it is the idea that there is no place in France for a people defined by their religion, that Muslims have every right to remain in France just so long as they cease to follow Islam, and should they fail to leave France, their Muslim behaviour entitles them to abuse or worse.[41]

The appeal to FN voters continued under Nicolas Sarkozy, first as Chirac's minister of the Interior from 2002 and then as President from 2007. On his appointment to the former role, Sarkozy declared, 'Presidential elections will not be won at the centre. If the right does not do its job, it will leave a road to the extreme right.' To prove his anti-immigrant credentials, in 2002, Sarkozy closed the refugee camp at Sangatte in Calais. The following year, he introduced an immigration law extending the residence period needed to claim a long-term residence authorisation to five years and criminalising marriages for immigration status. A further 2003 asylum law had the effect of limiting the period for which a refugee could be granted asylum to a single year, requiring the victims of wars in Afghanistan and Iraq to remain in a permanent legal limbo. As Interior Minister, Sarkozy was also responsible for the state's response to 21 days of rioting in October 2005. He promised to 'hose down' those involved, describing them as *racaille* (scum). Afterwards, he spoke again of appealing to the Front's electorate, 'I'm accused of trying to seduce Front National voters ... But that's exactly the case! Why do you want me to stop myself from addressing an electorate that used to be ours?'[42]

As President from 2007, Sarkozy grasped that the Front promised its voters not just racism but authoritarian leadership.

He recruited an adviser Patrick Buisson, a journalist from the far-right publication *Minute* and the author of a sympathetic biography of Jean-Marie Le Pen.[43] Another recruit was Guillaume Peltier, the previous leader of the Front's youth section. Sarkozy attacked the French left, blaming the events of May 1968 for the 'moral and intellectual permissiveness' of French society. He condemned the unemployed as fraudsters. He sought to present himself as an outsider, waging war against the French liberal elites. Sarkozy declared there were 'too many immigrants in France,' blaming them for crime, immigration and anti-social behaviour. A target was set of 25,000 deportations a year. The President travelled to Dakar where he declared that Africans were peasants who had for a thousand years lived by an 'eternal cycle of time' with no concept of progress.[44]

Sarkozy's shift to Islamophobia met little resistance from within the National Assembly. Éric Besson was his Immigration Minister and his law to criminalise the wearing of the Islamic niqab was welcomed from the far right to far left, with André Gerin of the Communist Party a key supporter of the new law. Arnaud Montebourg, a member of the Socialist Party, said that there was a consensus uniting his party, Sarkozy's UMP and the FN on questions of immigration. A wing of the Socialist Party, Gauche Populaire, spoke of France's 'little whites,' defined by François Kalfon as 'the heterosexual man … who lives with his classic family in a suburban house with a car and television'.[45] In order to woo such voters, it argued, the Party needed to turn away from causes such as multiculturalism. These Socialists accepted the Front's argument that its voters were the very essence of the electorate, not a minority of racist voters, but the representatives of the entire French nation.

Éric Besson predicted that a ban on the veil would show voters that the right was listening and will lead to the Front's 'political death'. Yet Sarkozy's economic liberalism failed to solve the longstanding problems of the French economy, its high unemployment rate, the shrinking of working-class living standards since 2008 and the increasing prosperity of the rich. A poll of FN voters in summer 2007 found that 90 per cent had confidence in the government's position on law and order. A year later the proportion had fallen to just 30 per cent.[46] Sarkozy had legitimised the Front's politics without creating an actual apartheid state for Muslims. Accordingly, FN voters ceased to support his government and the Front's vote began to increase again. In March 2010, it won 11.4 per cent of the vote; not the death Besson had predicted, but the party's best result since 2002.

One of the few politicians to have challenged the Front National in any sustained way is Jean-Luc Mélenchon, who stood in the 2012 Presidential elections as the 'Left Front' candidate, promising amongst other things a top rate of tax of 100 per cent for anyone earning more than 360,000 Euros. In the debates, Mélenchon termed Marine Le Pen a 'beast spitting hatred' and a 'dark presence'. Le Pen senior called Mélenchon a *voyou*, a yob. Mélenchon responded that Jean-Marie was 'a fat bourgeois who plays being a man of the people.' Afterwards, rather than standing for election to the National Assembly in a district where his Front de Gauche was ahead, Mélenchon chose to fight Marine Le Pen in the northern constituency of Hénin-Beaumont, which she had been cultivating for years.[47] Unfortunately, Mélenchon failed to beat Le Pen and since that time he appears to have calculated that it is better to ignore the Front's racism and to challenge the party indirectly, by raising economic and social demands and tailing the national consensus on culture and race.

In the run up to 2017, Mélenchon voted for the ban on the Muslim headscarf in schools. During the election, he criticised the European Union for the Posted Workers' directive which he said undercut the conditions of French workers, accepting the argument that immigration caused poverty. He stated that he had never been in favour of free movement and that migrants were 'stealing the bread' of French workers. If these equivocations were intended to broaden Mélenchon appeal, they instead made him seem opportunistic. During the first election debate, he criticised Le Pen's proposal to ban head-scarves from all public places. How could he attack her, she replied, when he had voted for the same ban in schools?[48]

Emmanuel Macron and the defeat of the left and right

By the second round of the 2017 Presidential election, leftists were faced with a similar choice to 2002 between two unwelcome candidates. Jean-Luc Mélenchon who, with 20 per cent of the vote had come within a fraction of making it to the final round, organised a referendum of his voters in his party, La France Insoumise. The largest group of whom said that they would spoil their ballot rather than vote for Emmanuel Macron, Le Pen's mainstream rival.[49] In contrast to others on the left, such as Robert Hue, the former National Secretary of the Communist Party, who called on voters to choose Macron over Le Pen, Mélenchon refused to say how he would vote in the second round. Critics accused him of betraying the left's anti-fascist tradition. Mélenchon's response was to deny that he had become an abstentionist, 'You don't have to be a great scholar to guess what I'm going to do. Is there a single person among you who doubts the fact that I'm not going to vote for the Front National? Everyone knows that.'[50]

Part of the problem for the left was that Macron made no secret of his economic liberalism or for his hostility to the normal trappings of parliamentary government. Both Macron and Le Pen described their politics as 'neither right nor left,' but they meant different things by the same words. For Le Pen, the phrase is part of the heritage of French fascism which the Front incorporates.[51] In Le Pen's worldview, the left and the right are both wrong, because neither shares her vision of converting the state into a mechanism for administering a new system of racial privilege. The right and the left are defective because neither of them is far right. Emmanuel Macron, by contrast, seeks to create a majority for the continuation of austerity policies. His appointments have included Edouard Philippe of the centre-right Republicans as his Prime Minister, and Bruno Le Maire and Gérald Darmanin from the same party as ministers of the economy and of public action and accounts. Macron himself had been the minister for the economy under Hollande. His is a militancy of the centre, not of the far right.

While far left candidates have had little success in national elections since the 2008 crisis, save for the ambiguous figure of Jean-Luc Mélenchon, France remains a country characterised by very high levels of social protest. The election of Jacques Chirac in 1995 and his announcement of pension reforms led to strikes by two million workers and compelled Chirac to withdraw, and attempts at pension reform in 2003 led to strikes on a similar scale. Attempts under Hollande to limit the 35-hour weeks and to make it easier for companies to dismiss workers led to a fresh wave of protests, the Nuit Debout campaign, which at its peak involved between half a million and a million demonstrators. Such has been the popular antagonism which has met previous anti-union laws and other regressive reforms, that a neoliberal majority can no longer be achieved by ruling through just the Republicans or just through the Socialists. Macron, it follows, has no choice but to cannibalise both the mainstream parties to find supporters who share his vision of permanent privatisation.[52]

The problem for French politics is that while left-associated social movements have been strong enough to operate a veto of sorts against the destruction of France's welfare state; without principled electoral representatives they have had no answer to the processes which are dragging politics successively to the right. It is in this context that the Front's ability to sustain a vote of 20 per cent or more is so dangerous. The Front may not be a majority party, but it takes up enough of the vote so as to diminish the authority of everyone else. Even without a further breakthrough, its consistent success operates as a recurring allurement to the mainstream. The mathematics seem to make the solution obvious. From the point of view of the centre right it is obvious that the disease destroying the French economy is the legacy (despite Sarkozy, despite Macron) of such ongoing reforms as the maximum 35-hour working week. The Front is not a neoliberal party, so while it agrees with the centre right that the people need to be subordinated to the nation, it disagrees with the centre as to which reforms are most urgently needed. But in a France where Muslims are already treated as less than second-class citizens, its policies of segregating black and white no longer seem extraordinary. It follows that a stable transition to a different kind of politics could be achieved, if only the Republican and Front electorates were to find an agreement. With every election the Front's residual taint grows a little less, and the incentive for the mainstream parties to compromise with the far right grow more.

Macron rejects this approach, and yet his alternative is hardly benign. From his first months in government, Macron's authoritarianism was clear. On being elected to the Presidency, he set up a new centre-right party La République en Marche composed of bankers, civil servants, graduates of the École Nationale d'Administration and recruits from tech industry. Muriel Pénicaud was recruited from a role as a senior manager at the multinational food business Danone, Élisabeth Borne from a similar position at the civil engineering company Eiffage. Buoyed by positive press coverage and defections from both left and right (and assisted by a wave of abstentions), Macron succeeded in winning a clear majority of elected delegates. This move would not have been possible save for the blackmail that Macron presented the French people. Once again, they had to choose between a crook and a fascist.

After Parliamentary elections in 2012, the two main parties had 519 out of 577 seats in France's National Assembly; by 2012 the share held by the centre left and centre right was reduced to 181, with Macron's supporters holding 350 seats or 60 per cent of the total. The creation of a Presidential party succeeded in destabilising France's existing left and right and enabling Macron to govern with little scrutiny from the National Assembly.[53] It came, however, at the cost of popular disengagement, with just one in three French voters participating in the second round of elections, the lowest figure in modern French history. Following his election Macron proposed to take this process still further, planning to reduce the size of the Assembly, reduce the time spent debating legislation and giving legislative powers to the President.

In common with previous mainstream governments which have sought to present themselves as above politics and the way to prevent fascism,[54] Macron's government rests upon the support of the police, the institutions of the state and the army. Its first reflex is to seek the repression of social protest. Labour laws introduced by decree in September 2017 weakened national collective bargaining, ended sector-wide union representation and made it cheaper once again for employers to dismiss workers. Then, as if determined to accept the popular jibe that he was the President of the rich, Macron followed up these decrees with a budget cutting corporation tax from 33 to 25 per cent, culling 120,000 public sector jobs and reducing housing benefits.[55]

Macron proposed for students, the introduction of selection for university education and the introduction of a system of 'competition' between universities. These, as with other key changes, were to be introduced by administrative decree made by the President, rather than through any normal legislative process. Meanwhile, immigrants have been made subject to a new imprisonment regime, extending the period they could be required to spend in detention centres from 45 to 90 days, reducing asylum seekers' rights to file an application or an appeal against rejection, and allowing the deportation of those whose cases are subject to appeal.[56]

Emmanuel Macron has matched his personal style to the authoritarian policies of his regime. During the Presidential campaign he said that he wished to see the return of an austere and powerful executive, what he called a 'Jupiterian presidency'. He has given interviews regretting the demise of the French monarchy. He has attempted to associate himself with the armed forces, insisting on being dangled from a helicopter while being filmed visiting a nuclear submarine and then being photographed from the deck, as if he was its military commander.[57]

From January 2015, France had been in a state of emergency, introduced following the murder of the journalists of *Charlie Hebdo*. Border controls were tightened, deportation normalised and police numbers increased. In the 2017 elections, Emmanuel Macron cast himself as a critic of these powers. In office, however, he sought to make them permanent. In October 2017, the Assembly passed a law to strengthen the fight against terrorism and internal security. This wrote into the statute book the most draconian features of the previous state of emergency, including powers for Prefects to close mosques or create security zones where law enforcement officials were permitted to exercise enhanced stop-and-search powers. The Minister of Interior was granted new powers to monitor individuals and restrict their freedom of movement. None of these measures required judicial approval.[58]

Macron is offering the French population a simulacrum of dictatorship: not the militant increase in the repressive powers of the state that would be needed to expel France's Muslim population, nor the system of direct racial preference which is the Front's programme, but a vision of authoritarian politics all the same. While Le Pen says that she would extend the power of the Presidency, it is Macron who has reduced parliament to a shadow of its former power. She promises to do away with both the left and the right, but Macron has removed their representatives from Parliament already.

In the aftermath of the 2017 elections, the Front National changed its name to Rassemblement National, or National Rally. Normally, when a party changes its name, it does so to mark a rejection with the past. Yet the name Rassemblement National, or something close to it, has been used on three previous occasions by the right. The word 'Rassemblement' had been the title of a previous appeal by Le Pen between 2010 and 2014 to other parties on the far right, under the banner of 'Rassemblement bleu Marine.' The name Rassemblement National was used in 1965 by far-right presidential candidate Jean-Louis Tixier-Vignancour's campaign to defend the French occupation of Algeria. Further back, in the 1940s, the title Rassemblement National Populaire had been chosen by Marcel Déat, a fascist advocate of collaboration with the German occupation. Once again, Le Pen's party neglected an opportunity to reject its fascist origins, choosing instead to emphasise its continuity with the past.

Yet with Le Pen in opposition, it is her enemies who are doing the greatest harm. Not for the first time, politicians in France are trying to prevent a far-right government by implementing illiberal policies. This process does not break the power of Le Pen, instead it serves to make her appear reasonable. Her party has been calling for an authoritarian Presidency for 30 years and, no matter how far Emmanuel Macron goes in that direction, Marine Le Pen will always be able to go further than he can.

CHAPTER SIX

The internationalism
of the far right

Six months after Steve Bannon's ejection from the Trump administration, the centre-right magazine, *National Review*, ran a piece questioning the appearance of Bannon at the Front National's annual convention in Lille. The author J. J. McCullough noted that this was far from the first occasion on which Bannon had given his support to European nationalists. A week before, he had been interviewed on the front page of Italy's *Corriere della Sera* newspaper, praising both Matteo Salvini of the League and Beppe Grillo's Five Star movement.[1] The French far-right campaigner Marion Maréchal-Le Pen of the Front National, McCulloch noted, had spoken at that year's CPAC conference, while Holland's Geert Wilders and Britain's Nigel Farage were often asked to comment on developments in America. Nationalism, McCullough noted, was being redefined in transnational fashion, not as the defence of the United States or Italy or France, but in terms of broader categories, such as 'Western civilization,' or 'the Judeo-Christian tradition'. 'It is not at all clear,' McCullough wrote, 'what pressing interest an unemployed Pennsylvania steelworker has in what party controls the French National Assembly, yet a great many professional anti-globalists seem much more interested in the latter than in the former, because it exists in a world they more easily understand and relate to.' If nationalism was supposed to be about protecting what was specific to a country from the encroachment of the global then the nationalists, he observed, were becoming a new cosmopolitan movement of their own:

> Increasingly, the self-declared leadership of the anti-globalist movement seems to be tottering on the precipice of *Animal Farm*–style decadence, in which the supposed heroes have evolved into an arrogant mirror of everything they purport to hate. There is very obviously an anti-globalist global elite these days, comprising a tight class of educated, wealthy, cosmopolitan politicians, journalists and Internet personalities who enjoy international travel and intellectual careers and usually have more in common with one another (and even their opponents) than with the forgotten men of the lower classes they purport to speak for.[2]

The magazine in which this criticism appeared, *National Review*, had been founded in 1955 by the oil heir William F. Buckley Jr., to spread the gospel of conservatism to a Republican right, which Buckley felt to be too moderate on economics and liberal on social questions when it should have taken its cue from Christian natural law. Over the following years, *National Review* has opened its pages to any number of conservatisms influenced by theorists from outside the United States: the *Review*'s long-term contributor Russell Kirk was moulded by the Anglo-Irish anti-revolutionism of Edmund Burke and by a social Catholicism of European origin. Another early contributor, James Burnham, was a former Marxist and a mainstream Republican on most matters, save for the extension of Soviet power, against which raged with all the bitterness of an apostate. Buckley's project was serious about dragging the Republican Party to the right, while gatekeeping its edges, excluding anti-semites and conspiracy theorists.[3] Post-war US conservatism was a milieu which knew its Trotsky from its Stalin, its Thomas Aquinas from its St Augustine. The right, as much as the left, has long exchanged ideas across borders.

That said, there was something new about the post-Brexit right and the way in which its successes in one country served to justify a new confidence and militancy elsewhere. The 'internationalism' of Le Pen or Bannon or Farage was not incidental to their political project but a key part of their break-through in 2016–17, and an asset that Bannon (who had now been dismissed by Trump) was desperate to reuse, in order to remain relevant to the new generation of nationalists.[4]

Nationalism as the politics of race and class

McCullough's scepticism related to the nationalism of these self-identified patriots. They could not be called nationalists, he suggested, once their frame of reference went beyond their country's borders. His arguments assume that nationalism has a meaning along the lines of what Bannon or Trump says it does. In other words, it is a philosophy which takes up the interests of everyone within a given nation state and defends them at the expense of everyone else. A more persuasive starting point would be to observe that while a clear majority of politicians employ a national rhetoric from time to time, only a much smaller number can be labelled nationalists. Almost every politician from the centre left to the far right speaks as if their audience is the country and this nation is a collective whole which has a single existence and a single history. Here, for example, is Labour's Tony Blair following his election victory in 1997,

> The British don't fear change. We are one of the great innovative peoples. From the Magna Carta to the first parliament to the industrial revolution to an empire that covered the world; we are by our nature and tradition innovators ... Great rewards [await] for all of us if we rise to them as we can. As one nation. Held together by our values and by the strength of our character.[5]

This, by way of comparison, is François Hollande's inauguration speech in May 2012, following his election to the French Presidency:

> We are a great country which, through its history, has always been able to brave the ordeals and take up the challenges facing it ... The first condition for new-found confidence is the nation's unity. Our differences mustn't become divisions or our diversity discord. The country needs calm, reconciliation and to come together.[6]

And here is Donald Trump campaigning during the Presidential election:

> We will be a country of generosity and warmth. But we will also be a country of law and order ... The most important difference between our plan and that of our opponents, is that our plan will put America First. Americanism, not globalism, will be our credo. As long as we are led by politi-

cians who will not put America First, then we can be assured that other nations will not treat America with respect. But this will all change in 2017.[7]

At a first reading, it is hard to distinguish between the three speeches. Each of them treats the nation as an organic whole, something whose virtue is beyond question but which faces external threats and which needs to change.

The point at which it starts to become meaningful to describe one of these politicians, but not the others, as nationalist is when national rhetoric becomes pervasive. The boundary is crossed when politicians appear to forget the obvious truth that a nation is only a metaphor, that society is in fact divided, and that different groups of people have different experiences of housing, education and employment. Nationalism is a means of suppressing the recognition of these class differences.

Any knowledge of the nationalist right in history suggests that its politics involve much more than a belief in the virtues of a nation. In the 1930s, for example, the British Union of Fascists was staffed by a generation of middle-aged men, many of whom had spent decades overseas either in the army or in the colonial civil service. Alone among the political parties in Britain in the 1930s, the branches of the British Union of Fascists asked the group's members to fill in a form specifying what languages they spoke, a practice which would have been pointless were it not for their shared experience outside Britain in her colonial territories.[8] The fascists had an idea of 'Britain' which they sought to generalise. It owed rather more to the overt racial hierarchies of Empire than it did to any positive identification with the actual conditions of England, Scotland, Northern Ireland or Wales.

In the 1970s, British nationalism was again a movement strongest among a white diaspora. The first Chairman of the National Front, A. K. Chesterton, had been born outside Johannesburg and returned there every year. He was funded by an expatriate millionaire, Robert Jeffery, who lived in Chile. Chesterton's successor John Tyndall was the son of an Irish Protestant policeman.[9] The Front's main public event was a Remembrance Day procession, held in support of white Rhodesia.

Even during the Brexit controversy, exiles and returnees were prevalent among the Leave campaigners. They included Patrick Robertson, the original founder of the Bruges Group who had lived almost all of his life in France and Italy save for attending a boarding school in England; vote Leave chairman Nigel Lawson, who prior to the referendum had left Britain permanently and settled in southwest France; Jimmy Goldsmith, who was born in France, retired to Mexico and died in Spain; Douglas Carswell who had lived in Uganda into his late teens; Arron Banks who grew up in South Africa before attending secondary school in Berkshire and at difficult moments during the referendum returned home to Pretoria.[10] The British nation for which these nationalists were fighting was a country they had known rarely and selectively; they were trying to take it back to an imagined characterisation of what it had been rather than fighting for the Britain that was there in front of their eyes.

Nationalism is, in other words, a recurring device whose purpose is to enable politicians to present themselves as speaking for everyone when in fact their programmes represent a strategy for distributing resources unequally between classes. This is the reason why Steve Bannon finds it easier to talk to Matteo Salvini or Nigel Farage than he does to a notional Pennsylvania steelworker; because Steve Bannon is motivated by a politics whose beliefs include the need to transfer wealth and power upwards rather than down. Indeed the more success Bannon and his kind have, the less the pay, the social benefits and the life expectancy of that steelworker will be.

The most sophisticated theory of how nationalism tries to change society appears in the work of the political scientists Stanley Payne, Roger Griffin and Roger Eatwell. For Griffin in particular, the defining aspect of fascism is its palingenetic ultra-nationalism. Fascists see the nation as an organic racial entity. In fascist discourse, the nation is under threat from a series of political and racial enemies and the nation must endure a violent rebirth, or 'palingenesis'. In Griffin's words:

> The mythic core that forms the basis of my ideal type of generic fascism is the vision of the (perceived) crisis of the nation as betokening the birth pangs of a new order. It crystallizes in the image of the national community, once purged and rejuvenated, rising phoenix-like from the ashes of a morally bankrupt state system and the decadent culture associated with it.[11]

The fact that someone uses nationalist language does not make them a fascist.[12] The examples just given of nationalist rhetoric include figures from the centre-left, as well as Donald Trump in his niche position straddling the centre- and far-right. Such non-fascists have used palingenetic language but without consistency and without the one-track fixation of a revolutionary nationalist.

One way to understand Griffin's analysis is to think of a series of positions from the political centre rightwards towards fascism, with the insistence on palingenesis growing more insistent at each point. Politicians at the centre mix up a language of national crisis with appeals to the basic goodness of the population, the possibilities present in any situation or the capacity of institutions to change. They speak in a language of hope, suggesting that the country is near to its ideal state and can find its way home through identifiable legal reforms. Among those on the centre right, the balance is similar but with a greater insistence on the actuality of an external threat. Supporters of the non-fascist far right use a language of crisis and rebirth, but mix it up with other ideas. For fascists, palingenesis is central. They speak in the most repetitive, obsessive, way about national decay and the need for rebirth.

I have argued in a previous book that Griffin over-emphasises the importance of language at the expense of the structure of the fascist parties; and that he is wrong to portray fascism as in essence a form of mass politics. Fascism is also a reactionary movement. It invites its adherents to destroy the organisations of social democracy: left-wing political parties and unions. It summons the people into politics in order to disenfranchise them.[13] However, one insight which Griffin's approach rightly emphasises is that, because fascism exists to promote certain groups and to push down others and because all the important distinctions of politics transcend borders, fascism shows a recurring tendency to organise on an international basis. In his words:

Fascism, though anti-internationalist in the sense of regarding national distinctiveness and identity as primordial values, is quite capable of generating its own form of universalism or internationalism by fostering a kindred spirit and bond with fascists in other countries engaged in an equivalent struggle for their own nation's palingenesis, often against common enemies (for example, liberals, communists and if they are white supremacists, non-white races). In Europe, this may well lead to a sense of fighting for a common European homeland on the basis of Europe's alleged cultural, historical or even genetic unity in contrast to non-Christian, non-Indo European/Aryan peoples.[14]

These dynamics are not limited to fascism but are shared with the non-fascist far-right, which after all is the successor to previous fascist internationals, which in the 1970s and 1980s, organised – in the same way as the contemporary non-fascist far-right – in defence of Western civilisation and the white race. The dynamics spotted by McCullough are not incidental to the far right, but recur throughout its history.

The relationship between internationalisation and radicalisation

So far, this book has treated the various successes of the newly aggressive right in 2016–17 as separate processes, taking place along national lines. Yet, convergence has meant more than an alliance between the Conservatives and UKIP or between the Republicans and Breitbart. It has also been a process which has taken place along parallel lines within several countries at once, with centre-right parties moving to the right in each of Austria, Poland, the Netherlands and so on. Indeed convergence has also seen right-wingers in different countries boosting each other, with Breitbart employing Milo Yiannopoulos as part of a plan to build an audience in Europe, former leader of the English Defence League Tommy Robinson being employed by Canada's Rebel Media, and Nigel Farage being favourably interviewed on Fox News.

These international ties have thickened in recent years and the right has become more radical as a consequence. This could be seen in the way that the radical right in the US and then its French counterpart latched on to the Brexit vote as a way of proving to American and French audiences that history was on their side.

In the first months of the 2017 French election, Breitbart ran sometimes several articles a day, each of them boosting the prospects of a Le Pen victory, claiming that the Front National was ahead in polling, describing her speeches as channelling the spirit of Brexit and Donald Trump. Just two days before the first round of voting began, Donald Trump declared Le Pen the candidate who was 'strongest on borders and she's the strongest on what's been going on in France,' in effect, endorsing her.[15]

Brexit was a major theme of the first Presidential debate in France, with the Conservative François Fillon criticising his rival Marine Le Pen for her anti-European stance. 'You want to drag the country into social and economic chaos,' he told Le Pen. 'That's called Project Fear,' she answered, 'it was used before Brexit.' During the final Presidential debate, the FN leader promised a referendum by September 2017 and said she would go to the people, calling for their support to negotiate the terms of France's membership in the EU. Macron asked if she would leave the Euro, saying that any such step would lose the French currency 20 per cent of its value overnight.

Answering defensively, Le Pen insisted that since Brexit, the UK's economy had boomed.[16]

In the same way that Brexit boosted Trump and Le Pen, so too the rise of Donald Trump was used by others on the international right to prove their own prospects of taking power. In Italy, Matteo Salvini of the League associated himself with Trump, meeting the Republican candidate in Philadelphia in April 2016, that is, before he had secured the Republican nomination and six months before the Presidential election. Salvini characterised Trump's victory as 'the triumph of the people against globalisation, against the mainstream press and the big economic interests.' Steve Bannon's endorsement of Salvini of the League and Luigi Di Maio of the Five Star Movement was front-page news on the day of the Italian elections.[17]

These international links changed the character of the right in each country, enabling it to acquire a deeper social layer of support and to advance more radical demands. Donald Trump's base in 2016 was a Republican electorate; a majority of his voters had voted four years before for the impeccably moderate and centre-right Mitt Romney. In choosing a Presidential candidate whose campaign was run by Steve Bannon, this conservative electorate was being pulled further to the right. Marine Le Pen was the leader of a party founded by fascists but ever since then a coalition of non-fascist far-rightists, Catholics, colonial and authoritarian nostalgists. In presenting herself as the leader of a party in the tradition of Brexit and Trump, she was trying to reposition herself closer to the centre than the Front ever previously had been and in that way win over voters who would never have chosen an ostensibly fascist party.

In working together in a permanent alliance, the mainstream and its outliers were converging at a mid-point somewhere between the centre and the far right.

Two models of right-wing internationalism

Among those who have lived through the events of 2016–17, there was a widespread feeling that the victories of the far right were not simply the success of one party in a particular country, but the signs of an epochal shift from one way of doing politics to another. '2017, fire and fascism,' the novelist Olivia Laing writes, 'that was how you defined eras, by death and dismemberment.' Yet the fascism her book *Crudo* describes is not the politics of the 1930s, but something less: not a system of government, but the numbness that millions felt as they looked in astonishment at an American President, different in the open contempt he had for everyone unlike him. 'She missed Obama. Everyone missed Obama. She missed the sense of time as something serious and diminishing, she didn't like living in the permanent sense of the id.'[18]

There are a number of historical analogies for the process in which right-wing parties have shared an approach across borders and became radicalised, moving further in an authoritarian direction as they have copied and competed with one another. One model is the alliance between Ronald Reagan and Margaret Thatcher following their election victories in May 1979 and November 1980. Indeed Nigel Farage made this comparison just four days after Trump's election. 'Brexit,' he claimed,

> was the first real kick back against the liberal establishment, which has with its friends in big business and the big

banks, dominated the world for the last couple of decades. What we have to do is follow the example given to us over 30 years ago by Reagan and Thatcher. They both won counter-revolution elections.[19]

The relationship between Regan and Thatcher preceded Ronald Reagan's election to the Presidency by several years. Reagan had first come to Thatcher's attention after a speech he gave to the Institute of Directors in London in 1969, warning against 'the inexorable march of government'. On her request, Reagan's office arranged for Thatcher to receive copies of the speech. They met again in 1975 and 1978. Within four days of Thatcher's election in May 1979, Reagan was the first foreign politician to congratulate her.[20] Even though he was still at that time a relatively minor figure in American politics, a mere potential candidate for the Republican nomination, he was her supporter and she was delighted to hear from him.

The similarities between the two governments in power were several and were a point of comparison for a sympathetic press. Both Thatcher and Reagan reduced taxes for the wealthy, while increasing taxes on consumption, which took money from the poor. Both rejected the use of price and income controls and the rescuing of failing businesses which had characterised the governments of Heath and Nixon, their predecessors on the right. Both administrations spoke of the need to reduce the scope of government. In both countries, however, total state spending rose between 1978 and 1992, both in real terms and as a proportion of GDP.[21] In each administration, the language of cuts was a code for refocussing government into new areas, significantly increasing spending on the army, prison and roads, while reducing subsidies for social welfare, manufacturing industry and public transport.

Both the Reagan and the Thatcher governments employed a language of moral restoration and national renewal. Both sought to bypass existing political structures (the civil service and the Tory grandees; Congress), in favour of a cadre of appointees from think tanks, including the Heritage Foundation and the Centre for Policy Studies.[22] Thatcher and Reagan each appealed to key groups of working-class supporters. Reagan promised to protect key parts of the welfare state (above all, pensions), receiving the support of the Teamsters Union, the National Maritime Union and (in a significant tactical misstep) the air traffic controllers' union, PATCO. Thatcher succeeding in 1979 in part because of her promises on unemployment and in 1983 and 1987, because of the sell-off of council housing which offered millions of people windfall profits in return for leaving the welfare state.[23] Both were skilled actors in the political game of persuading people to vote against their own most obvious interests. Under both administrations inequality between the rich and the poor was intended to increase rapidly; and did.

Both Reagan and Thatcher were monetarists, of a sort, with the ideas of Friedrich Hayek being used as an ideological justification for unpopular policies. In Britain, these ideas were simplified down to a rigid opposition to even medium level inflation, with anything more than a minimal increase in prices being (rightly) understood as a mechanism for wealth transfer from those who possessed to those who worked.[24] The war against inflation justified such policies as high interest rates and the welcoming of mass unemployment to discipline the unions and reduce the bargaining power of labour. It meant the proposals set out in Nicholas Ridley's 1977 Report (the recruitment of non-union lorry drivers, the closure of coal-based power plants, the equipment of a mobile squad of anti-union police officers)[25] and their implementation in the defeat of the 1984–5 miners' strike.

In America, there was a similar obsession with inflation which saw sharp increases in interest rates even before Reagan came into office. The war against rising prices shaped Reagan's response to the 1981 pay strike by the air traffic controllers' union, PATCO. He invoked decades-old anti-strike laws, instructing the union that if its members were not back at work within 48 hours, they would be dismissed from their employment. Between 1979 and 1982, some two and half million jobs were lost in US manufacturing. The unions, which had struck in the 1960s, were decimated and the number of private sector union jobs fell by 26 per cent.[26]

The two elections marked the starting point of a period of capital's ascendancy over labour. They were followed not just by PATCO and the miners, but by defeats for unions in many other countries, including car workers in Italy (1980) and textile workers in India (1982).[27] They ushered in a moment of capitalist advance which has long outlasted their terms in office.

The Thatcher and Reagan governments were the vanguard of a neoliberal assault. Their elections were sufficient to change the economic orthodoxy across Europe and the west, and to shift politics everywhere to the right. For the majority of the subsequent 40 years, all of us have lived in an age of neoliberalism (i.e. a moment in which economic policy has emphasised privatisation and the support of the interests of the super-rich), which has endured despite the replacement of Thatcher and Reagan's socially reactionary regimes with a subsequent generation of socially liberal privatisers (Clinton, Blair, Brown, Obama and so on).

There is also a second, older model familiar to historians of fascism and the far right. It is of what the German historian Ernst Nolte called an 'epoch of fascism'. Nolte began his account of the events of the 1920s and 1930s with the formation decades before, of a French anti-revolutionary movement, Action Française. The latter was a conservative and backward-looking campaign; its dominant politics were nostalgic, Catholic and reactionary. It became, he argued, a laboratory for the future development of fascism, with newspapers, intellectuals and a wing of former leftist recruits. It experimented with mass politics and in February 1934, a possible coup. As Action Française was succeeded by and adapted to Mussolini and Hitler, it changed. The original model of the far right gave way to something more focussed and destructive: fascism. In Spain and Romania, meanwhile, conservative movements that, unlike fascism, had originated within the state and the ruling class, converged with the fascist regimes, acting in a military alliance with them and taking on some of their character. Meanwhile, the relationship between Italian and German fascism was marked by moments of copying (Hitler's Beer Hall putsch was modelled on Mussolini's March on Rome), competition and mutual radicalisation. First, Italy began to act as a major European power, demanding the right to intercede in neighbouring states, including Austria. Then Germany copied her. Borrowing the idea of an epoch from the anti-fascist novelist Thomas Mann, Nolte developed the idea of an age of fascism, to describe how – through 20 years of crisis – the pre-1914 reactionary right could make way for the more militant fascist right of the interwar years.[28]

Behind these two models stands a single pattern. In any movement of historical change, a political movement deepens as it crosses borders. Its capacity to transform millions of people's lives is thus increased. This insight applies with equal conviction to processes demanding the revolutionary transformation of society[29] as to movements whose goals are inegalitarian and counter-revolutionary.

There are problems of course in drawing too close a comparison between either of these epochs and the period from summer 2016 to the end of 2017. The events which are the subject of this book were a period of 18 months rather than 10 or 20 years. Even if something like the same disturbance has been at work, it has (so far) gone less far. Its consequences have been felt in the election of right-wing parties straddling the mainstream and the far right, rather than (as in the 1920s and 1930s) the conversion of these countries into one-party dictatorships. The far right has been rising; it has, however, lacked the single-minded purpose of its predecessors.

As an instance of radicalisation through internationalisation, the period between 2016 and 2017 stands somewhere between these two models. In common with the politics of 1979–80, it was an electoral moment characterised by the success of right-wing candidates with significant popular support. Unlike the Reagan-Thatcher elections, however, this period saw a space opening up for politics beyond the limits of the parliamentary right, creating the opportunity for such outliers as Steve Bannon or Marine Le Pen, who had no direct comparison in 1979 or 1980.

In 2016–17, as in 1979–80, the international ties between forces at different points on the spectrum between centre and far right were part of the reason that the right succeeded.

The vote for Brexit raised the stakes for Trump's campaign, increasing his chances and requiring him to be more ambitious in his plans to change America. The success of Trump caused the likes of Bannon and Breitbart to believe that they were capable of remaking Europe as well as America. Trump's election gave Le Pen and her allies the confidence to believe that victory was possible. 'Their world is crumbling,' her advisor Florian Philippot told one journalist, 'Ours is being built.'[30] That self-belief was based on the right's victories in Britain and the United States.

CHAPTER SEVEN

Benefits and trade

The most common response to the success of Brexit and Trump or of the high support for the Front National has one of liberal mourning. According to one Labour MP Barry Sheerman, 'when you look at who voted Remain, most of them are the better educated people in our country.' The journalist Ian Dunt wrote that he was 'sick and tired of sending out cash to the rest of the country so they can whine about London and the immigrants.' Eighteen months after the referendum, David Aaronovitch told BBC's *Newsnight* that the Brexit vote was bound to be reversed, since 600,000 British people died each year and the old were Brexit's demographic. 'By the time we leave in 2020, we would have a Remain majority.' Following Trump's victory in 2016, the *Daily Kos* website, noted that one of the first acts of the Trump government had been to remove health insurance from retired miners, a social constituency which the author guessed had voted for Trump. 'Don't weep for these coal miners,' the anonymous author gloated, 'They are getting exactly the government that they voted for.'[1]

In this model, the success of the radical right has been driven by the decay of a series of institutions which have given working class people a stake in society. As these occupational and associational cultures have declined, the working class has been replaced by a new industrial poor which, facing the prospect of economic decay, rages against liberal society, voting for right wing extremists. If such liberalism is to be believed, the sole remaining purpose of the left is to watch and despair while the battles of the future are fought out between the centre and the far right.

It should be clear from previous chapters that this account fails to explain the success of either Brexit or Trump. It involves people with high social capital (usually journalists, academics or politicians) criticising the voting patterns of poorer voters and blaming them for unwelcome change. But Trump's voters were, on average, richer than Clinton's. The same dynamics could be seen in Brexit, with a majority of Brexit voters living in Southern England, nearly six out of ten Brexit voters coming from social classes, A, B and C1 and Brexit securing a majority despite low levels of working-class registration and voting.[2] It is a strange sociology which sees prejudice only in those below, when more of it is to be found among those at the top.

It is true that each of Brexit, Trump and Le Pen derived some support from working-class voters. But this needs to be placed in context. Elections in the US had been characterised for some time by both polarisation and a relative balance between the two main parties. In the four elections that preceded Trump's victory, the winning candidate out-polled the loser by 0.5 per cent of the vote (2000), 2.4 per cent (2004), 7.2 per cent (2008) and 2.9 per cent (2012). In circumstances where the support of the two main parties has been this close for over a decade and in an election determined not by the overall vote (which Clinton won), but by how the votes were distributed in the electoral college, it was crucial to his victory that Trump won in Wisconsin, Michigan and Pennsylvania, all states which had not voted Republican since 1992. There were working-class voters who did help to swing the votes in favour of Brexit and Trump; they were however a small minority within that class.

The starting point has to be the changes in the world economy since the Thatcher and Reagan elections in 1979–80. In the initial period of the mid-1980s, capital's ascendancy was made possible by open conflict: high unemployment (in the UK) and high interest rates (the US) were used to break the trade unions. Where they persisted in striking, the whole disciplinary power of the state was turned on the US air controllers and on the British miners. From the mid-1980s however, these set-piece conflicts have been replaced by slower, longer-term processes to increase the profitability of business and to discipline labour. These have included the growth of employment in service industries, much of it precarious and poorly-paid; the privatisation of state owned industries and parts of the service sector where unions once had a base; the privatisation of health and education; and the expansion of personal debt, which benefits the financial companies and disciplines workers paying the costs of education, housing, their own and their parents' care.[3]

The political loser from these processes has been social democracy, whose historic appeals to working class voters had come about successively from its emergence in the 1880s and 1890s; the memory of the Depression; the Second World War and its consolidation of politics into a conflict between the left and right wings of the anti-Nazi alliance; and the long post-war boom, during which time socialist parties had thrived by offering millions of voters practical solutions to the problems of poverty and unemployment. In far too many places since 1979, the centre-left has made peace with the super-rich. Where it has done so, it has gifted an opportunity to the right.

While liberals are wrong to blame poor voters for right-wing politics and exaggerate the decline of working class culture; on key indicators, workers' self-organisation has declined. In 1983, 20.1 per cent of US workers were members of unions, by 2017 this had fallen to 10.7 per cent. Union membership in the private sector stood at just 6.5 per cent. Trade union membership was at its highest in the UK at 13.2 million in 1979, by 2015–16, it had fallen to 6.2 million.[4] The demise of class organisation creates a structural problem for social democracy, which relies on trade unions, tenants associations and other working class organisations to formulate a programme for government and to mobilise voters behind it.

From 1979 to 2008, neoliberalism became the dominant way of doing politics on both the right and centre left. Behind its ascendancy was a widespread belief that there was simply no way of managing the economy except by giving the rich whatever they asked for. Moreover, economic liberalism seemed to prove its superiority in practice. Although in America where living standards have stagnated since the 1970s, this has been exceptional. British real household disposable incomes rose in every year between 1982 and 2008,[5] while increased trade saw middle-class living standards rise across much of the world. It was the banking crisis of 2008 which brought this long period of increased trade and rising incomes to an end.

There were two main ways in which the difficulties of neoliberalism shaped voting for the right in 2016 and 2017. First, through a stagnation in working class living standards and especially a reduction in welfare benefits payments, which delegitimised arguments for the maintenance of the status quo and gave some voters the confidence to switch to the people they saw as the most disruptive candidates; second, through a decline in the authority of proposals for increased trade, which influenced the debates around the European Union and Trump's policies of America First and gave credibility to the argument that globalisation needed to end.

Not rent or wages but benefits

The most striking feature of the economy in 2016–17 was the divergence between the wealth of the various richest and everyone else. This was the theme of Thomas Piketty's book, *Capital in the Twenty-First Century*, which argued that the very richest people were now as far away from those below them as their counterparts were during the 'Gilded Age' at the start of the twentieth century. The richest 1 per cent of the world, about 45 million people, now own an average wealth of €3 million per person or around half of all global wealth. One of the ways in which this international plutocracy has maintained its wealth has been through rent on historic capital, rather than through employing productive labour.[6] Our society has become one in which multi-billion web platforms survive by selling other businesses the right to advertise on their sites, where oil companies pay the owners of land for access to the sites on which they drill, and where the ownership of even small amounts of residential property can provide an income as generous as the best-paid work.

Donald Trump inherited a real estate empire of some 20,000 apartments from his father Fred; the value of that inherited wealth was already over $1 billion by 1987 and if all he had done was left that wealth invested in the Dow Jones average it would be worth more than $10 billion today. It was during the 1980s and 1990s that Trump's business (and indeed political) personality was formed. In his milieu, neither recklessness nor copious deceit are unusual qualities. According to one Trump supporter, Charles R. Kesler, 'He's never had to report regularly to a board of directors or to public shareholders ... He's used to being the boss, to following his intuition, to trying one thing and then another, to hiring and firing at will (and to hiring family members at will), to promoting his companies shamelessly.'[7]

As a result of successive bankruptcies, from the mid-1980s on, Donald Trump's ability to run his own building projects was significantly reduced. In 2004, his casino business was declared insolvent. In 2008, he defaulted on a $330 million loan from his New York creditor Deutsche Bank, which had been used to build the Trump International Hotel and Tower in Chicago, saying that as a result of the global banking crisis he could no longer afford to pay his debts. In 2011, Trump sold the Trump Castle casino for $38 million which may sound like an immense pay-off except that (even ignoring inflation) it was barely one-thirteenth of what Trump had paid for the casino 15 years before.[8] From 2008, Trump's personal difficulties were also shaped by the broader malaise in the economy, the ending of the speculative boom associated with the initial period of neoliberalism, the difficulty of making profits in the old bricks and mortar economy and the greater attractiveness of such new industries as information technology, programming and emerging media.

Trump's present status is the consequence of his decision after 2008 to reinvest the surplus profits of his father's rental business, not in further construction projects but in accumulating a position on television and social media. This is turn has led to a renewal of his commercial interests, save that these have increasingly depended on the investment of other people's money, with individuals in Latin America, Russia or the Middle East negotiating the right to build their own Trump Casinos or Towers. In Toronto, a *Financial Times* investigation found that the Trump Tower was largely financed by the Kremlin, with Trump's business partner Alex Shnaider paying a $100 million commission to Putin's allies and receiving in return finances of $850 million from the Russian state bank VEB. When challenged about this arrangement, a spokesmen for the Trump Organization denied that Trump had been involved in the building of the Tower and stated that: 'The Trump Organization['s] ... role was limited to licensing its brand and managing the hotel and residences.'[9] If so, then this was consistent with the general way in which Trump's business has operated for some time, which has been to co-operate with other people's capital investments. His business has long since ceased to be a matter of mere bricks and mortar.[10] The changing nature of his business is the context in which to understand Trump's bid for the Presidency: as a strategy to increase the value of the Trump brand. What is being rented out is not a physical property (land), not any sort of capital nor even an opportunity for others to work but simply the great golden egg that is Trump's own name.

The ability of the rich to increase their wealth much faster than before has not come about by coincidence. It is less a result of some unique talent belonging to this generation of the ultra-rich not shared by their predecessors, and more the inevitable consequence of nearly 40 years of changing American and European politics. For example, the primary response of governments to the 2008 crisis was to keep interest rates low, thereby protecting the owners of shares and housing. Centrist politicians of all varieties have reduced taxes, ostensibly to encourage economies to grow, but in reality, to protect the incomes of the wealthiest. They reflated their economies by spending trillions of dollars on quantitative easing, i.e. buying back their own assets from institutional lenders, with the lenders then using this money to purchase assets. According to the Bank of England, quantitative easing has increased the price of equities and house prices by 25 and 22 per cent respectively. It has been a boon for the wealthiest, and a waste of money for everyone else.[11]

From this perspective, the defining feature of 2016–17 is not the limited extent to which Donald Trump spoke about jobs, but the refusal of both Clinton and Trump to confront the advantages which wealth enjoys over everyone else.

Five months after his election victory, Donald Trump gave a speech in Pennsylvania. Consistent with his approach during the election, it emphasised the destruction of America by a cabal of the propertied, i.e. liberal Democrats. Where Trump broke from the majority of US business leaders and their allies in politics was in his insistence that one of the main victims of America's turn to globalisation over the past 40 or 50 years was the country's industrial working class:

> For decades, our country has lived through the greatest jobs theft in the history of the world. You people know it better than anybody in Pennsylvania. Our factories were shuttered. Our steel mills close down and our jobs were stolen away and shipped far away to other countries.[12]

The reason Trump's words resonated was not just because unemployment was high but because in the US over the past four decades, when manual jobs in production have gone, they have tended to be replaced by much worse paid work in services. When manufacturing employment was at its highest, in January 1973, the average hourly wage in the US was $4.03. That would have been the equivalent, with inflation, of an income of $23.61 by the end of 2017. But by that time the average hourly wage stood in fact at $22.42 per hour. Over the past 45 years, in other words, US hourly incomes have not risen in real terms at all; and if family incomes are a little higher than they were (which they are), this is only because many more women work and the combined hours worked by the typical family are much greater than they were.[13]

The response of the political centre, when faced by the right claiming to speak on behalf of the dispossessed, was to deny that there was anything wrong with capitalism. Employment rates were high and business was booming. This is Trump's Democratic opponent Madeleine Albright's response, in the course of a recent book warning of the threat of fascism, to Trump's speech in Pennsylvania:

> A speaker with a more objective approach might have noted the decline in Pennsylvania's unemployment to below five percent from eight percent a few years earlier … Trump inherited an economy that, among countries larger than Switzerland, was the world's most competitive.[14]

In comments like these we can see why since 2008, parties such as the Democrats (or the European social democrats who take a cue from them) have lost so many elections. For Americans who have lived through four decades of stagnant wages, it is no comfort to be told that the national economy is competitive

– in other words, that its factories are productive and that the wages paid to the workers are low. Competitiveness is not a soothing ointment but a legitimate reason for anger.

One reason why the centre left is unwilling to follow the right in questioning the dominant economic model of the past 40 years is that the former has been the recipient of significant donations from the very people who have benefited the most from neo-liberalism. This is easiest to see in the US. While the Democrats have always, in comparison to the classical European social democratic parties of 1930–60, been much more dependent on donations from businessmen rather than social movements such as trade unions, the imbalance has grown even greater in recent years. In 2016, three of the four largest donors to US political parties, hedge fund manager James Simons, Michael Bloomberg and George Soros, gave to the Democrats, not to the Republicans. When funders such as Bloomberg (a former Republican) donate to causes, they chose those which maintain progressive cultural values (i.e. gun control, climate change)[15] rather than those which encourage redistribution. Where the centre left draws its political inspiration from such allies, the result is an unequal conflict in which the left is allowed to speak only a language of culture while a right which marries cultural battles to economic grievances, wins.

In Britain and in France, the 2016–17 debates reflected processes of income inequality going back little further than the 2008 crash. Income growth in the UK fell behind inflation for the first time in decades after 2008 and since then inflation has kept ahead of wage growth. The contraction was so sharp that at the time of writing, wages were not expected to rise above their 2008 levels until 2020. British workers had not seen a pay squeeze of this depth for more than a century.[16]

In France, the 2008 crash saw the incomes of the poorest 10 per cent fall by €520 million. The wealth of the richest, meanwhile, grew by €14 billion. In 2013, 83 per cent of French voters said they expected the gap between rich and poor to widen.[17]

Yet while a stagnation in working class living standards was reflected in the Brexit debates and in both Presidential elections, in the US and in Britain it was not the main source of voting for the far right. As previous chapters have noted, Trump's social base was not poorer than Clinton's. If anything, it was slightly richer. In Britain, meanwhile, a majority of those in work voted to Remain. Brexit was not a vote of the poor in general, nor of all who worked. It was above all a ramp of the propertied. In so far as it did appeal to poorer voters, its pitch was to a specific part of this group.

While the living standards in Britain of waged workers have stagnated for ten years; those living on benefits have suffered even more than the average. Cuts to social benefits since 2010 have included a cap on housing benefit which is no longer allowed to pay more than 30 per cent of local private sector rents. That was followed by the abolition of the Education and Maintenance Allowance for poorer college students. There have been caps on housing benefit for single people aged 35 or under. The bedroom tax has reduced the housing benefit available to people living in homes containing more than one bedroom. A cap was introduced to limit total household benefits. This was followed by the abolition of Disability Living Allowance for disabled claimants. The government introduced a freeze from 2016 on all working age benefits. The backdating of housing benefit has been limited to one month. Additional child benefit is now refused to families with more than two children.[18]

The effect of all these changes has been to make those living on benefits much poorer, not just than those in full-time work, but even compared to their counterparts who were living on benefits ten years ago. The number of people evicted from their homes has risen, as have homelessness and rough sleeping. The number of people relying on food banks has also grown, with one provider, the Trussell Trust, feeding 14,000 in 2007–8, and 1,100,000 in 2016–17, just under half of whom were children.[19]

This has been the greatest transfer of resources away from the poor in Britain in more than a century. Inevitably, it causes people to distrust politicians.

The economist Thiemo Fetzer has studied UKIP voting between 2010 and 2016 and shown that it correlates very closely to experience of welfare cuts. In areas of the country where welfare reforms such as the bedroom tax affected an average or greater number of households, UKIP voting increased by 12 per cent between 2010 and 2015. Resentment of welfare cuts was, he concludes, the most important single factor underpinning the Leave victory in the 2016 referendum.[20]

Britain is an extreme case of austerity politics; but the processes underlying the events of 2016–17 affected a much wider set of countries. Brexit, Trump and Le Pen arrived at the transition point between two different ways of doing politics. In the first, between 2008 and 2015, the main response of the right to the economic crash had been the demand to balance budgets and to cut welfare programmes. At the point at which a message of austerity was first put, it had the advantage of

novelty and of a seeming strength of purpose. It acknowledged that the world economy was in trouble (which it was),
and promised a robust solution. In the previous era of welfare
spending, the state had overspent. Now it was time to insist
that budgets were balanced, which could not be done by
raising taxes on the rich but had to come through reduced
expenditure.

The problem with austerity was that it was ill-equipped to
provide any sort of lasting answers. After all, while the message
that cuts must happen to (someone else's benefits) can seem
to be mere common sense, eventually voters noticed that
their children's schools, their libraries, the hospitals their own
parents used were closing too. At that point, austerity ceased to
seem bold and seemed merely vindictive.

As the need for ever deeper cuts was pushed to an ever
further and bleaker future, there was every risk that voters
would reject it. A second response therefore came to dominate
on the right, a return to the protection of health services and
benefits, albeit by excluding foreigners' access to them.

In her book *Strangers in their Own Land,* based on several
years research among Tea Party voters, the anthropologist
Arlie Russell Hochschild has suggested that of all the ideological weapons available to the new right in recent years,
the most effective has been the belief that social security was
enabling racial others to sneak ahead of deserving whites. The
paradox, Hochschild found, was that the areas which have
seen the greatest industrial pollution, the greatest attacks on
unions and which have left workers most atomised were also
the ones where the greatest numbers of voters chose Trump.
Hochschild argues that for the troops of the new right, the
key issue has been the allocation of welfare. Families who

depend on state handouts have accepted the arguments that the benefits are going to someone else: 'women, immigrants, refugees, public-sector workers – where will it end? Your money is running through a liberal sympathy sieve you don't control or agree with.'[21]

As in Britain during Brexit, the right in America was latching on to a particular segment of the working class and one which was the worst placed to resist their ideological message. When politicians from the right try to sell a message to waged workers that the future lies in subordinating certain races, this message cuts against the experience of employment, which is that people from different groups are brought together and any collective campaigns require different groups of workers to meet and to unite. On the other hand, working-class people living on benefits have no workplace, no union and rarely any experience of joint struggle. It is therefore easier to persuade them that pensions, social security and other benefits can be sustained only be excluding others.

Racism, the East End doctor and pioneering anti-fascist Dave Widgery once wrote, is 'a simple answer ... an antidote to thought ... a blanket in your head to hide under'.[22] But if you see the world in 2016–17 from the perspective of those who lived on benefits, millions of whom were struggling to eat, you can begin to understand why that blanket – indeed any blanket – seemed attractive.

Trump's greatest success in Wisconsin, Michigan and Pennsylvania was not in persuading former Obama voters to vote for him, but in persuading enough of them not to vote. Similarly, Brexit's working class support was shallow among those who worked, but much deeper among pensioners and others who relied on benefits. In the absence of a plausible left-wing argument that politicians could be trusted to tax the rich and raise the money for shared services, the idea of restricting benefits to those with citizenship seemed a plausible way of making sure that benefits were paid.

Globalisation paused

Trump's politics of America First, Brexit and Marine Le Pen's success were also responses to the globalisation of trade. Since 1979–80, there has been an absolute consensus among politicians in the advanced world that it is better for trade borders to be kept to a minimum across the richer economies and between these economies and the developed world. It is said that free trade benefits the richer nations, who have higher levels of investment in technology. Free trade polarises production into high-technology and lower-technology sectors. The richer countries benefit as the exporters of high-technology goods, which poorer states desire, but lack the investment to produce. Richer countries also prosper as the importers of lower-tech goods, which are cheaper if they are produced by workers paid less elsewhere.

While Trump is often portrayed as an opportunist, a lifelong Democrat switching to the Republicans without any reasons of principle for adopting his new party, his hostility to the terms on which trade has been globalised is in fact longstanding. As long ago as 1987, Donald Trump paid for an advertisement in the *New York Times*, the *Washington Post* and the *Boston Globe*, criticising US foreign policy for sheltering American client states (Japan and Saudi Arabia) without requiring them to subsidise American defence spending. Part of the argument was that global terms of business were impacting unfairly on

America, which, as the world's military power, should have been able to force its allies to subsidise its hegemony:

> Over the years, the Japanese, unimpeded by the huge costs of defending themselves (as long as the United States will do it for free), have built a strong and vibrant economy with unprecedented surpluses. They have brilliantly managed to maintain a weak yen against a strong dollar. This, coupled with our monumental spending for their and others, defence, has moved Japan to the forefront of world economies.[23]

Trump followed up this manifesto with a 1990 interview for *Playboy* magazine, in which he complained of Japanese competitors 'screw[ing]' their US rivals, which the Japanese did first by selling their computer goods to Americans at inflated prices then buying real, physical assets (e.g. real estate) in the US. America's allies were able to profit because of two competitive advantages, first because of state protection which the US had wrongly eschewed in an epoch of free trade ('Their products are better because they have so much subsidy'); and second, because the US contributed more than it needed to NATO and other international bodies ('We Americans are laughed at around the world for losing $150 billion year after year, for defending wealthy nations for nothing'). Trump's solution was to threaten America's allies with trade wars, 'I'd throw a tax on every Mercedes-Benz rolling into this country and on all Japanese products and we'd have wonderful allies again.'[24] All of these ideas were restated during Trump's campaign for the Presidency in 2015–16.

For the sycophants of the new right, such as Fox News' Tucker Carlson, the political genius of the Trump campaign is that he was the first person in Western politics to have opposed 'trade deals that eliminated jobs'.[25] It would be more accurate to say that neoliberal globalisation has been declining in popularity and authority for some time, and long prior to 2016. Since the 2008 crisis, businesses have been unwilling to invest beyond their own borders. The consequences of the banking crisis have included tighter credit conditions and lower corporate profits, which triggered a sharp fall in global foreign direct investment (FDI). Since the banking crisis, FDI has remained at low levels, aggravated by the tendency for US and European companies to hoard excess capital, so that they were neither investing in their home country nor seeking opportunities abroad. According to the Organisation for Economic Co-operation and Development, global FDI reached its highest level in 2007 and as of 2016 was still 25 per cent below its peak.[26]

While businesses have been investing less abroad, political objections to cross-border free trade agreements have also been increasing. There have been significant protests against meetings of the World Trade Organisation in Seattle (1999), the A16 in Washington (2000), the G8 at Genoa (2001), the IMF and World Bank in Washington (2002), and meetings of the G20 in London (2009).

In a context of stagnant investment and increasing public criticism, it has become ever harder to negotiate new international trade treaties. The Multilateral Agreement on Investment, a proposal to protect foreign investments, was vetoed by its host, France, in 1998. The Free Trade Area of the Americas, intended to extend NAFTA to Central America, collapsed in 2005. The Doha Development Round of the WTO, a ten-year attempt to negotiate lower tariffs on agriculture, industry and services, stalled without agreement in 2008. CETA, the free trade agreement between the European Union and Canada, took five years to negotiate between 2009 and 2014 and came close to collapse in 2016, when vetoed by the Walloon regional parliament. By the end of 2017, just eight European Union states had ratified it.[27]

By 2016, there were any number of institutional voices arguing that neoliberal globalisation was responsible for instability and inequality and needed to change. In November 2016, for example, 13 economists met to sign a shared declaration (the 'Stockholm Statement') saying that globalisation had gone awry. Among the initial signatories were no fewer than four former Chief Economists of the World Bank.[28]

It was because globalisation was already unpopular that Trump and Brexit received backing from significant parts of the business world. Thomas Ferguson, Paul Jorgensen and Jie Chen's study of the millionaires who gave to Trump's campaign shows how the source of donations changed over time. In spring 2016, when Trump won the Republican nomination, he received support from coal mining companies, the major pharmaceutical companies (Hillary Clinton had been threatening to regulate drug prices), tobacco, chemical companies, oil producers including Chevron and Exxon, telecommunications (principally AT&T, which had a merger pending), banks (Bank of America, J. P. Morgan Chase, Morgan Stanley and Wells Fargo) and even some modest donations from Silicon Valley. At around the same time, Trump also appears to have negotiated an agreement with the United States' largest owner of TV stations, the Sinclair Broadcast Group. What these donors had in common was that they were frequent historic contributors to the Republican Party.

From August 2016, when Bannon was appointed as Trump's campaign manager and the slogan America First came to the fore, the nature of Trump's backing shifted. One new group of Trump investors consisted of steel, rubber, and the manufacturers of industrial machines. The other main group of Bannon-era donors were the billionaire owners of private equity firms, Michael Milken (once instrumental to the development of junk bonds, but in 1989 convicted of serious fraud),[29] Nelson Peltz (owner of Trian Fund Management and part-owner of US food companies Heinz and Cadbury's) and Carl Icahn (a corporate raider, specialising in taking over failing businesses, such as the TWA airline and selling off their property and machinery for windfall profits). While business donations to Trump's campaign were overall at a lower level than donations to Clinton, there were parts of US capital for whom Trump was the preferred candidate.[30] Donations from sectors such as steel and machine tools are best explained in terms of Trump's policies of using tariffs to protect industry.

Brexit saw a similar polarisation within British business circles. While senior politicians and a majority of firms favoured Remain, there were also a number of businesses which favoured Brexit, including high street brands (Next, Dixons, Weatherspoon's) and the owners of some hedge funds (Asset Management, CQS and C Hoare and Co).[31] By far the most important backers of Brexit were the Anglo-Atlantic owners of the UK press, with six out of ten of Britain's daily newspapers (the *Daily Mail,* the *Daily Express*, the *Telegraph*, the *Sun,* the *Daily Star* and *The Times)* running significantly more pro-Leave than pro-Remain articles.[32] As with Trump in the US, Brexit was never the majority demand of British business; it just needed to have enough support to appear credible.

The effect of these processes was to change the balance of politics. Austerity's sharp attack on benefits neutralised a long tradition of working class opposition to the far right. Meanwhile, the disagreements within the super-rich as to whether or not to continue with globalisation enabled Trump, Brexit and Le Pen to present themselves as equal combatants in a struggle between a globalised left and a nationalist right.

CHAPTER EIGHT

Could the far right change back?

This book has argued that we are in a post-fascist moment. In other words, that fascism remains a despised tradition and that the most successful recent movements on the right have been those which have acknowledged fascism's unpopularity and based their politics on more recent events: on 9/11 rather than Hitler or Mussolini. This chapter asks whether that shift within the far right is permanent, whether a far right which has turned away from fascism might turn back in years to come. If this question is addressed from the perspective of today's leaders, then the answer is straightforward: none of Donald Trump, Nigel Farage or Marine Le Pen envisage a revolutionary war against the liberal state; their approach is solely electoral and this is likely to remain the case for any foreseeable future. The leaders of the converged right and far right are well aware that the dominant values of our time remain hostile to fascism. This is one reason why, for example, the League was able to form a government in Italy while the Front failed in France. The former was not founded as a fascist party, its adoption of Italian nationalism has made it a hybrid party, combining nationalism with its earlier regional politics. The party was mobile, heterogeneous and hard to pin down. It was in these ways different from the Front and better equipped for power.

This chapter approaches the question of whether under the next generation of leaders on the right, the direction of travel might yet be reversed. This question is approached in two ways: first, historically, through a study of the street movements of the far right and in particular the British EDL and its successors, and then politically, by asking what the far right loses from the subordination of its fascist element.

Street movements

The fascist parties of the 1920s and 1930s were committed to street politics at the expense of electoralism. They were serious about purging the liberal state and replacing the existing structures with their own appointees. This approach is incompatible with parliamentary politics, in which any victory is only temporary, and large parts of the state (the judiciary, the army, the civil service) are immune to political control. For that reason, if there is going to be a fascist party in the future, it is most likely to emerge out of those far right movements which reject conventional politics in favour of the street. The typical street parties of recent years have been groups such as Britain's English Defence League or Germany's Patriotic Europeans Against the Islamisation of the West (Pegida). As yet, neither of these has become a party, still less a fascist party. These are principally racists, organised in a protest movement, with few cadres, with no conception of political or cultural revolution, and no model of personal leadership or of the spiritual renewal of the nation. For the most part, the leaders of these groups have had little knowledge of or interest in the fascist ideology of 70 years ago, and yet they have shared with historic fascism a profound hostility to conventional politics and to the existing state.

The politics of such movements can be illustrated by the text of the Prague Declaration which Pegida signed in 2016 along with a series of allies, the Czech Blok proti islámu, Estonia's Conservative People's Party, Lega Nord, Poland's National Movement and Pegida groups in Austria, Bulgaria and Holland:[1]

> Being aware of the fact that the thousand-year history of Western civilisation could soon come to an end through Islam conquering Europe and the fact that the political elites have betrayed us, we, representatives of different European nations, declare the following: We will not surrender Europe to our enemies. We are prepared to stand up and oppose political Islam, extreme Islamic regimes and their European collaborators.[2]

On the face of it, the Prague Declaration offered little more than a radical hostility to Islam, in other words, much the same politics as the dominant Western response to 9/11, except in a more concentrated form. Here were various figures on the right taking ideas from the mainstream and pushing them further.

Yet even in this short passage there were hints that the step rightwards from mainstream to margin represented a change of substance as well as form. To speak of Islam's 'collaborators' was to suggest that there were Europeans who had outstepped the limits of acceptable behaviour and should themselves be jailed or expelled. The signatories went on to explain who their enemies were: 'the Central European government ... the global elites [whose rules] have brought ... corruption, chaos and moral collapse.' Mere Islamophobia followed to its logical conclusion required a cultural war against politicians (in Pegida's case, the 'traitor' Angela Merkel) and their business cronies. It meant the re-establishment of Europe as a mono-ethnic one party space, purged of anyone who equivocated in the face of the Islamic threat.

The origins of the English Defence League were similar to Pegida's. It was a street movement, mainly composed of newcomers to far right politics. Its dominant politics were anti-Muslim and post-9/11 rather than directly fascist. The formation to the EDL represented a rejection of previous models of far-right organising. Between 2001 and 2009, the far right in Britain had been dominated by two main parties, UKIP and the British National Party. The latter's successes included the election of three councillors in Burnley in 2002, further gains until the party reached 58 councillors in 2009, and in the same year the election of Andrew Brons and Nick Griffin to seats in the European Parliament. During this period, the BNP modelled itself on the electoral Euro-fascists of the FN and the AN, naming its magazine *Identity* after the Front's publication of the same name. Despite its growth, the BNP suffered a very large number of splits, with elected councillors in different parts of the country quitting on contact with the national leadership. With its disavowal of any sort of street politics and its insistence on electoralism, the BNP seemed to be no more than half of a 'proper' fascist party.[3] By 2009, the BNP had recruited members across the country, but many of its branches were in decline and this process accelerated from October 2009 when BNP leader Nick Griffin was invited onto

Question Time. Confronted by the other panellists, Griffin gave a series of shallow answers, claiming for example that he had ceased to be a Holocaust Denier but was prevented by European law from explaining what he now believed. Griffin failed to connect with his audience and his answers cemented his party's public reputation as a party of unreformed fascists.[4]

The roots of the EDL go back to a campaign by Luton football casuals angered by Anjem Choudary and his provocative group Islam4UK. Choudary held a demonstration in Luton against a homecoming march by the Royal Anglian Regiment, at which placards called the soldiers cowards and killers. In response, groups of football casuals demanded a physical reaction against Choudary and against Muslims. The result was a series of demonstrations, ostensibly against Islamic extremism, but often resulting in physical attacks on British Muslims.

The EDL was boosted by an influx of BNP members or former members. Nigel Copsey has listed the BNP figures who participated in the nascent EDL, including Peter Fehr, the BNP's Luton organiser, who asked the members of his group to attend the EDL's first protest, Laurence Jones from Dunstable and Chris Mitchell, an organiser for Young BNP who also attended. The EDL website organiser 'John Sheridan' (Chris Renton) was a BNP member, as was Davy Cooling, administrator of the EDL's Luton Facebook group. By autumn 2009, Stephen Yaxley-Lennon ('Tommy Robinson') had emerged as the EDL's leader. Robinson was a former member of the BNP, and photographs exist of him attending meetings addressed by the Holocaust denier Richard Edmonds. Other BNP stalwarts to have joined EDL events included Karen Otty, the BNP's Merseyside Secretary, Wakefield BNP organiser, John

Aveyward and Stuart Bates and Michael Fritz from the BNP's West Midlands security team.[5] They brought organising experience, but the BNP's support was in other ways a liability, since the BNP leadership was widely perceived as out of touch, obsessed with ideology and tied to the past. By contrast, the EDL was trying to be something new.

The first point at which the English Defence League distinguished itself from the British National Party was through holding demonstrations, often in smaller towns and typically from the railway station to a central square where speeches would be held. This was different from the BNP for whom demonstrations were a rarity and the main local event was a private meeting with a single speaker. BNP members were expected to read and sell a magazine drafted by the party's leaders, reflecting a culture in which the membership served to communicate the leader's politics. The League did not have a list of approved publications. The EDL's events were public rather than private, active rather than passive. They were supplemented by Facebook discussions and a website with a calendar of upcoming demonstrations. From the perspective of Muslims in the affected towns, an EDL presence meant racist language and physical attacks such as in Luton in May 2009, when an Asian man was assaulted, numerous car windscreens were smashed and the window of a restaurant smashed in.[6]

Different groups within the EDL distanced themselves from the BNP, as a way of seeking to imprint their own personalities on the movement. The largest group were football fans,[7] many from Luton where the group had been formed. One early recruit was the pseudonymous 'Billy Blake' whose book *Coming down the Road*, provides a diary of the demonstrations held during the EDL's first two years. Blake tried to portray the EDL as the inheritor of a socialist tradition, comprising such unlikely figures as Bessie Braddock, the Labour MP for Liverpool Exchange from 1945, a one-time Communist who became a hammer of the Labour left, and Dave Nellist the Militant supporter and Labour MP for Coventry South East from 1983 to 1992. Even the name Billy Blake was a tribute of sorts to the eighteenth century radical poet. For Blake, it was significant that the EDL marched carrying English flags, not the Union Jack, and called itself the English Defence League:

> [T]he English working class is a distinct ethnic group, with its own tradition and culture ... The English working class are traditionally proud people who lead tough lives and operate on a system of core beliefs and values: patriotism, loyalty, a black and white view of right and wrong and an ingrained support of the underdog ... Even though they might not necessarily support a particular war, the English working class will still support the military while they are risking their lives for Queen and Country ... With this in mind it is obvious to see how the protest by the radicals [Islam4UK] was perceived as a direct challenge by English working class males who took to the streets believing it was their duty to respond and defend the soldiers.[8]

A second group seeking to shape the English Defence League were people who wanted to tie the group to an international milieu of far-rightists. In 2009–10, these included 'Alan Lake' (Alan Ayling), a computer technician who spoke at an anti-Islamic conference on 6 September 2009 in Malmö organised by the far right Swedish Democrats and on his return was widely reported in the press to be the EDL's financier and chief strategist. On 11 September, a group known as Stop Islamisation of Europe (SIOE) called an event to oppose the building of a mosque in Harrow. The EDL was reported to have co-sponsored the event and at this stage it seemed likely that the EDL might evolve into the UK chapter of an anti-Islam international. Others arguing for an 'international' strategy, included Roberta Moore, a Brazilian-born Jewish Islamophobe who founded an EDL Jewish division and was pushed forward by the EDL leadership as a way of proving that the group had a wide range of supporters. In February 2011, Moore announced that she was in discussions with Victor Vancier, a pro-Israeli terrorist who had been jailed in 1978 and 1986 for fire bombings of cars, homes and concert halls associated in his mind with Israel's Egyptian and Soviet enemies. Despite the controversy surrounding Moore's association with a convicted terrorist, the leadership asked her to represent the EDL in discussions with the SIOE, including at conference in Strasbourg in June 2011.[9]

The history of the right includes various proterozoic stages, when new political forms emerged, capable of developing in different directions, including towards the creation of an authoritarian party. The violence and racism of the Ku Klux Klan has an obvious affinity to the politics of the 1920s and 1930s; and yet the Klan never developed the ideological coherence of classical fascism. The British Brothers League, which campaigned against Jewish migration from 1901 to 1905, can also be seen as a precursor to fascism, although it emerged with mainstream (i.e. Conservative) support and had little programme other than anti-migrant racism. The post-1918 German Freikorps, characterised by nostalgia for the war, anti-Communism and an intense and violent misogyny, trained many future leaders of the NSDAP, Heinrich Himmler of the SS, Ernst Röhm of the SA and Rudolf Höß, the Commandant at Auschwitz. In Robert Paxton's history of fascism, groups of this sort form a first stage, giving way later to the more familiar faces of fascism as a mass movement and then as a regime.[10]

Pegida and the EDL on their foundation had a similar capacity of evolving into a fully formed political party with a worked-out political programme borrowed from the past (i.e. from fascism), although this was only one of several possible outcomes. There were other directions in which the EDL could have turned. Another might have been for the group to shed its origins as a social movement and to become an electoral party. Something like this happened in Germany where Pegida was at its height for a year after October 2014, after which the movement shifted in an electoral direction, with several of its former supporters going over to the Alternative for Germany, which won 92 seats in federal elections, securing its highest votes in the southern districts of the old East Germany (the exact area, in other words, where Pegida had been strongest).[11] Alternatively, the English Defence League could have followed the Billy Blake model, deepening its social content and formulating a wider ideological programme. This could have included drawing on the EDL's past as a group of working-class football supporters, but developing a wider project. Or the group could have become a British affiliate of SIOE or any of the other mini-internationals of the right.

Tommy Robinson, Kevin Carroll and the leaders of the EDL proved incapable of choosing between these strategies, but attempted all of them at different times. In September

2009, Robinson staged a press conference in front of journalists from *Newsnight* for which he and a dozen others dressed up in black balaclavas and produced a swastika, which they then burned. While this seemed to be an attempt – albeit an inept one – to separate the EDL from any far-right association, by the following April, EDL supporters were seen attending a demonstration in support of Geert Wilders outside the Dutch embassy called by the Pax Europa Citizens Movement. In November 2011, Robinson announced he was ending the EDL in favour of an electoral alliance with the British Freedom Party, a splinter from the BNP. The move was criticised by the EDL's members and ultimately dropped, despite Kevin Carroll's success in winning 8,500 votes in the election for Luton's Police and Crime Commissioner in 2012.

In 2013, Tommy Robinson announced that he was quitting the far right in order to work with the anti-Islamist Quilliam Foundation. Within a couple of years, however, he was back with the far right, offering to be the leader of a UK offshoot of the Pegida campaign.[12] When this failed to break through, Robinson sought to reinvent himself as an independent journalist and social media celebrity. He was paid a salary of just under £100,000 a year by the Canadian far-right social media site Rebel Media, to film himself carrying out stunts in which he would confront advocates of multiculturalism. These were followed up by obsessive tweets in which Robinson claimed to know of undocumented Islamic outrages. In June 2017, Darren Osborne, drove a van at Finsbury Park Mosque, killing Markram Ali, a grandfather from Haringey. Osborne was radicalised in part by reading posts from Robinson. Following Osborne's trial for murder, Twitter closed down Robinson's account.[13]

Through the course of 2017, the English Defence League was superseded by a new organisation, the Football Lads Alliance, which mobilised a similar demographic of football hooligans and first-time supports of the far right. At least initially, the FLA's cadre was older than their counterparts among the EDL and ostensibly even more hostile to all organised politics, even right-wing politics. It made strenuous efforts to ban chanting, slogans, banners, flags (save for the St George's flag and the Union Jack), even alcohol, all of which it associated with the EDL. In its first few months, the FLA sought to exclude Robinson. The FLA also found new allies, notably in Birmingham, where a 'Justice4the21' campaign group had been set up to demand a fair inquest for the victims of the 1974 pub bombings. The Football Lads Alliance split in an argument concerning John Meighan, the FLA's founder and the steps he had made to set up a private company to profit from FLA merchandise, giving rise to a Democratic FLA (DFLA) successor. For the DFLA, like the EDL, the target was not just 'extremists' (in other words, Muslims) but their allies: all of liberal society.

Having lost his Twitter account, Tommy Robinson forced his way to the leadership of the movement, speaking at DFLA events and confronting the state, filming trials of Muslim suspects and risking the collapse of those cases. He had already received a suspended sentence for contempt of court in 2017, after attempting to film from the court building where (he said) Muslim rape suspects were being tried. Robinson did the same again a year later, pleading guilty to contempt charges and received a 13-month sentence, which he then successfully appealed.

Through these events, and in particular a mass campaign demanding Robinson's release from prison, a new far-right milieu was built, combining supporters of electoral projects (Gerard Batten, the new leader of UKIP), Canadian and American funders, British allies of Steve Bannon (Raheem Kassam, formerly of Breitbart London), the supporters of the Football Lads Alliance and people brought in by Robinson's social media presence. Once again, different parts of the right were converging in defiance of their seeming political differences. The parliamentarianism of UKIP and the street approach of Tommy Robinson were no obstacle to a sustained collaboration.[14] What the final result would be of this convergence was far from clear.

One theme of Klaus Theweleit's study of a previous generation of proto-rightists, the German Freikorps of 1918–20, is that they were equipped as much by misogyny as by racism. In their imagination, women might be 'white', that is nurses or aristocrats, beautiful and passive; or they might be 'red', the castrating women who led Communist gangs and who deserved to be met with rape or murder.[15]

A similar contempt for women has informed parts of the emergent British far right since 2017. Tommy Robinson portrays his movement as a campaign to save white women and children from what would otherwise be their inevitable rape at the hands of Muslims. This is a discourse in which even at its most 'heroic', women are never more than the subjects of other people's decisions. In Sunderland, the DFLA has organised under the banner of 'Justice for women and children'. The men who are supposed to be protecting women turn out themselves to be no paragons of virtue. Far-right supporters John Broomfield of Britain First and Richard Price of the EDL have been convicted for downloading, and making, child pornography. Kristopher Allan of the EDL's Scottish affiliate was convicted of sending indecent images to and having sexual contact with a 13-year-old child.[16] It is not surprising that the men who claim to be defending women turn out to be sexual predators. Even at its most 'feminist', their politics treats women as the objects and not the subjects of their own lives.

In her book *Angry White People*, the journalist Hsiao-Hung Pai spent several years shadowing members of the EDL, including 'Darren' a founding member of the group who had taken part in early EDL marches, carrying a 'black and white unite' banner, and was fiercely loyal to the group's origins in terrace culture. Darren was Kevin Carroll's cousin and, like him, of Irish ancestry. A key moment came when Darren saw Carroll taking his grandfather's wartime medal to an EDL protest, in order to ward off criticisms that he came from an Irish background. 'Grandad went through all that war, for Kev to stand in the Midlands somewhere, to try and prove to the EDL crowd that he's British. I'll never forgive him for that.'[17] Darren believed that the leaders of the EDL presented themselves as the representatives of the working class but that, unlike the people who lived on Luton's housing estates, Carroll and Robinson had no belief in the underdog and were not loyal even to their own families.

Darren's story should not be taken as a sign that the EDL and its successors had a continuing problem with the war, or that they were simply a stage in what was the inevitable re-emergence of a fascist street culture. One of the EDL's favourite pub songs was Ten German Bombers ('and the RAF from England shot them down'), with the word 'Muslim' substituted for German. The supporters of the EDL left wreaths at war memorials.[18] Tommy Robinson himself has a Churchill quote on his arm. As a group, the EDL was at ease with its sense of history, and more than capable of presenting itself as the successor to the British patriotic glory of 1939–45.

While the street orientation of the EDL and its successors and their rejection of democratic politics might be said to open the door to a more aggressive street politics of the right, there is very little else that points in the same direction. Tommy Robinson's alliances have been with the various anti-Islamic internationals (SIOE and Pegida) rather than with parties of fascist origin. The movements he has built have remained just that, social movements rather than parties. The unifying factor is anti-Islamic racism rather than a fascist programme. The method of fascism was not to reject parliament in favour of the street but to combine both. Fascism is a coherent form of politics with a worked out strategy for confronting the state and a programme for government. Robinson's success is by contrast defiantly anti-political. The politics of an epoch of conservative far-right convergence have assisted the far right; but what they had not yet done is produce growing numbers of fascists.

Can the far right return to fascism?

The far right has grown; its fascist component has withered. These two statements are both true, yet their combination is unstable. After all, fascism is a part of the far right; so the more that the right grows, you would expect fascism to flourish. Another reason you would expect the fascist component of the far right to grow in future is connected to the very category 'far right'. While this term has a changing meaning, it has a certain recurring logic, which shapes all the groups which belong to it. At different points in the last 100 years the far right has been principally nostalgic (in the 1900s, with Action Française), a party of anti-black racists (the Klan), anti-semitic (Dreyfus, the British Brother Leagues) counter-revolutionary (after 1917), and so on. Despite this discontinuity of ideas, the people involved in the different far right projects are coherent enough to be worth treating as a single group. People can inhabit a similar point on the political spectrum to those who went before, even while the projects which motivate them change. Indeed the logic of occupying the same political space causes parties to find different routes to the same solutions: opposing democracy, opposing social reforms, using rhetorical and physical violence against their opponents.

The metaphor of a genealogical tree suggests that the effective content of political tradition can be recreated even while the surface forms are changed. Under capitalism, it is possible to have parties that call for greater or lesser equality (the left and the right); it is possible to have parties that call for stability or transformation (the mainstream and the extremes). If and when there are in future mass parties calling for a counter-revolutionary war to re-establish fading social hierarchies, the chances are that these parties will behave something like a fascist party, even if they have not copied the ideas of previous fascists, but have found their own way to them.

While the ideas of fascism were opportunistic and the speeches contained a very high degree of verbiage and promises which no leader intended to keep, there were certain recurring themes which equipped fascists in their project of fighting a social and cultural war against their enemies. Some examples of these core ideas include the idealisation of struggle, the use of anti-socialism and of anti-semitism.

The fascists maintained that they were fighting a cultural and political war against the society around them and that the outcome of their war would be an entirely different system. They presented themselves as revolutionaries (in the sense of being violently opposed to the status quo in Europe) and in that way, were able to appeal to some of the most impoverished people in the world around them, including many unemployed workers. Anti-socialism was another core idea, which gave the fascists a purpose and a source of allies among the mainstream right.

Anti-Jewish racism fitted closely with the way in which German and Italian fascists saw themselves. They were against the Russian Communists, who (they said) were led by a generation of left-wing Jews, and against the Western Communists who were leading strikes that threatened to destroy the nation. Anti-semitism provided the fascists with a series of enemies below them. Yet the fascists were also (in their own eyes) militant advocates of change. In their understanding of the world, the Jews were not merely in the USSR, they were also in America, where they dominated Wall Street. Anti-semitism gave the interwar right a critique of capitalism as well as communism and enabled the fascists to appear neither left nor right. This dual positioning was essential to the project of mass counter-revolutionary politics.

Over the past two decades, the right has renounced these ideas. Rather than teaching their supporters to prepare for a struggle, literal or metaphorical, the dominant style of the contemporary right is to present their messages as a series of provocations.[19] Supporters of the far right like to say that they speak ironically. This is, as one right-wing blogger, Mytheos Holt, puts it, 'an ironic pose: a way to stick their thumbs in the eyes of the moralists and orthodoxy-enforcers of both Right and Left'.[20] This style can be a successful way for unpopular groups to win a hearing. But when a moment acquires any sort of power, it must take a responsibility for its supporters and for other people's lives. At a certain point it has to acknowledge its obligations and has to start planning for what it will do with its newfound authority. It needs a programme. In order to acquire a programme, the right is compelled to join up the dots between the different positions that it holds, and to argue its ideas strategically.

The far right of recent years has replaced socialism as its great enemy with social liberalism, and even liberalism is fought intermittently (so that the 'feminism' which justifies the subordination of Muslims is supported, while the politics that rejects all male violence is despised). Again, this weakens the far right compared to its ideological ancestors, leaving it ideologically vague, and shorn of any long-term coherence.

As for anti-Islamic racism, this is a widespread and popular opinion, whose adoption by the far right serves to normalise and legitimise parties which were previously considered unacceptable. But it is hard to see how – even from the paranoid perspective of the right – anti-Muslim racism could be used to explain the 2008 crash in the way that Jews were once blamed for the Wall Street Crash and the Great Depression. Anti-Muslim racism is an ideology which kicks down, which condemns migrants and the racialised poor of the inner cities. It provides the right with narrower opportunities than the racism which dominated the right in the past.

Fascism has a functional utility to the far right, which motivates people to revert to it. For 20 years, this has been a weaker tendency than the sustained move to keep the right clear of the stigma still attached to Hitler and Mussolini. However, as the far right has grown, in particular since 2016, we have started to see initial signs of parts of the politics of the 1930s returning.

During the 2016 election campaign, Donald Trump counterposed his message of America First to the risks posed by the 'global' power structure, manifested in the 'international banks' that he accused of holding covert meetings with Hillary Clinton.[21] Trump was echoing a group of his far-right allies, for whom globalisation is an error in late capitalism, which is in all ways the perfect economic system save for its supposed takeover by Jews. Under the impact of his campaign, anti-semitic images and themes became widespread on social media, with websites such as Andrew Anglin's Daily Stormer calling on their readers to denounce their opponents as Jewish Communists, and to confront them with twitter hashtags such as #HitlerWasRight. Indeed, Trump himself was not shy of using anti-Jewish symbols, for example, by tweeting images of Hillary Clinton with a pile of money, the words 'Most Corrupt Candidate ever,' and a six-pointed Jewish star. The Anti-Defamation League counted 2.6 million anti-semitic worldwide tweets between summer 2016 and summer 2017. These dynamics have continued after Trump's victory. In the year starting 29 January 2017, for example, the number of anti-semitic tweets increased to 4.2 million.[22]

The return of old forms of politics has not been limited to social media. In areas of far-right strength, such as the southeastern corner of Germany which has been the base for Pegida and more recently the AfD, attacks on Jewish-owned shops have increased. Racism, in all its forms, has become more pervasive.[23]

As the international far right has grown in strength since 2016, its participants have shown a greater willingness to use violence, and have become more likely to identify the left as their chief antagonist. In October 2018, Jair Bolsonaro was elected President of Brazil. Although Bolsonaro chooses his targets widely (to include Brazil's LGBT community, anti-Zionist Jews, political women and many others beside); key to his campaign was the promise to destroy his opponents on the left. 'These red outlaws,' he promised, 'will be banished from our homeland. It will be a clean-up the likes of which has never been seen in Brazilian history.'[24]

From the perspective of those who identify with the far right, fascism is a 'tight' ideology, which provides a series of positions which justify the adoption of violence and offer its supporters not just the excitement of military struggle and race war but in the final stages a new society and a new fascist mandate. Nothing developed by the far right in the past decade, in the US or in Europe, offers the same coherence. This is why fascism may yet return; because unlike the non-fascist far right, fascism has a clear goal; and because the supporters of the right will increasingly need one.

'The revolution of the nineteenth century must let the dead bury their dead in order to arrive at its own content,' Karl Marx once wrote.[25] In a similar spirit, this book argues that today's anti-fascists have to confront the far right on the basis of what the parties are now, not for what their ideological ancestors did.

That said, it is also true that an increasing number of states and right-wing parties combine the forms of political democracy with a style of leadership which is authoritarian and nationalist and hostile to opposition. If this politics continues to succeed in a space to the right of mainstream conservatism, the likelihood grows that we will face new and still more aggressive configurations of the right, evolving their own politics in ever more aggressive directions. Indeed, the financial catastrophe of 2007–8 was so intense, and the collective learning from it has been so shallow,[26] that it is hard not to believe that some sort of economic crisis will recur. When it does, and if the right continues to mutate and produce new political forms, then its new partisans will emerge into a world where the far right will have many more supporters than it did ten or 20 years ago. Fascism will remain an option for them, and it will satisfy certain needs that even a militant conservatism cannot answer.

Stopping the right

The argument of this book can be summarised in a few propositions:

The left needs to expose the new right as racists. The convergence of the centre- and far-right has led to a vast increase in cruelty and suffering. In Britain, refugee children have been detained in prisons; landlords, doctors, even marriage registrars have been turned into unpaid immigration police. The number of deportations has increased, from 300 people a year at the end of the 1970s to 40–45,000 a year in 2010–15.[1]

Politicians on the right portray the increasingly violent policing of borders as a dissuasive act from which no one suffers, since it works by preventing people from leaving their homes where they are (by definition) content, or even as a kindness, since it brings an end to what would otherwise be indefinite cuts to social welfare. Yet, as Enoch Powell observed 50 years ago during his 'Rivers of Blood' speech, it would be impossible for the state to control the numbers of people migrating to Britain or the US without considering the people who were already here; a process he referred to euphemistically as, 'stopping, further inflow … promoting the maximum outflow.'[2]

After the 2016 referendum in Britain, the Home Office attempted to deport first several thousand European migrants and then members of the Windrush Generation, UK citizens who had been living in the UK for decades.[3] Many of the latter had worked in the NHS, in transport or in care, before being dragged from their homes. The deportation of these British citizens was the result of the rise of nationalism and the introduction of policies intended to create a hostile environment for all migrants, irrespective of how they had come to Britain, or of what they had contributed here.

In the US, Donald Trump's hostility to immigration took the form of a policy of separating migrants from their children and holding both groups in metal cages within detention camps. Within a year of his election, thousands of children were living in prison camps, most of them barely distinguishable from prisons. Clips were being played on news programmes of young children sobbing aloud at the realisation that they might never see their parents again.[4]

The left must challenge all the discriminatory ideas on which the far right thrives. The militant right of recent years has also turned back to other forms of prejudice. Among the examples given in previous chapters have been the re-emergence in Britain and Poland of arguments for the restriction of abortion, the introduction in Europe of laws against the wearing of Islamic headscarves, and the use of the debate around the veil as a mechanism by which small but vocal groups of leftists in France have gone over to the far right. In autumn 2016, when Trump's presidential campaign appeared on the verge of collapse following the candidate's boasts of having sexually assaulted women, the far right responded by challenging the very idea of women's consent, insisting that sex was natural and sexual harassment an impossibility.

Fascism is a minority position within today's far right. The right has succeeded as a result of alliances between the mainstream right and the non-fascist far right; the typical space at which these politics have converged has been one which is poised between the mainstream and its extremists. Neither Donald Trump, Steve Bannon nor Nigel Farage is a fascist. Even Marine Le Pen's electoral success has depended on a 40-year project in which the Front has repeatedly distanced itself from fascism.

When the left confronted the right in Europe, 40 years ago, it was an effective strategy to condemn our opponents as fascists. If a new member of the MSI or of the National Front heard that criticism and looked at their party with open eyes, they would see countless examples of fascists: the children of Hitler's admirers in local leadership roles, fascist literature on sale in their party bookshops. Showing that these parties were as fascist was an effective strategy because fascism remained stigmatised, because the parties were evolving away from fascism in the direction of electoralism and because the process had only gone so far: the leaders were equivocating and unwilling to commit to it. Calling them fascists was a genuine threat to the right.

When today the left cries fascist at people who are at a different point of the political spectrum, we waste an opportunity to challenge them. We make ourselves appear to be the ones who are fixated on the past.

There are other problems, as well, with exaggerating the fascist component of today's right. In the aftermath of Donald Trump's victory, the Italian socialist activist Cinzia Arruzza observed the large number of people taking to the streets to call for Trump's defeat. She also noted the broad similarities between Trump's campaign and those of Silvio Berlusconi, Italy's recent Prime Minister. Like Trump, Berlusconi had been a businessman for many years before going into politics. Both had used their inexperience to present themselves as something new in politics, both had promised in Trump's phrase to 'drain the swamp'. Each of them used their wealth and supposed entrepreneurial success to prove their suitability for high office. Both were aggressive to their opponents; both indulged in misogynist and racist jokes. In each case, their success was based on alliances with the far right: Trump with Steve Bannon, Berlusconi with the National Alliance. The purpose of Arruzza's article was, however, not to dwell on the similarities of the two demagogues, but on the tactics of their opponents. It was essential, she warned, that anti-Trump campaigners did not replicate the mistakes of their Italian predecessors.

In Italy, Arruzza recalled, Berlusconi's first 1994 government had lasted in power for no more than seven months. It collapsed because Berlusconi relied on votes from the Northern League while Berlusconi himself wanted to centralise power in the Italian state and was not willing to compromise with the League's regionalist policies. Moreover, Berlusconi was a committed neoliberal and set out to reduce the Italian welfare state, above all pensions. The working class component of the Northern League's cross-class support was antagonistic to this measure. The split within the centre-right government gave confidence to its critics outside. In October 1994, Italy's largest trade unions called a general strike, with three million people marching in opposition to pension reform and Berlusconi had no choice but to resign.

During the months that followed, the Italian left enjoyed the chance to build a popular, stable, centre-left alternative. Yet this opportunity was squandered by the 1995–6 government of Lamberto Dini which introduced its own, still more devastating, changes to the pension system. The organisations which were best placed to be the mainstay of an anti-Berlusconi government saw their task as being above all to prevent Berlusconi's return to power, and collaboration with malign reforms. These politics continued after 1996, with a centre-left government which eroded workers' rights, privatised public companies, strengthened anti-immigration laws and worked with Berlusconi to strengthen the executive at the expense of Parliament:

> In the anti-Berlusconian imaginary, Berlusconi's rule lasted 20 long years rather than nine, Berlusconi was a fascist, Italian democracy was in danger, the radical left helped consolidate Berlusconi's power because of its sectarianism and unwillingness to cooperate with the centre left, Berlusconi's voters were all racist and misogynistic uneducated losers, the country was constitutively right-wing ... [E]ven moderate Keynesian policies were impossible and the left needed to ally with all kinds of neoliberal technocrats, in the name of preventing Berlusconi's return to power at all costs.[5]

The approach Arruzza was criticising might be termed a 'militant and meek' answer to the emboldened right. It is militant in its verbal commitment to democracy and its rhetorical anger against the far right, which it blames for cuts and which it condemns as imminent fascism. Yet this verbal self-confidence is in no way supported by its policies in government, which have been to fight an economic and social war against its own voters. This politics is in fact meek because for all its confidence and seeming bluster when faced with the poor, it has been fawning and weak when faced with capital and the super-rich whose interests it has repeatedly conciliated.

Part of the reason why the left has fallen behind centrist politicians offering nothing to the poor has been the fatalism which follows from the sense that these are the final days and anything at all is preferable to what would otherwise be fascism. By mentally resetting our own internal clocks away from five minutes to midnight, we can place the threat in context. A durable resistance to the likes of Trump or Le Pen will be the work of years, and emotional survival is hardest in perpetual crisis mode.

We need to break the alliance between centre- and far-right. One effective place to challenge the right is by exposing the alliance between parliamentary and street politics. Most people in America and Europe are hostile to the right's drift towards anti-democratic politics and its willingness to use violence against its opponents. By attacking the right for its tendency towards authoritarianism, it is possible to sever the alliance between politicians of the centre right and the margins.

The clearest recent example of the left breaking the constituent elements of the far right coalition apart came in the United States, in Charlottesville in 2017 when the right took to the streets and President Trump repeatedly refused to condemn the violence of the far right responsible as it was for the death of Heather Heyer. By overplaying its hand, the street right forced Trump to break his alliance with it. The result has been the isolation of the likes of Spencer and Yiannopoulos.

The broader the alliance becomes between different parts of the right, and the more that an anti-parliamentary right takes to the street, the more the opportunities are for the left to expose the incompatibility between these two wings of the right.

Because the right is repeatedly violent, the left must defend itself. In the face of a purely electoral right, the most effective tactics are the ordinary dynamics of popular protest: demonstrating against its leaders, objecting to their politics. With fascists or other supporters of the street right, physical self-defence is often necessary. At times, it can even force the far right back. As well as Charlottesville, another example was the moment, outside the inauguration of Donald Trump as President, when Richard Spencer was confronted by protesters. 'Are you a neo-Nazi?' they asked. 'No, I'm not a neo-Nazi,' he answered, glaring contemptuously at them. 'Do you like black people?' they asked. 'Why not?' he said, smiling at his own response. 'Sure,' he continued. Moments later, a member of the crowd punched him. The verbal exchanges between Spencer and his critics made him seem dishonest and insincere. The physical confrontation was in consequence an immensely popular piece of visual propaganda and film of the attack was shared by tens of millions of people online.[6]

We need the electoral left to provide an alternative. Where the right prioritises elections over street politics, it is capable of making itself seem a mass force. The left must be equally serious about speaking to an audience of tens and hundreds of thousands of people, to the unpolitical and the newly politicised. When the right presents itself as the champions of the dispossessed, its enemies cannot cede that ground by arguing that the workers are, in the terms used by Cinzia Arruzza, 'racist and misogynistic uneducated losers'. Rather, what the left needs to do is expose the bizarre idea that only a group of millionaire right-wing politicians and property speculators can speak for workers and for the victims of welfare cuts.

In a world of static incomes and in a context of attacks on welfare, voting will continue to polarise. It is for the right's opponents to show that pensions can be increased and welfare protected without the racism of a Trump or a Le Pen.

In the US, France and Britain in 2016–17 the right has faced challengers on the left. Bernie Sanders won 13 million votes for the Democratic nomination. He showed that it was possible to win, relying on small donations from hundreds of thousands of supporters and without rich backers. In France, Jean-Luc Mélenchon came first among voters aged 18–24, and won also among the unemployed, a group which the mainstream press had predicted would vote overwhelmingly for the Front.

When the left has given the impression of being both serious about redistribution and capable of winning office, this combination has done serious damage to the alliances on which the contemporary right has sustained itself. Under pressure from the left, the link between the authoritarian treatment of migrants and increased prosperity has ceased to be an axiom, so obvious that it barely needed justification. The people who believe that there is such a relationship have had to argue publicly for it. When voters were given a meaningful choice between welfare and authoritarianism, millions preferred welfare, including millions of the most vulnerable. The politics can be seen in the 2017 general election in Britain.

Like any number of right-wing politicians, when they set about wooing working-class voters for the first time, the Conservatives seemed to believe that everyone who left school at 16 believes in get-on-your-bike hard graft, patriotism and deference to their superiors and will pass on their values to their children. The working class was assumed to be made up of millions of families, all dominated by a white middle-aged man of unlimited authority. But working-class life contains any number of other experiences; the working class is also female, black and young.

The Conservatives were trying to win votes from UKIP, a party whose vote was age-segregated, attractive to home-owning older voters, but not to their children, a difference which had been apparent in several years of polling.[7] In pitching to this audience, the party failed to grasp the extent to which working-class experience varies by age. The right's politics since Thatcherism, the 1980s policy of right to buy for council tenants, and the minimal interest rates for borrowers since 2010, have protected voters who inherited little wealth but have been able to buy their own home. They have been a great boon for the old. A programme of maintaining house prices indefinitely was, by contrast, a high barrier to the increasing number of voters who did not own their home and who paid an ever-higher portion of their income in rent.

During the 2017 election, the groups of people most likely to vote Labour were black voters aged under 25, women aged under 25 and poorer young voters, with Labour winning 70 per cent of the vote in each of these three categories. In other words, the convergence of the centre and far right created the social base for its resistance: a generation of 20- and 30-year-olds who prized redistribution over the exclusion of migrants. 'Even though the Conservatives did well among the segment of the population on low incomes who were relatively pro-Brexit, Labour did even better among the segment who were relatively left wing … their preference for redistribution outweighed their preference for immigration control.'[8]

But the left needs to do better than it has at challenging all forms of oppression. All three of Corbyn, Sanders and Mélenchon have grasped that, as Corbyn has told his fellow European socialists, they must reject neoliberalism or voters will reject them. All three have been weaker at understanding the other half of any strategy for survival, which requires a sustained hostility to the misogyny and racism which underpin the new right.[9] In a France which remains obsessed by Islam, a new unifying figure needs to emerge, closer in anti-racist sensibility to the Mélenchon of 2012 than the candidate of 2017 with his repeated concessions to anti-Muslim racism.

In the US, the best hope for the future has to be the emergence of a left without the ties to business which have caused the Democrats to compromise with Donald Trump. The social forces of a potential mass movement against Trump already exist: they could be seen in the people who drove to their local airport to protest against the Muslim ban, in the school students who demanded gun control, in the #metoo campaign, and in the strikes led by teachers' unions, including in the very Red States whose working-class voters were often blamed for having chosen Trump.

The institutional supports of Corbynism come from the existing British left, including an anti-war milieu which is nostalgic for the politics of the 1980s, a trade union leadership whose tolerance of dissenters is limited, and a far left, key parts of which have been badly compromised by their indifference to sexism.[10] They are the best that those previous generations of the left which emerged between 1968 and 1989 can supply;

the emerging egalitarian and redistributive left needs to create new bases of support which go much further than any of them will allow.

What the left needs above all is its own process of renewal, in which centre-left parties take on people and ideas from their outliers. To some extent, this is what has been happening, with the demise of the Socialists and the rise of La France Insoumise, or the replacement of Ed Miliband by Jeremy Corbyn. But the process needs to go much further. The right has grown by taking on ideas from its militant wing; equally, the left needs to learn from those of its outliers who do not see the present distribution of wealth as the best of all possible outcomes. In most of Europe and in the United States, the control of the left-wing parties is still held by social liberals nostalgic for a period where any improvements to health or education were done by stealth, and the left was able to prosper even while conceding to the right on the terrain of economics.

In a society where the long-term funding of welfare is at risk, in part through the determination of the rich to conceal their resources, the option of just leaving the wealthy to their own devices is no longer compatible with the survival of social reforms.

The left needs to learn again how to attack the obscene disparities of wealth between those who own capital and those who do not. We need to defend at the same time the equality of women, migrants and every other victim of systemic injustice. We need to see both tasks as one process. It is only by offering that vision of expanded welfare provision and justice for all that the left will be able to break apart today's alliance of conservatives and those further to their right.

Notes

Introduction

1. A. de Jong, 'National-populism in the Netherlands,' in F. Leplat (ed), *The Far Right in Europe* (London: Resistance Books, 2015) pp. 266–310, 284, 290; C. Mudde, 'The PVV at 10! Writing Dutch Political History One Insult at A Time,' *Huffington Post*, 6 December 2017.

2. C. Mudde, *The Far Right in America* (London: Routledge, 2018), p. 115; E. van den Hemel, 'The Dutch War on Easter: Secular Passion for Religious Culture and National Rituals,' *Yearbook for Ritual and Liturgical Studies* 33 (2017), pp. 1–19; A. J. Rubin and C. F. Schuetze, 'To Hold Off the Right, New Dutch Coalition Partly Embraces It,' *New York Times*, 26 October 2017.

3. L. Al-Serori and O. Das Gupta, 'The Strache files,' *Süddeutsche Zeitung*, 15 October 2017; 'Austria's far-right party hit by yet another Nazi scandal,' *Times of Israel*, 23 March 2018; E. Schultheis. 'A New Right-Wing Movement Rises in Austria,' *The Atlantic*, 16 October 2017; T. Szyskowitz, 'Austria Swings Right and How,' *Carnegie Europe*, 16 October 2017.

4. M. Eirmann, Y. Mounk and L. Gultchin, *European Populism: Trends, Threats and Future Prospects* (London: Tony Blair Institute for Global Change, 2018).

5. O. Holmes, 'Rodrigo Duterte vows to kill three million drug dealers and likens himself to Hitler,' *Guardian*, 30 September 2016.

6. H. Agerholm, 'Donald Trump calls Turkey's president to congratulate him on winning referendum,' *Independent*, 18 April 2017.

7. M. Peel and J. Shotter, 'EU rebukes Poland over judicial reforms,' *Financial Times*, 20 December 2017; R. Pankowski, *The Populist Radical Right in Poland: The Patriots* (London: Routledge, 2010), p. 178.

8. J. Meek, 'Somerdale to Skarbimierz,' *London Review of Books*, 20 April 2017.

9. A. Bozóki, 'Broken Democracy, Predatory State and Nationalist Populism,' in P. Krasztev and J. van Til, *The Hungarian Patient: Social*

Opposition to an Illiberal Democracy (Budapest: Central European University Press, 2015), pp. 28–9.

10. 'Hungary passes a law to shut down a bothersome university,' *Economist*, 8 April 2017; P. Wilkin, *Hungary's Crisis of Democracy: The Road to Serfdom* (New York: Lexington Books, 2016), pp. 49–82; L. Marsili and N. Milanese, *Citizens of Nowhere: How Europe Can Be Save from Itself* (London: Zed, 2018), pp. 67–9.

11. S. Walker, 'Hungary's Viktor Orbán secures another term with resounding win,' *Guardian*, 8 April 2018; 'Viktor Orbán: Our duty is to protect Hungary's Christian culture,' *Guardian*, 7 May 2018; Z. Kovács, 'A stronger, more rigorous Stop Soros bill is now in front of the Parliament: here's a look at the details,' *About Hungary*, 31 May 2018; S. Walker, 'No entry: Hungary's crackdown on helping refugees,' *Guardian*, 4 June 2018; ADL, *Quantifying Hate: A Year of Anti-Semitism on Twitter* (New York: Anti-Defamation League, 2018); J. Atkinson, 'I will continue to fight against the EU, to deliver Brexit and make a lot of noise in the chamber,' *Voice of Europe*, 15 June 2018.

12. Human Rights Watch, *We have no Orders to Save You: State Participation and Complicity in Communal Violence in Gujarat* (London: Human Rights Watch, 2002), pp. 4, 6.

13. M.S. Golwalkar, *We Or Our Nationhood Defined* (Nagpur: Bharat Prakashan, 1939), p. 88; M. Mann, *Fascists* (Cambridge: Cambridge University Press, 2004), p. 372; S. Pendse, *Fascism and Communalism: Considerations* (Mumbai: Centre for Education and Documentation, 2007), pp. 55–6; M. Casolari, 'Hindutva's Foreign Tie-up in the 1930s,' *Economic and Political Weekly*, 22 January 2000; A. Vanaik, 'The John McCain of India,' *Jacobin*, 30 August 2018.

14. K. Nag, *The Saffron Tide* (New Delhi: Rupa Publications, 2014), pp. 194–7; A. Tikku, 'Over 11,000 NGOs lose license for foreign funding,' *Hindustan Times*, 4 November 2016; Z. Hasan, 'Govt. is restricting protests, stifling dissent,' *The Hindu*, 26 June 2017; A. Vanaik, *The Rise of Hindu Authoritarianism: Secular Claims, Communal Realities* (London: Verso, 2017), pp. 356–65; J. Banaji, 'Trajectories of Fascism: Extreme-Right Movements in India and Elsewhere,' in M. Jal, *Challenges for the Indian Left* (New Delhi: Aakar Books, 2017), pp. 555–70, 567.

15. C. Clover, *Black Wind, White Snow: The Rise of Russia's New Nationalism* (New Haven: Yale University Press, 2016); T. Snyder, *The Road to Unfreedom* (London: Bodley Head, 2018); M. Specia, 'How Syria's Death Toll is Lost in the Fog of War,' *New York Times*, 13 April 2018.

16. M. H. Van Herpen, *Putinism: The Slow Rise of a Radical Right Regime in Russia* (Basingstoke: Palgrave Macmillan, 2013), pp. 137–53; O. J. Reuter, *The Origins of Dominant Parties: Building Authoritarian Institutions in Post-Soviet Russia* (Cambridge: Cambridge University Press, 2017).

17. M. H. Van Herpen, *Putin's Propaganda Machine: Soft Power and Russian Foreign Policy* (London: Rowman & Littlefield, 2016), pp. 101–2, 104–5; C. Cadwalladr, 'Brexit, the ministers, the professor and the spy: how Russia pulls strings in UK,' *Guardian*, 4 November 2017; C. Wheeler, '"Putin crony" banker Lubov Chernukhin gifts Tories £161,000,' *Times*, 3 December 2017.

18. H. Beirich and S. Buchanan, '2017 the Year in Hate and Extremism,' *Southern Poverty Law Center Intelligence Report*, 11 February 2018; Anti-Defamation League, *Anti-Semitic Targeting of Journalists During the 2016 Presidential Campaign, A report from ADL's Task Force on Harassment and Journalism* (New York: ADL, 2016), p. 6.

19. N. Bobbio, *The Left and the Right: The Significance of a Distinction* (Cambridge: Polity, 1995), p. 66.

20. C. Robin, *The Reactionary Mind: Conservatism from Edmund Burke to Sarah Palin* (Oxford: Oxford University Press, 2011), p. 10.

21. D. Mack Smith, *Mussolini* (London: Orion, 1994), pp. 24–7.

22. N. Davidson et al, 'The Longue durée of the Far-right: an introduction,' in R. Saull, A. Anievas, N. Davidson and A. Fabry, *The Longue Durée of the Far-Right: An international historical sociology* (London: Routledge, 2015), pp. 4–5.

23. A. Mondon, *A Populist Hegemony? The Mainstreaming of the Extreme Right in France and Australia* (Farnham: Ashgate, 2013), p. 21; A. Mondon and A. Winter, 'Understanding the mainstreaming of the far right,' *Open Democracy*, 26 August 2018.

24. N. Davidson, 'The far-right and the "needs of capital",' in Saull, Anievas, Davidson and Fabry, *The Longue durée*, pp. 129–52, 140–41; Robin, *The Reactionary Mind*, pp. 24–5.

25. G. Souvlis, 'The National Question, Class and the European Union: An Interview with Neil Davidson,' *Salvage*, 22 July 2017.

26. Levitsky and Ziblatt, *How Democracies Die*, pp. 33–52.

27. D. Renton, *Fascism: Theory and Practice* (London: Pluto, 1999).

28. D. Renton, 'On Benjamin's Theses or the utility of the concept of historical time,' *European Journal of Political Theory* (2012) 11/4, pp. 380–93.

29. A. Gramsci, 'On Fàscism, 1921,' in D. Beetham (ed), *Marxists in Face of Fascism* (Manchester: Manchester University Press, 1983), pp. 82–7, 82.

30. Davidson, 'The far-right and the "needs of capital", pp. 140–41.

31. K. Kautsky, *Erläuterungen zum Stammbaum des modernen Sozialismus* (Stuttgart: J. H. W. Dietz, 1898); K. Kautsky, *Die Vorläufer des neueren Sozialismus: Erster Band, erster Theil: Von Plato bis zu den Wiedertäusern* (Stuttgart: Verlag von J.H.W. Dietz, 1895).

32. P. Nilsson, 'Opening the Door to the Far Right,' *Jacobin*, 9 June 2018.

33. A. Gramsci, 'Reactionary subversiveness,' *L'Ordine Nuovo*, 22 June 1921, in Q. Hoare (ed) *Selections from political writings 1921–1926* (London: Lawrence and Wishart, 1978), pp. 272–3.

Chapter 1: The subordination of the war

1. In the final stages of finishing this chapter, a friend urged me to read Dan Stone's history of 1945 Europe: D. Stone, *Goodbye to All That? The Story of Europe since 1945* (Oxford: Oxford University Press, 2014). Stone sees the history of 1945 differently to me, as a slow unravelling of a post-war consensus, whereas my argument is that the consensus had first of all to be established, and that this process was three decades in the making. That said, our approaches significantly overlap in emphasising the fall of that consensus in recent years.

2. R. Griffin, *Fascism: An Introduction to Comparative Fascist Studies* (Cambridge: Polity, 2018), pp. 106–8.

3. 'Hungary's Jobbik party tries to sound less extreme,' *Economist*, 15 November 2017; Reuters, 'Hungarian far right launches new party,' *Guardian*, 8 July 2017; C. Mudde, 'Orbán's Hungary is not the future of Europe: it represents a dying past,' *Guardian*, 8 July 2017; 'Hungary: Nationalists Split from Jobbik, form New Party,' *The New Observer*, 27 June 2018.

4. P. Sotiris, 'Political crisis and the rise of the far right in Greece: Racism, nationalism, authoritarianism and conservatism in the discourse of Golden Dawn,' in M. Kopytowska (ed), *Contemporary Discourses of Hate and Radicalism across Space and Genres* (Philadelphia: John Benjamins Publishing Company, 2017), pp. 215–42; P. Strickland, 'What is the future of Greece's neo-fascist Golden Dawn?' *Aljazeera*, 17 April 2018.

5. Associated Press, 'Rise of proudly neo-Nazi party unnerves a European nation,' *CBS News*, 18 November 2016; H. Agerholm, 'Far-right party crushed in Slovakia elections,' *Independent*, 5 November 2017.

6. F. J. Simonelli, *American Fuehrer, George Lincoln Rockwell and the American Nazi Party* (Chicago: University of Illinois Press, 1999), pp. 21–4.

7. 'L'intervista a Orsi, il cosiddetto "sosia" di Valpreda (dieci mesi fa),' *Paolo Brogi*, 16 March 2012; P. Biondani, G. Tizian and S. Vergine, 'I segreti di Roberto Fiore, il fascista a capo di Forza Nuova,' *L'Espresso*, 20 December 2017; F. Germinarlo, *L'altra memoria. L'estrema destra, Salò e la Resistenza* (Torino: Bollati Boringhieri, 1999).

8. S. and N. Lebert, *My Father's Keeper: Children of Nazi Leaders – An Intimate History of Damage and Denial* (Boston: Little, Brown and Co., 2001).

9. H. Rosen, *Are You Still Circumcised? East End Memories* (Nottingham: Five Leaves Publications, 1999), p. 105.

10. M. Halbwachs, *On Collective Memory* (Chicago: University of Chicago Press, 1992).

11. J. Foot, *The Archipelago: Italy since 1945* (London: Bloomsbury, 2018), p. 4; P. Sands, 'Primo Levi's If This is a Man at 70,' *Guardian*, 22 April 2017.

12. M. Beckman, *The Forty Three Group* (London: Centreprise, 1993); D. Renton, *Fascism, Anti-Fascism and Britain in the 1940s* (Basingstoke: Palgrave Macmillan, 1999).

13. T. Kushner, *The Holocaust and the Liberal Imagination: A Social and Cultural History* (Oxford: Blackwell, 1994), pp. 206–8, 213; T. Kushner, *The Persistence of Prejudice: Anti-Semitism in British Society during the Second World War* (Manchester: Manchester University Press, 1989).

14. T. Judt, *Postwar: A History of Europe since 1945* (London: Vintage Books, 2010), p. 47; M. Gebhardt, *Crimes Unspoken: The Rape of German Women at the End of the Second World War* (Cambridge: Polity, 2016).

15. H. Rousso, *The Vichy Syndrome: History and Memory in France since 1944* (Boston: Harvard University Press, 1994); G. Schwarz, *After Mussolini: Jewish Life and Jewish Memories in Post-Fascist Italy* (London: Valentine Mitchell, 2012), pp. 109–20.

16. H. B. Poulsen, '77 The Year of Punk and New Wave* (London: South Bank House 2005), p. 28.

17. J. Savage, *The England's Dreaming Tapes* (London: Faber and Faber, 2009), p. 340.

18. P. Novick, *The Holocaust in American Life* (Boston: Mariner, 2000).

19. E. Faux, T. Legrand and G. Perez, *La main droite de Dieu* (Paris: Éditions du Seuil, 1994).

20. B. M. Gordon, 'World War II France Half a Century After,' in R. J. Golsan (ed), *Fascism's Return: Scandal, Revision and Ideology since 1980* (Lincoln: University of Nebraska Press, 1995), pp. 152–81,

155–7; Z. Sternhell, 'Ce passé qui refuse de passer,' *Le Monde*, 21 September 1994; L. Baier, 'Un Acharnement décontertant,' *Le Monde*, 21 September 1994; Foot, *Archipelago*, pp. 320–25.

21. M. G. Knox, 'The Fascist Regime, its Foreign Policy and Its Wars: An Anti-Anti-Fascist Orthodoxy,' *Contemporary European History* 4/3 (1995), pp 347–65; D. Mack Smith, 'Mussolini; reservations about Renzo De Felice's biography', *Modern Italy* 5/2 (2000), pp. 193–210; A. Stille, 'Kinder, Gentler Fascism,' *New York Times*, 28 September 2002; J. Hooper, 'Mussolini wasn't that bad, says Berlusconi,' *Guardian*, 12 September 2003.

22. Judt, *Postwar*, pp. 803–4.

23. Stone, *Goodbye to All That?*, p. 279; E. Zuroff, 'Lithuania's Shame,' *Jerusalem Post*, 15 May 2012.

24. Act of 26 January 2018 amending the Act on the Institute of National Remembrance; D. Tilles and J. Richardson, 'Poland and the Holocaust,' *History Today*, 24 April 2018.

25. Jan Grabowski, *Murder in German-Occupied Poland* (Bloomington: Indiana University Press, 2013) M. Mann, *The Dark Side of Democracy* (Cambridge: Cambridge University Press, 2005), pp. 280–81; J. Gunter, 'Holocaust law wields a "blunt instrument" against Poland's past,' *BBC News*, 3 February 2018; R. Mackey, 'Polish Law on Holocaust Draws New Attention to Anti-Semitism in Poland's Past and Present,' *The Intercept*, 3 March 2018.

26. A. Bokhari and M. Yiannopoulos, 'An Establishment Conservative's Guide to the Alt-Right,' *Breitbart*, 29 March 2016.

27. M. Astor, 'Holocaust is Fading from Memory, Survey finds,' *New York Times*, 12 April 2018; S. Sontag, 'Fascinating Fascism,' *New York Times*, 6 February 1975.

28. R. Seymour, *The Liberal Defence of Murder* (London: Verso, 2008), p. 4.

29. M. Amis, *The Second Plane: September 11, 2001–2007* (London: Vintage, 2007), p. 3.

30. Foot, *Archipelago*, pp. 338–43; 'Elections, migrants, and a fascist renaissance in Italy,' *Middle East Eye*, 4 March 2018.

31. Robin, *The Reactionary Mind*, p. 167; R. Seymour, *Unhitched: The Trial of Christopher Hitchens* (London: Verso, 2012); A. Nagle, *Kill All Normies: Online Culture Wars from 4Chan and Tumblr to Trump and the Alt-Right* (London: Zero Books, 2017), p. 109.

32. M. Kennedy, 'Enough, says Amis, in Eagleton feud,' *Guardian*, 13 October 2007.

33. K. Kalfus, *A Disorder Peculiar to the Country* (London: Simon & Schuster, 2007), p. 154.

34. B. Lewis, 'The Roots of Muslim Rage,' *The Atlantic*, September 1990; S. P. Huntington, 'The Clash of Civilizations?' *Foreign Affairs*, summer 1993.

35. C. Robin, *The Reactionary Mind: Conservatism from Edmund Burke to Sarah Palin* (Oxford: Oxford University Press, 2011), pp. 161–8.

36. L. Bond, *Frames of Memory after 9/11: Culture, Criticism, Politics and Law* (Basingstoke: Palgrave Macmillan, 2015), p. 91.

37. J. Kampfner, *Blair's Wars* (London: Simon & Schuster, 2004), p. 89.

38. Bond, *Frames of Memory*, pp. 96–7.

39. S. Erickson's *Shadowbahn* (New York: Blue Rider Press, 2017).

40. A. Kundnani, *The Muslims are Coming: Islamophobia, Extremism and the Domestic War on Terror* (London: Verso, 2014), p. 15.

41. T. Teitze and G. Rundle (ed), *On Utøya: Anders Breivik, Right Terror, Racism and Europe* (Sydney: Elguta Press, 2011).

42. R. K. Ghanash, 'A Most American Terrorist: The Making of Dylann Roof,' *GQ*, 21 August 2017.

43. United States Governmental Accountability Office, 'Countering Violent Extremism: Actions Needed to Define Strategy and Assess Progress of Federal Efforts,' 6 April 2017.

44. N. Kapoor. *Deport, Deprive, Extradite: 21ˢᵗ Century State Extremism* (London: Verso, 2018), pp. 55–6.

45. Kundnani, *The Muslims are Coming*, p. 11; J. Hammer, 'Center Stage: Gendered Islamophobia and Muslim Women,' in C. W. Ernst, *Islamophobia in America: The Anatomy of Intolerance* (Basingstoke: Palgrave Macmillan, 2013), pp. 107–45, 118–19, 133–4.

46. J. Huggler, 'AfD politician faces criminal investigation over "barbarian Muslim gang-raping hordes" tweet,' 2 January 2018; F. Thompson, 'Women's march on Sunderland's streets draws in hundreds,' *Sunderland Echo*, 30 June 2018.

47. S. Berman, 'Why identity politics benefits the right more than the left,' *Guardian*, 14 July 2018; 'PM's speech at Munich Security Conference,' *gov.uk*, 5 February 2011.

48. PM's speech at Munich Security Conference.

49. N. Gordon, 'The "New Anti-Semitism,"' *London Review of Books*, 4 January 2018; A. Topolski, 'Good Jew, bad Jew ... good Muslim, bad Muslim: "managing" Europe's others,' *Ethnic and Racial Studies* 41/12, pp. 2179–96.

50. A. Browne, 'Britain is losing Britain,' *The Times*, 7 August 2002.

51. G. Monbiot, 'A 9/11 conspiracy virus is sweeping the world but it has no basis in fact,' *Guardian*, 6 February 2007; G. Monbiot, '9/11 fantasists pose a mortal danger to popular oppositional campaigns,' *Guardian*, 20 February 2007.

52. A. Kaczynski, 'Trump pick for UN migration job shared tweets warning of creeping Sharia, pushed fringe view of Islam', *CNN Politics*, 15 March 2018.

53. Kundnani, *The Muslims are Coming*, p. 55–89.

54. W. Maclean and C. Hornby, 'Analysis: Europe far right shuns Breivik's acts, flirts with ideas,' *Reuters*, 26 August 2012; J. Wilson, '"Cultural Marxism": a uniting theory for right-wingers who love to play the victim,' *Guardian*, 19 January 2015; J. B. Peterson, 'Postmodernism and Cultural Marxism,' *YouTube*, 6 July 2017.

55. C. Schofield, *Enoch Powell and the Making of Postcolonial Britain* (Cambridge: Cambridge University Press, 2013), pp. 7, 9, 15.

56. R. Burden, 'Bin The Conspiracy Theories, From Whichever Quarter They Come,' *Huff Post*, 24 April 2018; 'An Investigation Into Red-Brown Alliances: Third Positionism, Russia, Ukraine, Syria, And The Western Left,' *Libcom.org*, 1 February 2018; R. Hensman, *Indefensible: Democracy, Counterrevolution, and the Rhetoric of Anti-Imperialism* (Chicago: Haymarket Books, 2018).

Chapter 2: When right-wing parties change

1. 'Generation Identity book review of the Strange Death of Europe,' *Generation Identity*, 27 August 2018.

2. D. Murray, 'Is Marine Le Pen really far-right?' *Spectator*, 6 May 2017; D. Murray, *The Strange Death of Europe: Immigration, Identity, Islam* (London: Bloomsbury, 2017).

3. This is how many of the Front National's left-wing critics, including notably the political scientist Jim Wolfreys, read its recent development. Chapter 5 of this book addresses the Front in more detail.

4. This is how I describe the development of the National Front in 1970s Britain. D. Renton, *Never Again: Rock Against Racism and the Anti-Nazi League 1976–1982* (London: Routledge, 2019).

5. The recent history of Jobbik corresponds broadly to this model; as does the MSI prior to 1960; after which it was closer to the first of these models.

6. T. Hunt, *The Frock-Coated Communist: The Revolutionary Life of Friedrich Engels* (London: Allen Lane, 2009), pp. 340–1.

7. M. Salvadori, *Karl Kautsky and the Socialist Revolution 1880–1938* (London: Verso, 1990), pp. 48–90; G. Eley, *Forging Democracy: The History of the Left in Europe, 1850–2000* (Oxford: Oxford University Press, 2000), pp. 314–18; T. Judt, *Postwar: A History of Europe since 1945* (London: Vintage Books, 2010), pp. 268–9; D. Beetham, *Marxists in Face of Fascism* (Manchester: Manchester University Press, 1983), p. 42.

8. J. Foot, *The Archipelago: Italy since 1945* (London: Bloomsbury, 2018), p. 71.

9. T. Behan, *The Long Awaited Moment: The Working Class and the Italian Communist Party in Milan, 1943–1948* (New York: Peter Lang, 1997), pp. 78–82; E. Hobsbawm, *Interesting Times: A Twentieth Century Life* (London: Allen Lane, 2002), pp. 346–61; Judt, *Postwar*, pp. 495–6.

10. J. Horowitz, 'Steve Bannon Cited Italian Thinker Who Inspired Fascists,' *New York Times*, 10 February 2017;' J. Bernstein, 'Here's How Breitbart and Milo Smuggled Nazi and White Nationalist Ideas Into The Mainstream,' *BuzzFeed News*, 5 October 2017.

11. C. Schaeffer, 'How Hungary Became a Haven for the Alt-Right,' *The Atlantic*, 28 May 2017; J. Lester Feder and P. Buet, 'The Man Who Gave White Nationalism A New Life,' *Buzzfeed*, 26 December 2017.

12. J. Evola, *A Traditionalist Confronts Fascism* (Budapest: Arktos, 2015), p. xxiv.

13. J. Evola, *Saggi sull'idealismo magico* (Rome: Atanor, 1925).

14. P. Furlong, *Social and Political Thought of Julius Evola* (London: Routledge, 2011), pp. 101–2.

15. 'Evola's Autodifesa,' in J. Evola, *Men Among the Ruins* (Rochester, Vermont: Inner Traditions, 2002), pp. 287–97; Furlong, *Social and Political*, pp. 1–2.

16. Evola, *Men among the Ruins*, p. 240; Furlong, *Social and Political*, p. 37.

17. J. Evola, *Revolt Against the Modern World* (Rochester, Vermont: Inner Traditions, 1995).

18. J. Evola, *The Path of Cinnabar: An Intellectual Autobiography* (London: Integral Tradition, 2009), pp. 111–14.

19. U. Eco, 'The poisonous Protocols,' *Guardian*, 17 August 2002; Evola, *Men among the Ruins*, pp. 239–51.

20. S. Garau, 'Between "Spirit" and "Science": The Emergence of Italian Fascist Antisemitism through the 1920s and 1930s,' in D. Tilles and S. Garau (Eds), *Fascism and the Jews: Italy and Britain* (London: Valentine Mitchell, 2011), pp. 41–65; L. B. Weinberg, *After Mussolini: Italian Neo-Fascism and the Nature of Fascism* (Washington: University Press of America, 1979), p. 16; K. Coogan, *Dreamer of the Day: Francis*

Parker Yockey and the Postwar Fascist International (Brooklyn, New York: Autonomedia, 1999), pp. 319–20.

21. Furlong, *Social and Political*, pp. 93–100.

22. H. T. 'Hansen' [Hakl], 'Introduction: Julius Evola's Political Endeavours,' in Evola, *Men among the Ruins*, pp. 1–105, 79–88; Furlong, *Social and Political*, p. 125.

23. J. Evola, *Sintesi di dottrina della razza* (Milan: Editore Ulrico Hoepli, 1941), p. 172–3; A. J. Gregor, *The search for Neofascism: The Use and Abuse of Social Science* (Cambridge: Cambridge University Press, 2006), p. 103.

24. Evola, *Men among the Ruins*, pp. 235, 237, 240, 241.

25. M. Mann, *The Dark Side of Democracy* (Cambridge: Cambridge University Press, 2005), pp. 288–92.

26. Evola, *Men among the Ruins*, p. 283.

27. J. Foot, *The Archipelago: Italy since 1945* (London: Bloomsbury, 2018), p. 4.

28. F. Ferraresi, *Threats to Democracy: The Radical Right in Italy After the War* (Princeton: Princeton University Press, 1996), pp. 86, 196; R. Griffin, *Fascism: An Introduction to Comparative Fascist Studies* (Cambridge: Polity, 2018), p. 103.

29. E. C. Wolff, 'The meaning and role of the concepts of democracy and corporatism in Italian neo-fascist ideology (1945–1953),' *Modern Italy* 16/3 (2011), pp. 295–313.

30. G. Parlato, 'Delegitimation and anticommunism in Italian neofascism,' *Journal of Modern Italian Studies* 22/1 (2017), pp. 43–56.

31. Weinberg, *After Mussolini*, pp. 16, 33; D. Eisenberg, *The Re-Emergence of Fascism* (London: MacGibbon & Kee, 1967), p. 151; Ferraresi, *The Radical Right*, p. 53.

32. J. Banaji, 'Trajectories of Fascism: Extreme-Right Movements in India and Elsewhere,' in M. Jal, *Challenges for the Indian Left* (New Delhi: Aakar Books, 2017), pp. 555–70; C. Ginsborg, *A History of Contemporary Italy 1943-1980* (London: Penguin, 1990), p. 336; R. Drake, *The Revolutionary Mystique and Terrorism in Contemporary Italy* (Bloomington and Indianapolis: Indiana University Press, 1989), pp. 130–31.

33. R. Griffin, 'Interregnum or end-game? The radical right in the 'post-fascist' era,' *Journal of Political Ideologies* (2000), pp. 163–78, 163; P. Ignazi, *Extreme Right Parties in Western Europe* (Oxford: Oxford University Press, 2003), p. 46; Foot, *Archipelago*, pp. 352–4.

34. S. Dechezelles, 'Renouncing Violence or Substituting for it? The Consequences of the Institutionalization of the *Alleanza Nationale* on the Culture of Young Neo-Fascist Activists in Italy,' in E. Leaman and

M. Wörsching, *Youth in Contemporary Europe* (London: Routledge, 2010), pp. 268–82; Foot, *The Archipelago*, p. 294; D. Albertazzi and D. McDonnell, 'The Parties of the Centre Right: Many Oppositions, One Leader,' in J. L. Newell (ed), *The Italian General Election of 2008; Berlusconi Strikes Back* (Basingstoke: Palgrave Macmillan, 2009), pp. 102–17.

35. V. Igounet, 'En avant pour un Nouveau Nom,' *Franceinfo*, 10 September 2017; V. Igounet and P. Picco, 'Histoire du logo de deux "partis frères" entre France et Italie (1972–2016),' *Histoire-Politique* 2016/2, pp. 220–35; G. Fini, 'Pourquoi nous avons rompu avec le FN', *Le Monde*, 26 June 1998.

36. A. Scianca, 'Il Front national cambia nome, ma occhio alla sindrome di Fiuggi,' *Il Primato Nazionale*, 8 May 2017; F. Deidda, 'L'ultimo Congresso del Front National,' *Ordine Futuro*, 14 March 2018.

37. C. Antonini, 'Italy: a resurgent far-right and fascism,' in F. Leplat (ed), *The Far Right in Europe* (London: Resistance Books, 2015) pp. 248–66; S. Martin, 'Football, fascism and fandom in modern Italy,' *Eurozine*, 5 September 2018.

38. A. Stille, 'How Matteo Salvini pulled Italy to the far right,' *Guardian*, 9 August 2018.

39. A. D'Arma, *Media and Politics in Contemporary Italy: From Berlusconi to Grillo* (London: Lexington Books, 2015), pp. 97–114; D. Broder, 'Italy's Terrible Alternatives,' *Jacobin*, 1 March 2018.

40. A. Giuffrida, 'Italy's immigrants fear tough times as populist coalition heads for power,' *Guardian*, 19 May 2018; C. Ruzza, *Re-inventing the Italian Right: Territorial Politics, Populism and 'Post-Fascism'* (London: Routledge, 2009), 91–3; M. Tarchi, 'Italy: A Country of Many Populisms,' in D. Albertazzi and D. McDonnell (eds), *Twenty-First Century Populism: The Spectre of Western European Democracy* (London: Routledge, 2008), pp. 84–99; T. Abse, 'Anti-fascists on the march,' *Weekly Worker*, 1 March 2018.

41. M. Holt, 'The Rise and Fall of the Alt Right,' *American Greatness*, 4 September 2018.

Chapter 3: Brexit and the prospect of convergence

1. M. Ashcroft and K. Culwick, *Well you did ask … Why the UK voted to leave the EU* (London: Biteback, 2016), pp. 108–9.

2. Following the Maastricht Treaty of 1992, the European Communities, including the European Economic Community (EEC or Common Market), became the European Community (EC), one of three

pillars of the European Union (EU). Since 2007, the name of EC has dropped out of use. For simplicity, this chapter refers to the EEC and the EC as the 'European Union' throughout.

3. D. Sandbrook, *Seasons in the Sun: The Battle for Britain, 1974–1979* (London: Penguin, 2013), pp. 323–4; M. Thatcher, *Europe as I see it* (Luxembourg: European Conservative Group, 1977), p. 6.

4. B. Grob-Fitzgibbon, *Continental Drift: Britain and Europe from the End of Empire to the Rise of Euroscepticism* (Cambridge: Cambridge University Press, 2016), pp. 416–17; K. Harris, *Thatcher* (London: Weidenfield and Nicolson, 1988), p. 99.

5. S. Hall, *Cultural Studies 1983* (Durham and London: Duke University Press, 2016), p. 178.

6. D. Macshane, *Brexit: How Britain Left Europe* (London: I. B. Tauris, 2016), p. 67; D. Renton, 'Britain and Europe after the general election: An interview with John Palmer,' *RS21*, 15 May 2015; J. Palmer, *Europe Without America: The Crisis in Atlantic Relations* (Oxford: Oxford University Press, 1987).

7. S. Wall, *A Stranger in Europe: Britain and the EU from Thatcher to Blair* (Oxford: Oxford University Press, 2008), p. 80; M. Thatcher, *The Autobiography* (London: Harper Press, 2013), p. 656.

8. A. Adonis, *Half In, Half Out: Prime Ministers on Europe* (London: Biteback, 2018).

9. N. Hopkins, 'Two sides line up for action after Pinochet ruling,' *Guardian*, 23 March 1999. For Pinochet's appeal to Thatcher and to the Thatcherites, C. Robin, *The Reactionary Mind: Conservatism from Edmund Burke to Sarah Palin* (Oxford: Oxford University Press, 2011), pp. 74–5.

10. The Bruges Group was later, together with UKIP, one of the main backers of the Leave.EU campaign: O. Bennett, *The Brexit Club: The Inside Story of the Leave Campaign's shock victory* (London: Biteback, 2016), p. 105.

11. R. Harris, 'Some issues in Political Economy,' in Institute of Economic Affairs, *Libraries: Free-for-All?* (London: IEA, 1962) pp. 7–18; R. Harris, *Ralph Harris in his own words* (London: IEA, 2008), pp. 199, 249; 'Lord Harris of High Cross,' *Telegraph*, 20 October 2006; Lord Harris, 'Foreword,' in *Health Wars: The Phantom Menace* (London: Forest, 2001), pp. 5–6.

12. G. Harris, *The Dark Side of Europe: The Extreme Right Today* (Edinburgh: Edinburgh University Press, 1994), p. 224.

13. Her Chief Whip acknowledges that Europe was the fatal problem: 'The Prime Minister's attitude was essentially one of looking

backwards to past history, whatever her personal success in bringing some sense into the European Community budget.' T. Renton, *Chief Whip: People, Power and Patronage in Westminster* (London: Politico's 2004), p. 116; J. Ramsden, *An Appetite for Power: A History of the Conservative Party* (London: Harper Collins, 198), pp. 480–81.

14. Bennett, *The Brexit Club*, p. ix; Grob-Fitzgibbon, *Continental Drift*, pp. 456–7; T. Heppell, *The Tories: From Winston Churchill to David Cameron* (London: Bloomsbury Academic Publishing, 2014), pp. 96–8; E. H. H. Green, *Thatcher* (London: Hodder Arnold, 2006), p. 191; M. Thatcher, *Statecraft* (London: Harper and Collins, 2002), p. 367.

15. P. Gardner, *Hard Pounding: The Story of the UK Independence Party* (Totnes: June Press, 2006), p. 29; 'Bruges Men from whom the Bell Tolls,' *Guardian*, 12 April 1991; A. Sked, 'Cheap Excuses or Life, Death and European Unity,' Target paper 1, Bruges Group, February 1991.

16. M. Goodwin and C. Milazzo, *UKIP: Inside the Campaign to Redraw the Map of British Politics* (Oxford: Oxford University Press, 2015), p. 2; M. Daniel, *Cranks and Gadflies: the Story of UKIP* (London: Timewell Press, 2005), p. 10; 'Kamikaze parties doomed to spend their lives in the fringes of politics,' *Daily Record*, 2 May 1997.

17. United Kingdom Independence Party, *Manifesto,* March 1997.

18. P. Hearse, 'UKIP and the politics of ultra-Thatcherism', in F. Leplat (ed), *The Far Right in Europe* (London: Resistance Books, 2015) pp. 34–63; A. Banks, *The Bad Boys of Brexit: Tales of Mischief, Mayhem and Guerrilla Warfare in the EU Referendum Campaign* (London: Biteback, 2017), p. xxii; N. Farage, *Flying Free* (London: Biteback, 2011), p. 31; 'Nigel Farage: I'm the only politician keeping the flame of Thatcherism alive,' *Sun*, 5 April 2016.

19. T. Shipman, *All Out War: The Full Story of How Brexit Sank Britain's Political Class* (London: HarperCollins, 2016), pp. 27–8; Bennett, *The Brexit Club*, p. 10.

20. A. Bilolikar, 'Brexit's humble beginnings in the Queen's Lane Coffee House,' *Cherwell*, 7 November 2017; Oxford University Campaign for an Independent Britain ephemeral papers, John Johnson collection, Bodleian library; R. Honeyford, 'Education and Race: An Alternative View,' *Salisbury Review*, winter 1984.

21. D. Hannan, *What Next?* (London: Head of Zeus, 2016) p. 205; R. Prince, 'Daniel Hannan risks angering David Cameron by praising Enoch Powell,' *Daily Telegraph*, 26 August 2009; D. Hannan, *The New*

Road to Serfdom: A Letter of Warning to America (New York: Harper-Collins, 2010), p. 89; Hannan, *What Next?*, p. xiv.

22. Bennett, *The Brexit Club*, p. 4.

23. M. Deavin, 'The Force to Save Britain,' *Spearhead*, July 1999; R. Merrick, 'Ukip: A timeline of the party's turbulent history,' *Independent*, 29 September 2017.

24. Farage, *Flying Free*, pp. 94–5, 97–8; N. Cohen, 'Hold On a Minute ... Will It Be Boots and Broadcasts at the BNP?', *Observer*, 5 January 1997; F. Wheen, 'The right revs up,' *Guardian*, 13 October 1999; Gardner, *Hard Pounding*, p. 72.

25. Farage, *Flying Free*, pp. 164–5.

26. A. Alderson and R. Watts, 'Revealed: UKIP official gave money to the BNP,' *Telegraph*, 4 March 2007; A. Porter, 'UKIP rejects pact with far right BNP,' *Telegraph*, 3 November 2008; 'Jan Moir talks to Baron Pearson,' *Daily Mail*, 29 December 2009; 'British National Party membership and contacts list, spread sheet, 2007–2008,' *Wikileaks*, accessed 7 June 2018.

27. I. Cobain and D. Pegg, 'Paul Nuttall's troubled relationship with the truth finally catches up with him,' *Guardian*, 25 February 2017.

28. A. Bienkov, 'The extreme right-wing views of new Ukip leader Paul Nuttall', *Politics.co.uk*, 28 November 2016; N. Griffin, *Who are the mind-benders?* (London: The Right Image, 1999 edn); P. Nuttall, 'Time for a revolution against the Marxists,' *Paul Nuttall MEP* (blog), 11 February 2015; J. Wilson, '"Cultural Marxism": a uniting theory for right-wingers who love to play the victim,' *Guardian*, 19 January 2015.

29. M. Goodwin and R. Ford. *Revolt on the Right: Explaining Support for the Radical Right in Britain* (London: Routledge, 2014), p. 97; also G. Macklin, 'Patterns of Far-Right and Anti-Muslim Mobilization,' in M. Fieitz and L. L. Laoire (eds), *Trouble on the Far Right: Contemporary Right-Wing Strategies and Practices in Europe* (Bielefeld: Transcript Verlag, 2016), pp. 165–9.

30. P. Stocker, *English Uprising: Brexit and the Mainstreaming of the Far Right* (London: Melville House, 2017), pp. 111–18; Bennett, *The Brexit Club*, p. 121; J. Elgot and R. Mason, 'Nigel Farage: migrant sex attacks to be "nuclear bomb" of EU referendum,' *Guardian*, 5 June 2016.

31. R. Harris, *The Challenge of a Radical Reactionary* (London: Centre for Policy Studies, 1980), p. 7.

32. 'UKIP leader Nigel Farage: "We want our country back",' *BBC News*, 25 September 2015.

33. I. Buruma, 'Steve Bannon's European Adventure,' *Project Syndicate*, 7 August 2018.

34. B. O. Hing, *Ethical Borders, NATFA, Globalization and Mexican Migration* (Philadelphia: Temple University Press, 2010), pp. 9, 98, 103–4.

35. D. Trilling, *Lights in the Distance: Exile and Refuge at the Borders of Europe* (London: Picador, 2018); *The Human Cost of Fortress Europe: Human Rights Violations against Migrants and Refugees at Europe's Borders* (London: Amnesty International, 2015); 'Refugee deaths in Mediterranean hit 10,000,' *Euractiv*, 8 June 2016.

36. Ashcroft and Culwick, *Well you did ask*, pp. 108–9; R. Ford and M. Goodwin, 'Britain after Brexit: A Nation Divided,' *Journal of Democracy* 28/1 (2017), pp. 17–30, 25.

37. C. Hore, 'Seeing the whole picture after the referendum,' *Socialist Worker (US)*, 28 June 2016.

38. R. Seymour, *Corbyn: The Strange Rebirth of Radical Politics* (London: Verso, 2017 edn), p. 189.

39. Ashcroft and Culwick, *Well you did ask*, p. 112; Banks, *The Bad Boys of Brexit*, p. 243.

40. Ashcroft and Culwick, *Well you did ask*, p. 108.

41. S. Virdee, *Racism, Class and the Racialized Outsider* (Basingstoke: Palgrave Macmillan, 2014), p. 5; C. Renwick, *Bread for All: The Origins of the Welfare State* (London: Allen Lane, 2017); R. J. Harrison, *The Life and Times of Sidney and Beatrice Webb 1858–1905 The Formative Years* (Basingstoke: Palgrave, 2001), pp. 318–20, 340; D. Paul, 'Eugenics and the left,' *Journal of the History of Ideas* 45/4 (1984), pp. 567–90, 567–8.

42. A. Kundnani, *The End of Tolerance: Racism in 21st Century Britain* (London: Pluto, 2007), pp. 74, 76; D. Garvie, *Far from home: The Housing of Asylum Seekers in Private Rented Accommodation* (London: Shelter, 2001), pp. 7, 8, 31; S. Cohen, *Standing on the Shoulders of Fascism: from Immigration Control to the Strong State* (Stoke-on-Trent: Trentham, 2006).

43. A. Kundnani, *The Muslims are Coming: Islamophobia, Extremism and the Domestic War on Terror* (London: Verso, 2014), p. 39.

44. 'Hostile environment: anatomy of a policy disaster,' *Guardian*, 27 August 2018.

45. T. Rutter, 'No place like the Home Office: former top officials on the department's unique challenges,' *Civil Service World*, 10 May 2018; A. Gentleman, 'The children of Windrush: "I'm here legally but they're asking me to prove I'm British,"' *Guardian*, 15 April 2018.

46. *A Guide to the Hostile Environment* (London: Liberty, 2018), pp. 12–15, 28–31.

47. Shipman, *All Out War*, pp. 298–9; Bennett, *The Brexit Club*, p. 296.

48. *R (On the Application of Gureckis and ors) v Secretary of State for the Home Department* [2017] EWHC 3298; *A Guide to the Hostile Environment*, p. 9.

49. A. Gentleman, 'Woman nearly deported after 50 years in UK wins leave to remain,' 11 January 2018'; A. Gentleman, '"They don't tell you why": threatened with removal after 52 years in the UK,' *Guardian*, 1 December 2017; A. Gentleman, 'Man who moved from Antigua 59 years ago told he is in UK illegally,' *Guardian*, 30 March 2018; P. Crear, A. Perkins and A. Gentleman, 'Windrush generation will get UK citizenship, says Amber Rudd,' *Guardian*, 23 April 2018; J. Tapsfield, '"I don't want them back": Javid says 32 Windrush migrants who committed serious offences and were deported are NOT welcome to return to the UK,' *Daily Mail*, 2 June 2018.

50. D. Foster. 'Citizens of the World, look out,' *LRB Blog*, 5 October 2016.

51. *R (on the application of Miller and another) v Secretary of State for Exiting the European Union* [2017] UKSC 5; J. Slack. 'Enemies of the People,' *Daily Mail*, 4 November 2016.

52. Conservative and Unionist Party, *Manifesto*, 18 May 2017, p. 54.

53. T. Shipman, *Fall Out: A Year of Political Mayhem* (London: Harper-Collins, 2017), p. 183; Shipman, *All Out War*, pp. 48–9.

54. 'Theresa May's general election statement,' *BBC News*, 18 April 2017; 'In a stunning move, Mrs May calls bluff of the "game-playing" Remoaners (including "unelected" Lords) with a snap election and vows to … Crush the Saboteurs,' *Daily Mail*, 19 April 2017.

55. S. Hannah, *A Party with Socialists in it: A History of the Labour Left* (London: Pluto Press, 2018), p. 233.

56. C. Curtis and M. Smith, 'How Did 2015 Voters Cast Their Ballot at the 2017 General Election?' *YouGov*, 22 June 2017; S. Sparks, 'The left and the rise of the far right: does Corbynism offer the solution?' *Transform*, November 2017.

57. Theresa May letter to David Davis, 8 July 2018.

58. 'MP Jacob Rees-Mogg: Dinner speech "a mistake,"' *BBC News*, 9 August 2013; M. Fletcher, 'The polite extremist: Jacob Rees-Mogg's seemingly unstoppable rise,' New Statesman, 20 February 2018.

59. B. Johnson, 'Britain Must Look "Beyond" the EU and Focus on Links with the Commonwealth,' *Daily Telegraph*, 25 August 2013.

60. O. Milman, 'Boris Johnson calls for Free Labour Exchange between UK and Australia,' *Guardian*, 26 August 2013.

61. A. Asthana and H. Stewart, 'Theresa May urged to accept more skilled Indian workers to help trade deal,' *Guardian*, 7 November 2016; I. Jack, 'Britain sees the Commonwealth as its trading empire. It is sadly deluded,' *Guardian*, 7 April 2018.

62. A. Asthana and H. Stewart, 'Theresa May urged to accept more skilled Indian workers to help trade deal,' *Guardian*, 7 November 2016; I. Jack, 'Britain sees the Commonwealth as its trading empire. It is sadly deluded,' *Guardian*, 7 April 2018; M. Gill, 'Don't wish for a new party to end the Brexit mess. It will be a far-right one,' *Guardian*, 23 July 2018.

Chapter 4: Remaking the G.O.P.

1. D. J. Trump, *Twitter*, 24 June 2016, 27 June 2016, 18 August 2016; D. Kellner, *American Horror Show: Election 2016 and the Ascent of Donald J. Trump* (Rotterdam: Sense Publishers, 2017), p. 42; J. Diamond, 'Trump gets boost from Brexit leader Farage as he aims for "American independence", *CNN*, 25 August 2018.

2. M. Yglesias, 'If you want to understand Donald Trump, look to the success of the European far-right,' *Vox*, 25 August 2015; D. Cole and M. Wachtell Stinnett (eds), *Rules for Resistance: Advice from Around the Globe for the Age of Trump* (London: New Press, 2017); C. Arruzza, 'Lessons from Italy: The Dangers of Anti-Trumpism,' *Verso*, 21 November 2016.

3. C. Berlet and M. N. Lyons, *Right-wing Populism: Too Close for Comfort* (New York: Guilford Press, 2000), p. 41; P. Kahan, *The Bank War: Andrew Jackson, Nicholas Biddle and the Fight for American Finance* (Yardley: Westholme, 2015).

4. J. Higham, *Strangers in the Land: Patterns of American Nativism 1860–1925* (New York: Atheneum, 1975), pp. 296–7; C. Mudde, *The Far Right in America* (London: Routledge, 2018), p. 5; D. H. Bennett, *The Party of Fear: From Nativist Movements to the New Right in American History* (New York: Vintage Books, 1988), pp. 199–237.

5. S. Diamond, *Roads to Dominion: Right-wing Movements and Political Power in the United States* (New York: Guilford Press, 1995), pp. 142–4; J. Lowndes, 'From Founding Violence to Political Hegemony: The Conservative Populism of George Wallace,' in F. Panizza (ed) *Populism and the Mirror of Democracy* (London; Verso, 2005), pp. 144–171; J. E. Lowndes, *From the New Deal to the New Right: Race and the Southern Origins of Modern Conservatism* (New Haven: Yale University Press, 2008), pp. 77–105.

6. M. Wolff, *Fire and Fury: Inside the Trump White House* (London: Little, Brown, 2018), pp. 44, 122.

7. C. Postel, 'The American Populist and Anti-Populist Legacy,' in J. Abromeit, *Transformations of Populism in Europe and the Americas* (London: Bloomsbury Academic, 2016) pp. 116–35, 119; T. Frank, *What's the Matter with America* (London: Secker and Warburg, 2004), p. 32; M. Kazin, *The Populist Persuasion: An American History* (Ithaca: Cornell University Press, 1998 edn), pp. 27–48; P. Le Blanc, *Left Americana: The Radical Heart of US History* (Chicago: Haymarket Books, 2017), pp. 13–14, 171; R. Hofstadter, *The Age of Reform* (New York: Knopf, 1955).

8. J. Y. Sexton, *The People are going to Rise like the Waters upon your Shore: A Study of American Rage* (Berkeley: Counterpoint, 2017), p. 89; R. Solnit, 'From Lying to Leering,' London Review of Books, 9 January 2017.

9. D. A. Hopkins, *Red Fighting Blue: How Geography and Electoral Rules Polarize American Politics* (Cambridge: Cambridge University Press, 2017); G, Hawley, 'America's Polarization Has Nothing to do with Ideology,' *American Conservative*, 24 April 2018; Mudde, *The Far Right in America*, p. 94; T. Piketty, 'Trump, Macron: same fight,' *Le Monde Blogs*, 12 December 2017.

10. C. Mudde and C. R. Kaltwasser, *Populism: A Very Short Introduction* (Oxford: Oxford University Press, 2017), p. 48.

11. S. Levitsky and D. Ziblatt, *How Democracies Die* (London: Penguin, 2018), pp. 3–5.

12. I. Errejón and C. Mouffe, *Podemos: In the Name of the People* (London: Lawrence & Wishart, 2016), pp. 93–108.

13. E. Schultheis. 'A New Right-Wing Movement Rises in Austria,' *The Atlantic*, 16 October 2017.

14. G. Passarelli, 'Populism and the Lega Nord,' in E. Jones and G. Pasquino, *The Oxford Handbook of Italian Politics* (Oxford: Oxford University Press, 2015), pp. 224–39.

15. M. Löwy, 'Ten theses on the far right in Europe,' in F. Leplat (ed), *The Far Right in Europe* (London: Resistance Books, 2015), pp. 28–33; E. Laclau, *On Populist Reason* (London: Verso. 2005), pp. 3–20, 157–73; E. Fassin, *Populisme: le grand ressentiment* (Paris: Textuel, 2017).

16. A. Sullivan, 'America Takes the Next Step toward Tyranny,' *New York Daily Intelligencer*, 23 March 2018.

17. A. S. Chaudhary and R. Chappe, 'The Supermanagerial Reich,' *Los Angeles Review of Books*, 7 November 2016.

18. D. Kean, 'Prescient about the president: which writers can help us read Trump?' *Guardian,* 24 January 2017; S. Lewis, *It Can't Happen Here* (New York: Doubleday, Doran & Company, 1935).

19. L. Green, '"Chasing Hillary": Clinton's "Deplorables" Was No One-Off Gaffe,' *American Conservative,* 23 April 2018; B. Jacobs, 'Joe Biden says European leader likened Trump to Mussolini,' *Guardian,* 17 October 2017; M. Albright, *Fascism: A Warning* (New York: Harper, 2018), p. 5.

20. N. Faulkner and S. Dathi, *Creeping Fascism* (London: Public Reading Rooms, 2017), p. 129; J. B. Foster, *Trump in the White House: Tragedy and Farce* (New York: Monthly Review Press, 2017), pp. 19–23.

21. C. Post, 'Fascism and Anti-Fascism: reflections on recent debates on the US Left,' *Salvage,* 10 October 2017.

22. N. Short, '*Passato e presente?* Gramsci's analysis of fascism and the far-right,' in R. Saull, A. Anievas, N. Davidson and A. Fabry, *The Longue durée of the Far-Right: An international historical sociology* (London: Routledge, 2015), pp. 106–28, 109.

23. R. O. Paxton, *The Anatomy of Fascism* (London: Allen Lane, 2004), p. 50; M. Mann, *Fascists* (Cambridge: Cambridge University Press, 2004), pp. 87–9.

24. D. Neiwert, *Alt-America: The Rise of the Radical Right in the Age of Trump* (London: Verso, 2017), pp. 362–3; 'Donald Trump announces a presidential bid,' *Washington Post,* 16 June 2015.

25. C. Pedersen. 'The Obama Dilemma: Confronting Race in the 21st Century,' in M. Ledwidge. K. Verney and I. Parmar (eds), *Barack Obama and the Myth of a Post-Racial America* (London: Routledge, 2014), pp. 27–43, 32; S. Alexander, 'You are still crying wolf,' *Slate Star Codex,* 16 November 2016; C. Hitchens, *No one Left to Lie to* (London: Verso, 1999), pp. 33–4.

26. S. V. Meyers, *Del Otro Lado: Literacy and Migration across the US-Mexico Border* (Carbondale: Southern Illinois University Press, 2014), p. 54.

27. T. Dart, '2,000 children separated from parents in six weeks under Trump policy,' *Guardian,* 16 June 2018.

28. *Patel v The Secretary of State for the Home Department* [2017] EWCA Civ 2028, paras 60, 84; *Harrison (Jamaica) v Secretary of State for the Home Department* [2012] EWCA Civ 1736, paras 56, 63; S. Singh, 'Theresa May's family separations would make Trump blush,' *Guardian,* 22 June 2018.

29. P. Buchanan, *A Republic, Not an Empire: Reclaiming America's Destiny* (Washington: Regnery, 1999), p. 262; G. Hawley, *Right-Wing Critics of*

American Conservatism (Lawrence: University Press of Kansas, 2016), pp. 58–60.

30. T. Stanley, *The Crusader: The Life and Tumultuous Times of Pat Buchanan* (New York: Thomas Dunne Books, 2012), pp. 332–7.

31. 'Trump again questions Obama's birthplace,' *Political Ticker,* 23 March 2011.

32. R. Tam, 'Rep. Farenthold says House could impeach Obama', *Washington Post,* 12 August 2013; M. A. Genovese, *The Trumping of American Politics: the Strange Case of the 2016 Presidential Election* (New York: Cambria Press, 2017), p. 61.

33. L. Douglas, 'Why Donald Trump pardoned the unpardonable Joe Arpaio,' *Guardian,* 26 August 2017; 'Andy Martin: 2012 Presidential Profile,' *Conservative Daily News,* 4 June 2011; J. H. Richardson, 'What really happens when you demand the President produce his birth certificate,' *Esquire,* 11 August 2009; G. Winant, 'What Orly Taitz believes,' *Salon* 13 August 2009; Neiwert, *Alt-America,* pp. 87–108.

34. Mudde, *The Far Right in America,* p. 19.

35. C. Mieville, '"One thinge that ouerthroweth all that were graunted before": On Being Presidential,' *Salvage,* 31 January 2018; T. Skocpol and V. Williamson, *The Tea Party and the Remaking of Modern Conservatism* (Oxford: Oxford University Press, 2012), p. 78; C. Robin, *The Reactionary Mind: Conservatism from Edmund Burke to Sarah Palin* (Oxford: Oxford University Press, 2011), p. 248.

36. C. S. Parker and M. A. Barreto, *Change They Can't Believe In: the Tea Party and Reactionary Politics in America* (Princeton: Princeton University Press, 2013), pp. 36–45; L. Grossberg, *Under the Cover of Chaos: Trump and the Battle for the American Right* (London: Pluto, 2018), p. 72.

37. A. R. Hochschild, *Strangers in their own Land: Anger and Mourning on the American Right* (New York: New Press, 2016), pp. 136–7.

38. J. Green, *Devil's Bargain: Steve Bannon, Donald Trump and the Storming of the Presidency* (New York: Penguin, 2017), p. 40.

39. M. Coppins, *The Wilderness: Deep inside the Republican Party's Combative, Contentious, Chaotic Quest to Take Back the White House* (New York: Little, Brown and Company, 2015), p. 25; M. Preston and A. Silverleib, 'Trump endorses Romney,' *CNN Politics,* 3 February 2012.

40. A. Breitbart, *Righteous Indignation: Excuse Me While I Save the World!* (New York: Hachette Books, 2012), pp. 106–36, 230.

41. Coppins, *The Wilderness*, p. 232; L. Kaufman, 'Breitbart Network Plans Global Expansion,' *New York Times*, 16 February 2014; Green, *Devil's Bargain*, pp. 148–9.

42. J. Feldman, 'Breitbart Now Donald Trump's PR Firm,' *Media-ite*, 18 February 2014; C. Malone, 'Trump made Breitbart Great Again,' *FiveThirtyEight*, 18 August 2016.

43. Green, *Devil's Bargain*, p. 83.

44. E. Gjoni, 'Why does this post exist?' *The Zoe Post*, 12 September 2014; B. Stuart, '#Gamergate: the misogynist movement blighting the video games industry,' *Daily Telegraph*, 24 October 2014.

45. Z. Quinn, *Crash Override: How Gamergate (nearly) Destroyed my Life and how we can Win the Fight against Online Hate* (New York: Public Affairs, 2017), pp. 18–19.

46. B. Stuart, 'Brianna Wu and the human cost of Gamergate: "every woman I know in the industry is scared,"' *Guardian*, 17 October 2014.

47. M. Yiannopoulos, 'Feminist bullies tearing the video game industry apart,' *Breitbart*, 1 September 2014.

48. V. Tenold, *Everything You Love Will Burn: Inside the Rebirth of White Nationalism in America* (New York: Nation Books, 2018); J. Harkinson, 'The Push to Enlist 'Alt-Right' Recruits on College Campuses,' *Mother Jones*, 6 December 2016.

49. J. C. Pan, 'Money Troubles,' *Dissent*, 3 February 2016; N. Fraser, 'Crisis of Care? On the Social Reproductive Contradictions of Consumer Capitalism,' in T. Bhattacharya (ed), *Social Reproduction Theory: Remapping Class, Recentering Oppression* (London: Pluto, 2017), pp. 21–36, 32.

50. Gjoni, 'Why does this post.'

51. G. Hawley, 'The Demography of the Alt-Right,' *Institute for Family Studies*. 10 August 2018; J. Reitman, 'All-American Nazis,' *Rolling Stone*, 2 May 2018; B. Zadrozny, 'Milo Yiannopoulos' charity for "white boys" winds down as mystery remains over the $100,000 raised,' *NBC News*, 29 March 2018.

52. 'Queer Fascism: Why White Nationalists are Trying to Drop Homophobia,' *Anti-Fascist News*, 6 November 2015; A. Nagle, *Kill All Normies: Online Culture Wars from 4Chan and Tumblr to Trump and the Alt-Right* (London: Zero Books, 2017), pp. 58–66; D. Penny, '#Milosexual and the Aesthetics of Fascism,' *Boston Review*, 24 January 2017; M. Rose, 'The Anti-Christian Alt-Right,' *First Things*, 12 February 2018; P. MacDougald, 'Fascists and Revolutionaries,' *American Affairs*, 20 February 2018.

53. Green, *Devil's Bargain*, p. 148; R. E. Gutsche Jr, *The Trump Presidency, Journalism and Democracy* (London: Routledge, 2018), pp. 119, 151.

54. A. Bokhari and M. Yiannopoulos, 'An Establishment Conservative's Guide to the Alt-Right,' *Breitbart*, 29 March 2016; J. Bernstein, 'Here's How Breitbart and Milo Smuggled Nazi and White Nationalist Ideas Into The Mainstream,' *BuzzFeed News*, 5 October 2017.

55. 'Donald Trump's jobs plan speech,' *Politico*, 28 June 2016.

56. D. Frank, *Buy American: The Untold Story of Economic Nationalism* (Boston: Beacon Press, 1999); F. Witsil, 'UAW group: Racial incidents need to stop, be condemned by leadership,' *Detroit Free Press*, 8 February 2018; K. Fox-Hodess, 'Tariffs Aren't the Best Way To Protect U.S. Steelworkers. Global Solidarity Is,' *In These Times*, 10 April 2018.

57. D. Lind, 'What we know about attacks on police,' *Vox*, 8 July 2016; R. Balko, 'Police Fatality Statistics Show 2012 On Pace To Be Safest Year For Police In 60 Years,' *HuffPost*, 6 December 2017.

58. T. Ferguson, P. Jorgensen and J. Chen, 'Industrial Structure and Party Competition in an Age of Hunger Games: Donald Trump and the 2016 Presidential Election,' Institute for New Economic Thinking, Working Paper 66, January 2018, pp. 4, 19, 50.

59. J. Mayer, *Dark Money: How a Secretive Group of Billionaires is Trying to Buy Political Control in the US* (London: Scribe, 2016), p. 373; N. MacLean, *Democracy in Chains: The Deep History of the Radical Right's Stealth Plan for America* (London: Scribe, 2017).

60. D. Katch, *Why Bad Governments Happen to Good People* (Chicago: Haymarket, 2018), pp. 15–18; D. Kaufman, 'Notes on the Cheddar Revolution,' *New Yorker*, 22 February 2011.

61. B. Shor, 'Polarization in American State Legislatures,' in J. A. Thurber and A. Yoshinaka (eds), *American Gridlock: The Sources, Character and Impact of Political Polarization* (Cambridge: Cambridge University Press, 2015), pp. 203–21, 209.

62. This chapter sets out some problems of using education as a proxy for class; the self-reporting of economic decline is even less persuasive. Given that the best indicator of a person's likelihood to vote Trump in 2016 was whether or not they had voted for Mitt Romney in 2012, and the very high reporting of Trump voters' that they had suffered relative economic loss, the only plausible conclusion would be that tens of millions of America's registered Republicans had seen their incomes crash since 2012, when we know from the economic data that this had simply not happened. N. Silver, 'Education, Not Income, Predicted Who Would Vote For Trump,' *538*, 22 November 2016; S.

McElwee and J. McDaniel, 'Economic Anxiety Didn't Make People Vote Trump, Racism Did,' *The Nation*, 8 May 2017.

63. K. Moody, *On New Terrain: How Capital is Reshaping the Battleground of the Class War* (Chicago: Haymarket Books, 2017), p. 176.

64. Grossberg, *Under the Cover of Chaos*, pp. 26–7; J. T. Rothwell and P. Diego-Rosell, 'Explaining Nationalist Political Views: The Case of Donald Trump,' *Social Science Research Network*, 29 December 2017, p. 23; Moody, *On New Terrain*, p. 175.

65. C. Post, 'We got Trumped,' *International Socialist Review* 104, spring 2017; G. Palast, 'The GOP's Stealth War on Voters,' *Rolling Stone*, 24 August 2016; Moody, *On New Terrain*, p. 184.

66. D. Merica, 'Clinton dismisses reinstating Glass-Steagall,' *CNN Politics*, 6 October 2015; S. Condon, 'Hillary Clinton: Single-payer health care will "never, ever" happen,' *CBS News*, 29 January 2016; A. Marchevsky and J. Theoharis, 'Why It Matters That Hillary Clinton Championed Welfare Reform,' *The Nation*, 1 March 2016.

67. C. Sittenfeld, *You Think It I'll See It* (London: Penguin, Doubleday, 2018), pp. 3–16.

68. M. Nelson, 'The 2016 Election in Print,' *Claremont Review*, 10 April 2018.

69. J. Nolte, '8 Reasons Why #NeverTrump Failed,' *Daily Wire*, 6 June 2016; E. Stewart, 'Donald Trump Rode $5 Billion in Free Media to the White House,' *The Street*, 20 November 2016; M. Cooper, 'A Message from Trump's America,' *US News*, 9 March 2016.

70. 'Donald Trump and Hillary Clinton's final campaign spending revealed,' *Guardian*, 9 December 2016; 'Political party spending at previous elections,' *Electoral Commission*, 19 March 2018.

71. M. L. Sifry, 'Why America Is Stuck With Only Two Parties,' *New Republic*, 2 February 2008; L. J. Disch, *The Tyranny of the Two-Party System* (New York: Columbia University Press, 2002).

72. B. Sanders, *Our Revolution: A Future to Believe in* (London: Penguin, 2017), pp. 129–31; 'Elizabeth Warren agrees Democratic race "rigged" for Clinton', *BBC News*, 3 November 2017; E. Schultz, 'Leaked document shows the DNC wanted Clinton from start,' *New York Post*, 16 June 2016; N. Allen, 'Hillary Clinton faces mass dissent over "dirty tricks" on Bernie Sanders,' *Daily Telegraph*, 25 July 2016.

73. D. O'Sullivan, 'Vengeance is mine,' *Jacobin*, 18 November 2016.

74. R. Shabad, 'Why more than 100 gun control proposals in Congress since 2011 have failed', *CBS News*, 20 June 2016; D. French, 'How Progressive Radicals Move the Country Left and Right,' *National Review*, 15 February 2018.

75. C. Mathias, 'Reminder: Ben Carson Is An Anti-Muslim Conspiracy Theorist Who Thinks Islam Isn't A Religion,' *Huffpost*, 6 December 2016; M. Crowley, 'On torture, Cruz stands alone,' *Politico*, 21 January 2016; A. D. Sorkin, 'Bush's Befuddled Goodbye and Risks of Trump Denialism,' *New Yorker*, 21 February 2016.

76. R. Leber, 'Ben Carson on Climate Change: "Gravity, Where did it Come From?"' *New Republic*, 1 October 2015; D. Allott, 'Marco Rubio's brilliant answer on abortion,' *Washington Examiner*, 7 February 2016; Southern Poverty Law Center, *Intelligence Report*, 27 October 2015.

77. A. Mahdawi. 'The Bill Clinton rape shirt: what anti-Hillary merch says about this election,' *Guardian*, 20 July 2016; M. Wendling, *Alt Right: From 4chan to the White House* (London: Pluto, 2018), p. 172.

78. Levitsky and Ziblatt, *How Democracies Die*, pp. 62–4.

79. Wolff, *Fire and Fury*, p. 13.

80. S. Posner, 'Meet the "Spokesman" of the Alt-Right,' *The Investigative Fund*, 18 October 2016; R. Stockman, '"That's What Mammals Do!" Alex Jones' Comments Supporting Trump "Pussy" Video Rear Head in Court', *Law & Crime*, 22 April 2017; M. Taibbi, 'Milo Yiannopoulos Isn't Going Away,' *Rolling Stone*, 21 February 2017.

81. F. Morse, 'What women have to say about Donald Trump's comments on 2005 tape,' *Independent*, 8 October 2016; M. Willstein, 'The Sad Surrogates Still Spinning for Trump,' *Daily Beast*, 10 August 2018.

82. Ferguson, Jorgensen and Chen, 'Industrial Structure,' pp. 19–20.

83. Green, *Devil's Bargain*, pp. 196-7; Wolff, *Fire and Fury*, p. 59.

84. A. Kelly, 'Clinton: Trump Is 'Taking Hate Groups Mainstream,' *National Public Radio*, 25 August 2016.

85. R. Cornwell, 'Where have the Never Trumpers gone? Republicans are abandoning their integrity to get into government,' *Independent*, 18 November 2016.

86. 'Trump assembles America's "richest cabinet",' *BBC News*, 1 December 2016.

87. L. Bayer, 'Controversial Trump Aide Sebastian Gorka backed violent anti-semitic militia,' *Forward*, 3 April 2017.

88. Wolff, *Fire and Fury*, p. 118.

89. 'The full text of Donald Trump's inauguration speech,' *Guardian*, 20 January 2017.

90. Wolff, *Fire and Fury*, p. 65.

91. 'Remarks by President Trump to the People of Poland,' *whitehouse.gov*, 6 July 2017; N. Nougayrède, 'Steve Bannon is on a far-right mission to radicalize Europe,' *Guardian*, 6 June 2018.

92. J. A. Bloom, 'How to Destroy the Alt-Right,' *Jacobite*, 28 February 2018.

93. J. Harkinson, 'Meet the White Nationalist Trying To Ride The Trump Train to Lasting Power,' *Mother Jones*, 27 October 2016; V. Tenold, *Everything You Love Will Burn: Inside the Rebirth of White Nationalism in America* (New York: Nation Books, 2018), p. 226.

94. D. Lombroso and Y. Applebaum, '"Hail Trump!" White Nationalists Salute the President-Elect,' *The Atlantic*, 21 November 2016.

95. T. Williams, 'The French influence of "You will not replace us",' *New Yorker*, 4 December 2017.

96. Hunton and Williams LLP, *Final report: Independent Review of the events in Charlottesville, Virginia* (Richmond: Hunton and Williams, 2017).

97. J. Wilson, 'Charlottesville: man charged with murder was pictured at neo-Nazi rally,' *Guardian*, 13 August 2017; Wendling, *Alt-Right*, p. 174; S. Hendrix, 'It's still hard to look at,' *Washington Post*, 10 August 2018.

98. J. Johnson and J. Wagner, 'Trump condemns Charlottesville violence but doesn't single out white nationalists,' *Washington Post*, 13 August 2017.

99. B. Jacobs and O. Laughland, 'Charlottesville: Trump reverts to blaming both sides including "violent alt-left",' *Guardian*, 16 August 2017.

100. Remaining supporters of the far right in Trump's administration included the more junior figures of Stephen Miller, Trump's speech-writer and advisor, and Ian Smith, an official at the Department of Homeland Security. M. Coppins, 'Trump's Right-hand Troll,' *The Atlantic*, 28 May 2018; R. Gray, 'Emails Link Former Homeland Security Official to White Nationalists,' *The Atlantic*, 28 August 2018.

101. G. Krieg, 'Rally Trump vs Teleprompter Trump,' *CNN politics*, 23 August 2017.

102. J. Butler, 'Milo's Stumble,' *LRB blog*, 22 February 2017; Wolff, *Fire and Fury*, p. 129; G. Worgaftik, 'Milo Yiannopoulos has been reduced to shilling "supplements" on InfoWars,' *AV Club*, 21 February 2018;' T. Gold, 'The fall of Milo Yiannopoulos,' *Spectator USA*, 6 April 2018; D. Levesley, 'Milo Yiannopoulos says he has lost "literally millions of dollars" on events that went on to be cancelled,' *Independent*, 26 August 2018.

103. K. Weill, 'The Alt-Right is self-destructing,' *Daily Beast*, 29 March 2018; J. Wilson, 'The alt-right is in decline. Has anti-fascist activism

worked?', *Guardian*, 19 March 2018; T. Kupfer, 'A Look at the Alt-Right One Year after Charlottesville,' *National Review*, 13 August 2018.

104. M. Holt, 'The Rise and Fall of the Alt Right,' *American Greatness*, 4 September 2018.

105. J. Flake, *Conscience of a Conservative: A Rejection of Destructive Politics and A Return to Principle* (New York: Random House, 2017), pp. 29, 51.

106. 'Tracking Congress in the Age of Trump,' *FiveThirtyEight*, accessed 15 April 2018; R. Douthat, 'How Trump is Winning,' *New York Times*, 5 May 2018.

107. J. Coaston, 'Self-described Nazis and white supremacists are running as Republicans across the country. The GOP is terrified,' *Vox*, 9 July 2018.

108. Hochschild, *Strangers in their own Land,* p. 7.

109. E. Green, 'The End of Trump Won't Be the End of Trumpism,' *The Atlantic*, 21 May 2018.

110. Tucker Carlson, speech to 2017 IAFF Legislative Conference, *YouTube*, 6 March 2017.

Chapter 5: Breaking the centre: the Front National and its rivals

1. M. Le Pen, *Twitter*, 24 June 2016, 28 June 2016, 28 June 2016, 16 October 2016.

2. V. Friedman, 'Le Pen Hits back at Hollande's anti-Populist NYE Speech,' *Breitbart*, 1 January 2017; '"Made in France": Marine Le Pen unveils election platform,' *Breitbart*, 4 February 2017; 'Le Pen: I will quit office if French reject Eurozone exit,' *Breitbart*, 27 March 2017.

3. J. Rydgren, *Political Protest and Ethno-Nationalist Mobilization: The Case of the French Front National* (Stockholm: Stockholm University, 2002), pp. 288–90; J. Marcus, *The National Front and French Politics: The Resistible Rise of Jean-Marie Le Pen* (Basingstoke: Macmillan, 1995), pp. 9–10.

4. J. Esterbrook, 'Chirac Is Mightier Than Le Pen,' *CBS News*, 6 May 2002; N. Vinocur, 'Riot police injured at anti-Marine Le Pen protest in Paris,' *Politico.EU*, 1 May 2017.

5. E. Ivarsflaten, 'Reputational Shields: Why Most Anti-Immigrant Parties Failed in Western Europe, 1980–2005,' paper prepared for the 2006 Annual Meeting of the American Political Science Association; N. Copsey, '"Fascism… but with an open mind," Reflections on the

Contemporary Far Right in (Western) Europe,' *Fascism* 2/1 (2013), pp. 1–17.

6. 'Torturés par Le Pen. Cinq témoignages accablants pour un homme politique qui a toujours nié les faits,' *Libération*, 12 February 1985; Marcus, *National Front*, p. 32; L. A. Higgins, 'The Barbie Affair and the Trials of Memory,' in R. J. Golsan (ed), *Fascism's Return: Scandal, Revision and Ideology since 1980* (Lincoln: University of Nebraska Press, 1995), pp. 200–218, 204.

7. '"Détail de l'histoire": Jean-Marie Le Pen à nouveau condamné,' *L'Humanité*, 6 April 2016.

8. A.-E. Moutet, 'Marine Le Pen becomes Front National leader: a Pivotal Moment for French politics?' *Daily Telegraph*, 16 January 2011; J. Wolfreys, 'The European Extreme Right in Comparative Perspective,' in A. Mammone, E. Godin and B. Jenkins, *Varieties of Right-Wing Extremism in Europe* (London: Routledge, 2013), pp. 19–38, 25; 'French National Front expels founder Jean-Marie Le Pen,' *BBC News*, 20 August 2015; G. Ivaldi and M. E. Lanzone, 'The French Front National: Organizational Change and Adaptation from Jean-Marie to Marine Le Pen,' in R. Heinisch and O. Mazzoleni, *Understanding Populist Party Organisation: The Radical Right in Western Europe* (Basingstoke: Palgrave Macmillan, 2016), p. 148.

9. A. Chrisafis, 'The Man Who Could Make Marine Le Pen President of France,' *Guardian*, 31 January 2017; J. Wolfreys, *Republic of Islamophobia: The Rise of Respectable Racism in France* (London: Hurst and Company, 2018), p. 76; NPA Anti-fascist Commission, 'France: Pétain's Children,' in F. Leplat (ed), *The Far Right in Europe* (London: Resistance Books, 2015), pp. 113–202, 138–9.

10. '"Jamais je n'aurais fait alliance avec Jean-Marie Le Pen", assure Nicolas Dupont-Aignan,' *E1*, 8 February 2018.

11. V. Vinocur, 'Marine Le Pen to borrow €6 million from father's lender,' *Politico.EU*, 31 December 2016; Agence-France Press, 'Marine Le Pen denies French role in wartime roundup of Paris Jews,' *Guardian*, 9 April 2017.

12. T. Bar-On, *Where have all the Fascists Gone?* (Aldershot: Ashgate, 2007), p. 31; D. Venner, 'Pour une critique positive,' *Europe-Action* 5 (May 1963), 3–80; D. Venner, *For a Positive Critique* (Budapest: Arktos Media, 2017); J. G. Shields, *The Extreme Right in France: From Pétain to Le Pen* (London: Routledge, 2007), pp. 119–20.

13. N. Lebourg and J. Beauregard, *François Duprat: L'homme qui inventa le Front National* (Paris: Éditions Denoël, 2012), p. 27; F. Duprat, *Les Mouvements d'extrême-droite en France depuis 1944* (Paris: Albatros,

1972), p. 122; P. Fysh and J. Wolfreys, *The Politics of Racism in France* (Basingstoke: Macmillan, 1998), pp. 93–4; Marcus, *The National Front*, p. 20; J. Rydgren, *The Populist Challenge: Political Protest and Ethno-nationalist Mobilization in France* (Oxford: Berghahn, 2003), p. 18.

14. N. Lebourg, J. Preda and J. Beauregard, *Aux racines du FN: L'histoire du mouvement Ordre Nouveau* (Paris: Fondation Jean-Jaurès, 2014), pp. 57, 82.

15. Fysh and Wolfreys, *The Politics*, pp. 95–6, 100; D. Gordon, *Immigrants and Intellectuals: May '68 and the Rise of Anti-Racism in France* (London: Merlin Press, 2012), p. 144; NPA, 'France,' p. 117; S. E. Atkins, *Holocaust Denial as an International Movement* (Toronto: Praeger, 2009), p. 91.

16. Lebourg and Beauregard, *François Duprat*, p. 49; S. François, 'Alain de Benoist: Mémoire vive,' *Fascism* 1/2 (2012), pp. 155–7; M. A. Lee, *The Beast Reawakens* (London: Little, Brown and Company, 1997), p. 209; P.-A. Taguieff, *Sur la Nouvelle Droite: jalons d'une analyse critique* (Paris: Descartes & Cie, 1994), pp. 116–43; J. Lester Feder and P. Buet, 'The Man Who Gave White Nationalism A New Life,' *Buzzfeed*, 27 December 2017.

17. A. de Benoist, 'Regenerating History,' in R. Griffin (ed), *Fascism* (Oxford: Oxford University Press, 1995), pp. 346–7; R. Griffin, 'Plus ça change! The Fascist Pedigree of the Nouvelle Droite,' in E. J. Arnold (ed), *The Development of the Radical Right in France* (Basingstoke: Palgrave Macmillan, 2000), pp. 217–52, 222–3; T. McCulloch, 'The Nouvelle Droite in the 1980s and 1990s: Ideology and Entryism, the Relationship with the Front National,' *French Politics* 2006/4 pp. 158–78; C. Flood, 'Organizing Fear and Indignation: The Front National in France,' in R. J. Golsan (ed), *Fascism's Return: Scandal, Revision and Ideology since 1980* (Lincoln: University of Nebraska Press, 1995), pp. 19–47, 27.

18. Bar-On, *Where have all the Fascists Gone*, p. 170; R. Wolin, 'Designer Fascism,' in Golsan (ed), *Fascism's Return*, pp. 48–62, 55; Fish and Wolfreys, *The Politics*, p. 111.

19. Flood, 'Organizing,' p. 36.

20. G. Harris, *The Dark Side of Europe: The Extreme Right Today* (Edinburgh: Edinburgh University Press, 1994 edn), pp. 64–6; Lee, *Beast Awakens*, p. 368; H. G. Simmons, *The French National Front: The Extremist Challenge to Democracy* (Boulder: Westview Press, 1996), p. 94; Wolfreys, 'The European extreme right,' p. 24.

21. 'La mairie FN veut rebaptiser plusieurs rues de Vitrolles,' *L'Humanité*, 25 September 1997; NPA, 'France,' pp. 121–2.

22. J. Guintard, '1989: la première fois que *Le Monde* a écrit "dédiabolisation",' *Le Monde*, 17 December 2015; V. Igounet, 'La dédiabolisation, c'est quoi au juste?' *France Info*, 26 June 2015.

23. 'Mégret annetue sa tentative de récuperation du gaullisme par le Front national,' *Le Monde*, 12 May 1998; C. Fieschi, *Fascism, Populism and the French Fifth Republic: In the shadow of democracy* (Manchester: Manchester University Press, 2004), p. 143.

24. K. L. Marcus, *The Definition of Anti-Semitism* (Oxford: Oxford University Press, 2015), pp. 1–2.

25. A. Benveniste and E. Pingaud, 'Far-right Movements in France: The Principal Role of Front National and the Rise of Islamophobia,' in G. Lazaridis et al (eds), *The Rise of the Far Right in Europe: Populist Shifts and 'Othering'* (Basingstoke: Palgrave Macmillan, 2016), pp. 55–80, 63–4; 'How 'identitarian' politics is changing Europe,' *Economist*, 28 March 2018; 'France,' *Hope not Hate*, accessed 9 August 2018.

26. P. Verduzier, 'Pierre Cassen et Christine Tasin, de la gauche à la haine de l'islam,' JDD, 5 June 2015; 8 May 2017; 'Philippe de Villiers, vous avez gravement fauté,' *Riposte Laïque*, 8 May 2017.

27. A. Mondon, *A Populist Hegemony? The Mainstreaming of the Extreme Right in France and Australia* (Farnham: Ashgate, 2013), p. 89; 'Leader of France's Jewish Defence League on run in Israel after conviction in Paris,' *Middle East Monitor*, 1 June 2016; C. Tomlinson, 'Firebrand Israeli Politician Endorses Marine Le Pen,' *Breitbart*, 5 May 2017; 'Marche blanche: la LDJ sort Mélenchon et escorte Le Pen,' *Politis*, 28 March 2018.

28. 'Premier tour présidentielle 2017: sociologie de l'électorat,' *Ipsos France*, 23 April 2017; D. Eribon, *Returning to Reims* (Massachusetts: MIT Press, 2018).

29. K. Willsher, 'Marine Le Pen sparks row over new name for Front National,' *Guardian*, 12 March 2018.

30. J. Lichfield, 'Far-right French historian, 78-year-old Dominique Venner, commits suicide in Notre Dame in protest against gay marriage,' *Independent*, 21 May 2013; 'La manif du 26 mai et Heidegger,' *Dominique Venner*, 21 May 2013; Marine Le Pen, Twitter, 21 May 2013.

31. NPA, 'France,' p. 125.

32. J. Wolfreys, 'Neither Right Nor left? Towards an Integrated Analysis of the Front National,' in N. Atkin and F. Tallett, *The Right in France: From Revolution to Le Pen* (London: I. B. Tauris, 2003), pp. 261–76, 262–3; NPA, 'France,' pp. 140–41, 173.

33. Marcus, *National Front*, p. 135; K. Hullot-Guiot, 'Le "front républicain", une longue histoire,' *Libération*, 24 April 2017.

34. Gordon, *Immigrants*, p. 215.

35. Marcus, *National Front*, pp. 141, 144.

36. NPA, 'France,' pp. 128, 150–51; B. M. Meguid, 'Competition Between Unequals: The Role of Mainstream Party Strategy in Niche Party Success,' *American Political Science Review* 99/3 (2005), pp. 347–59.

37. E. Bastié, 'Vie et mort du "Front républicain",' *Figaro*, 1 May 2017; E. Faux, T. Legrand and G. Perez, *La main droite de Dieu* (Paris: Éditions du Seuil, 1994); Simmons, *The French National Front*, pp. 77–8; NPA, 'France,' p. 119.

38. B. Winter, *Hijab and the Republic: Uncovering the French Headscarf Debate* (New York: Syracuse University Press, 2008), pp. 135–6; Fysh and Wolfreys, *The Politics*, pp. 175, 184–5; Wolin, 'Designer Fascism,' p. 57; Marcus, *National Front*, pp. 150–51.

39. R. Redeker, 'Face aux intimidations islamistes, que doit faire le monde libre?' *Le Figaro*, 19 September 2006; S. Sands, *The End of the French Intellectual: From Zola to Houuellebecq* (London: Verso, 2018), pp. 245–7.

40. A. Finkielkraut, *The Imaginary Jew* (Lincoln: University of Nebraska Press, 1997), pp. 17–18; E. Badinter, *Dead End Feminism* (Cambridge: Polity Press, 2006); A. Glucksmann, *The Master-Thinkers* (Brighton: Harvester Press, 1980), pp. 71–2, 170–71.

41. Wolfreys, *Republic of Islamophobia*, pp. 5–6, 37–41.

42. J. Carvalho, *Impact of Extreme Right Parties on Immigration Policy: Comparing Britain, France and Italy* (London: Routledge, 2014), p. 111; J. A. Selby, *Questioning French Secularism: Gender Politics and Islam in a Parisian Suburb* (Basingstoke: Palgrave Macmillan, 2012) pp. 63–5; NPA, 'France,' p. 151; P. Marlière, '"Sarkozyism": From Political Ambivalence to Hard Right', in G. G. Raymond (ed), *The Sarkozy Presidency: Breaking the Mould* (Basingstoke: Palgrave Macmillan, 2013), pp. 28–56, 33.

43. A. Renault and P. Buisson, *L'Album Le Pen* (Écully: Intervalles, 1984).

44. Marlière, 'Sarkozyism', p. 47.

45. C. Mathiot, 'Immigration: Montebourg et le "consensus" PS-UMP-FN,' *Libération*, 24 April 2012; Wolfreys, *Republic of Islamophobia*, p. 143.

46. 'Besson relance le débat sur l'identité nationale,' *Le Monde*, 26 October 2009; Wolfreys, *Republic of Islamophobia*, pp. 16, 81.

47. K. Willsher, 'French presidential election: the gloves are off,' *Guardian*, 16 April 2012; J. Gaffney, *France in the Hollande Presidency:*

The Unhappy Republic (Basingstoke: Palgrave Macmillan, 2015), pp. 17–18; 'Mélenchon va défier Le Pen à Hénin-Beaumont,' *SudOuest.fr,* 12 May 2012; K. Willsher. 'France's champion of the left sends a challenge to Marine Le Pen,' *Observer,* 26 May 2012.

48. Wolfreys, *Republic of Islamophobia,* pp. 5–6; G. Bekhtari, 'The Meaning of France Insoumise,' Jacobin, 23 April 2017; J. Dettmer, 'Red-Brown Alignments Unnerve Europe's Centrists,' *Voa News,* 27 August 2018.

49. B. Sim, '"You can't fight fascism every five years with a piece of paper",' *Open Democracy,* 14 May 2017.

50. D. Birnbaum, 'Le 4 août de Mélenchon, ou l'antifascisme trahi,' *Le Monde,* 2 May 2017; J. Henley and M. Belam, 'French election: Marine Le Pen and Emmanuel Macron lock horns in TV debate – as it happened,' *Guardian,* 4 May 2017.

51. Z. Sternhell, *Ni droite, ni gauche : L'Idéologie fasciste en France* (Paris: Folio Histoire, 2012).

52. B. Amble and S. Palombarini, *L'illusion du bloc bourgeois: Alliances sociales et avenir du modèle français* (Paris: Raisons d'agir, 2017), pp. 106, 115; Wolfreys, *Republic of Islamophobia,* p. 9.

53. 'The movement that Emmanuel Macron rode to power needs a new role,' *Economist,* 18 January 2018.

54. L. Trotsky, 'Bonapartism and Fascism,' in D. Beetham (ed), *Marxists in Face of Fascism* (Manchester: Manchester University Press, 1983), pp. 214–21.

55. T. Piketty, 'Trump, Macron: same fight,' *Le Monde Blogs,* 12 December 2017.

56. J. Legendre, 'Emmanuel Macron Was Supposed to Be the Anti-Trump. He's Not,' *Foreign Policy in Focus,* 12 February 2018; N. Selim, 'France: The Meaning of Macron – New forms of racism, authoritarianism, neoliberalism,' *Europe-Solidaires,* 19 October 2017; J. Hambly, 'Court on strike: French asylum reforms trigger months of action,' *Socialist Lawyer,* June 2018.

57. 'French President Emmanuel Macron Dangles From Helicopter Over Sub,' *NBC News,* 5 July 2017.

58. M. Perolini, 'Pourquoi la loi antiterroriste qui remplacera l'état d'urgence pose problème,' *Huffington Post.Fr,* 26 September 2017.

Chapter 6: The internationalism of the far right

1. V. Mazza, 'Steve Bannon a Roma: "Una coalizione Lega-M5S? Fantastica, trafiggerebbe al cuore Bruxelles",' *Corriere della Sera,* 4 March 2018.

2. J. J. McCullough, 'The Globalism of the Anti-Globalists,' *National Review*, 15 March 2018.

3. C. T. Bogus, *Buckley: William F. Buckley Jr. and the Rise of American Conservatism* (New York: Bloomsbury Press, 2011), pp. 109–10; J. O'Sullivan, 'Did William F. Buckley's Conservative Project End in Failure?' *National Review*, 20 July 2017; T. Mitchell, *Carbon Democracy: Political Power in the Age of Oil* (London: Verso, 2011), pp. 197–8; G. Hawley, 'Lee Edwards' Just Right and the Lessons of Movement Politics,' *Law and Liberty*, 16 April 2018; M. Holt, 'The Rise and Fall of the Alt Right,' *American Greatness*, 4 September 2018.

4. C. Mudde, 'Europe shouldn't fear Steve Bannon. It should fear the hype that surrounds him,' *Guardian*, 30 July 2018; I. Buruma, 'Steve Bannon's European Adventure,' *Project Syndicate*, 7 August 2018.

5. A. Finlayson, 'Tony Blair and the jargon of modernisation,' *Soundings* 10 (1998), pp. 11–27; G. Wheatcroft, 'Both Blair and Howard echo the rhetoric of fascism,' *Guardian*, 31 March 2005; C. Brooke, 'Tony Blair, petainiste?' paper presented at Cerberus, the PPE Society at Balliol College, Oxford, January 2007.

6. 'President François Hollande's Inauguration Speech,' *France in the United States*, 15 May 2012; E. Fassin, *Gauche: L'avenir d'une désillusion* (Paris: Éditions Textuel, 2014).

7. A. Blake, 'Donald Trump's strategy in three words: "Americanism, not globalism,"' *Washington Post*, 22 July 2016.

8. W. F. Mandle, 'The Leadership of the British Union of Fascists,' *The Australian Journal of Politics and History* 12/3 (1966), pp. 360–83; for the impact of colonialism on an earlier generation of race theorists, H. Arendt, *The Origins of Totalitarianism* (London: André Deutsch, 1986 edn), pp. 180–83.

9. J. Tyndall, *The Eleventh Hour: A Call for British Rebirth* (London: Albion Press, 1988), p. 11.

10. 'Growing up with Europe – A Memoir,' in P. Robertson (ed), *Reshaping Europe in the Twenty-First Century* (London: Macmillan, 1992), pp. 254–62; D. Levesley, 'Nigel Lawson, leading Brexit campaigner is applying for residency in France,' *Guardian*, 31 May 2018; S. Knight, 'The man who brought you Brexit', *Guardian*, 29 September 2016; A. Banks, *The Bad Boys of Brexit: Tales of Mischief, Mayhem and Guerrilla Warfare in the EU Referendum Campaign* (London: Biteback, 2017), p. 266.

11. R. Griffin (ed), *Fascism* (Oxford: Oxford University Press, 1995), p. 3; also R. Griffin (ed), *International Fascism: Theories, Causes and the New Consensus* (London: Hodder Headline, 1998), pp. 13–15; R.

Griffin, 'Studying Fascism in a Postfascist Age. From New Consensus to New Wave?' *Fascism* 1/1 (2012), pp. 1–17.

12. R. Griffin, *Fascism: An Introduction to Comparative Fascist Studies* (Cambridge: Polity, 2018), p. 32.

13. D. Renton, *Fascism: Theory and Practice* (London: Pluto, 1999), pp. 8–16; also R. O. Paxton, *The Anatomy of Fascism* (London: Allen Lane, 2004), p. 5; and M. Mann, *Fascists* (Cambridge: Cambridge University Press, 2004), pp. 11–13.

14. Griffin, *Fascism*, p. 8.

15. N. Hallett, 'Channelling Trump, Le Pen vows to make France the "model national-state"', *Breitbart*, 27 February 2017; N. Hallett, 'Le Pen Maintains First Round Lead in Latest Polling,' *Breitbart*, 6 March 2017; V. Friedman, 'Le Pen: "I Will Bring Islamist Fundamentalism to Its Knees,"' *Breitbart*, 4 April 2017; C. Tomlinson, 'Trump touts Le Pen as 'Strongest' Candidate in French Presidential Race,' *Breitbart*, 21 April 2017.

16. A. Chrisafis, 'French presidential debate: Le Pen comes under fire from rivals,' *Guardian*, 21 March 2017; J. Henley and M. Belam, 'French election: Marine Le Pen and Emmanuel Macron lock horns in TV debate – as it happened,' *Guardian*, 4 May 2017.

17. A. Stille, 'How Matteo Salvini pulled Italy to the far right,' *Guardian*, 9 August 2018; Mazza, 'Steve Bannon a Roma.'

18. O. Laing, *Crudo* (London: Picador, 2018), pp. 43, 86–7.

19. E. Helmore and M. Pengelly, 'Nigel Farage discusses "freedom and winning" in meeting with Trump,' *Guardian*, 13 November 2016.

20. N. Wapshott, *Ronald Reagan and Margaret Thatcher: A Political Marriage* (London: Sentinel, 2007), pp. 87, 120; S. A. Treharne, *Reagan and Thatcher's Special Relationship: Latin America and Anglo-American Relations* (Edinburgh: Edinburgh University Press, 2015), pp. 2–4; R. Reagan, *An American Life* (London: Arrow Books, 1990), p. 204.

21. P. Pierson, *Dismantling the Welfare State? Reagan, Thatcher and the Politics of Retrenchment* (Cambridge: Cambridge University Press, 1994), p. 144.

22. J. Krieger, *Reagan, Thatcher and the Politics of Decline* (Cambridge: Polity Press, 1986), pp. 17–35; P. Riddell, 'Ideology in practice,' in A. Adonis and T. Hames (eds), *A Conservative Revolution? The Thatcher-Reagan decade in perspective* (Manchester: Manchester University Press, 1994), pp. 19–41, 24.

23. J. Fund, 'The Reagan Strategy,' *National Review*, 31 July 2017; W. J. Antle III, 'Working Man Blues,' *Modern Age*, spring 2018; A. E. Busch, *Reagan's Victory: The Presidential Election of 1980 and the Rise of the*

Right (Lawrence: University Press of Kansas, 2005), p. 105; L. Hanley, 'Who's Ruling Whom?' *Guardian,* 11 June 2011.

24. D. Harvey, *A Brief History of Neoliberalism* (Oxford: Oxford University Press, 2005), pp. 60–61; R. Aldous, *Reagan and Thatcher: The Difficult Relationship* (London and Hutchinson), p. 24; S. Hall, *The Hard Road to Renewal: Thatcherism and the Crisis of the Left* (London: Verso, 1988), p. 271; A. Gallas, *The Thatcherite Offensive: A Neo-Poulantzasian Analysis* (Leiden: Brill, 2015), pp. 124-132; T. Piketty, *Capital in the Twenty-First Century* (Boston: Harvard University Press, 2014), p. 452.

25. 'Appomattox or Civil War,' *Economist,* 27 May 1978; J. Saville, 'An Open Conspiracy Conservative Politics and the Miners' Strike 1984–5,' *Socialist Register* 1985–6, pp. 295–329.

26. J. A. McCartin, *Collision Course: Ronald Reagan, The Air Traffic Controllers and the Strike that Changed America* (Oxford: Oxford University Press, 2011); K. Moody, *On New Terrain: How Capital is Reshaping the Battleground of the Class War* (Chicago: Haymarket Books, 2017), p. 14.

27. N. Davidson, 'The neoliberal era in Britain: Historical developments and current perspectives,' *International Socialism,* 5 July 2013.

28. T. Mann, *This Peace* (New York: Alfred A. Knopf, 1938); E. Nolte, *Three Faces of Fascism: Action Française. Italian Fascism. National Socialism* (London: Weidenfeld & Nicolson, 1965), p. 21.

29. 'Europe and Revolution,' in L. Trotsky, *The Permanent Revolution: Results and Prospects* (New York: Pathfinder Press, 1972), pp. 251–6.

30. A. Chrisafis, 'The man who could make Marine Le Pen president of France,' *Guardian,* 31 January 2017.

Chapter 7: Benefits and trade

1. R. Seymour, 'What's the Matter with the "White Working Class"?' *Salvage,* 2 February 2017; G. Stuart, 'Leave voters can't be dismissed as "old, racist and stupid,"' *New Statesman,* 3 November 2017; A. Wilkinson, 'Leave voters are not all idiots – some Londoners still don't get it,' *Guardian,* 14 February 2017; J. Carey, 'We will have Remain majority by 2020 – 450,000 Brexiteers die yearly Slams Newsnight guest,' *Daily Express,* 5 January 2018; D. Young, 'This Is What White Supremacy Looks Like,' *The Nation,* 9 November 2016; M. Moulitsas, 'Be happy for coal miners losing their health insurance. They're getting exactly what they voted for,' *Daily Kos,* 12 December 2017.

2. J. T. Rothwell and P. Diego-Rosell, 'Explaining Nationalist Political Views: The Case of Donald Trump,' *SSRN,* 29 December 2017, p. 23;

D. Dorling, 'Brexit: the decision of a divided country,' *British Medical Journal,* 6 July 2016.

3. N. Davidson, 'The neoliberal era in Britain: Historical developments and current perspectives,' *International Socialism,* 5 July 2013.

4. Bureau of Labor Statistics, 'Union Members,' news release, 19 January 2018; K. Moody, *On New Terrain: How Capital is Reshaping the Battleground of the Class War* (Chicago: Haymarket Books, 2017), pp. 2, 14, 98; A. Topping, 'Union membership has plunged to an all-time low, says DBEIS,' *Guardian,* 1 June 2017.

5. 'How UK incomes have risen (and fallen) since 1948,' *Daily Telegraph,* 30 March 2011.

6. T. Piketty, *Capital in the Twenty-First Century* (Boston: Harvard University Press, 2014), pp. 438–40.

7. K. Phillips-Fein, *Fear City: New York's Fiscal Crisis and the Rise of Austerity Politics* (New York: Metropolitan Books, 2017), p. 257–8; C. R. Kesler, 'Thinking About Trump,' *Claremont Review,* 7 May 2018.

8. L. Harding, *Collusion: How Russia helped Trump with the White House* (London: Guardian, 2017), pp. 299–301.

9. 'Tower of secrets: the Russian money behind a Donald Trump skyscraper,' *Financial Times,* 12 July 2018.

10. M. Kranish and M. Fisher, *Trump Revealed: An American Journey of Ambition, Ego, Money and Power* (London: Simon & Schuster, 2016), pp. 304–5; A. Davidson, 'The Inconvenient Legal Troubles That Lie Ahead for the Trump Foundation,' *New Yorker,* 27 June 2018.

11. J. Lanchester, 'After the Fall,' *London Review of Books,* 5 July 2018; Piketty, *Capital in the Twenty-First Century,* p. 259.

12. 'President Trump Speaks at Rally in Pennsylvania,' *CNN,* 29 April 2017.

13. D. Desilver, 'For most workers, real wages have barely budged for decades,' *Pew Research Centre,* 9 October 2014.

14. M. Albright, *Fascism: A Warning* (New York: Harper, 2018), p. 216.

15. J. Kotkin, 'Watch Out! Here Come the "Woke" Tech Oligarchs,' *Daily Beast,* 7 July 2018.

16. 'Pay squeeze worst since Victorian age, study finds,' *Guardian,* 11 October 2014; Lanchester, 'After the Fall.'

17. J. Wolfreys, *Republic of Islamophobia: The Rise of Respectable Racism in France* (London: Hurst and Company, 2018), pp. 16–17.

18. NAWRA Welfare Reform / Benefits Changes Chart, accessed 22 April 2018.

19. Trusell Trust, 'Biggest ever increase in UK foodbank use,' press release, 24 April 2013; Trussell Trust, 'End of year stats,' accessed 19 April 2018.

20. T. Fetzer, 'Did Austerity Cause Brexit,' working paper, Warwick University Centre for Competitive Advantage in the Global Economy, June 2018, pp. 23–6.

21. A. R. Hochschild, *Strangers in their own Land: Anger and Mourning on the American Right* (New York: New Press, 2016), p. 136–7.

22. D. Widgery, *Against Miserabilism: Writings 1968–1992* (Glasgow: Vagabond Voices, 2017), p. 125.

23. J. R. O'Donnell and J. Rutherford, *Trumped! The Inside Story of the Real Donald Trump - His Cunning Rise and Spectacular Fall* (London: Simon & Schuster, 1991), pp. 86–7.

24. J. Khan, 'What a 1990 Playboy Interview Tells Us about Trump's Economics,' *National Review*, 24 April 2018.

25. T. Carlson, 'Donald Trump Is Shocking, Vulgar and Right,' *Politico*, 28 January 2016.

26. 'FDI flows,' *Organisation for Economic Co-operation and Development*, accessed 20 April 2018.

27. European Parliament, 'Legislative Train Schedule,' press release, 20 March 2018; Canadian Press, '5 reasons Belgium's Walloons won't sign the Canada-EU trade pact,' *The Star*, 24 October 2016.

28. J. Stiglitz, *Globalisation and its Discontents* (London: Penguin, 2017 edn), p. 351.

29. W. D. Cohan, 'Michael Milken invented the modern junk bond, went to prison and then became one of the most respected people on Wall Street,' *UK Business Insider*, 2 May 2017.

30. T. Ferguson, P. Jorgensen and J. Chen, 'Industrial Structure and Party Competition in an Age of Hunger Games: Donald Trump and the 2016 Presidential Election,' Institute for New Economic Thinking Working Paper 66, January 2018, pp. 43–5.

31. M. Bow, 'EU referendum: Hedge fund managers backing "Out" campaign set to make millions from Brexit,' *Independent*, 25 October 2016.

32. While a leader in the *Times* backed Remain, the paper ran more articles calling for a Leave vote (36 per cent of its article on the referendum, compared to 22 per cent for Remain). D. A. L. Levy, B. Aslan, D. Bironzo, *UK Press Coverage of the EU Referendum* (Oxford: Reuters Institute for the Study of Journalism, 2016), pp. 16–17.

Chapter 8: Could the far right change back?

1. Pegida UK was not officially launched until the following month.

2. J. Bartlett, *Radicals: Outsides Changing the World* (London: William Heinemann, 2017), p. 48.

3. Roger Griffin terms the EDL (and Pegida) 'the activist faction' of a radical right-wing populist party. R. Griffin, *Fascism: An Introduction to Comparative Fascist Studies* (Cambridge: Polity, 2018), p. 99. But the EDL and Pegida (prior to the recent success of the AfD) have been the external factions of an *absent* right-wing party. The EDL kept apart from the BNP and UKIP. Robinson failed in his attempts to turn the British Freedom Party into a vote-gathering machine.

4. P. Stocker, *English Uprising: Brexit and the Mainstreaming of the Far Right* (London: Melville House, 2017), pp. 104–6.

5. N. Copsey, *The English Defence League: Challenging our country and our Values of Social Inclusion, Fairness and Equality* (London: Faith Matters, 2010), pp. 12–15; H.-H. Pai, *Angry White People: Coming Face-to-Face with the British Far Right* (London: Zed Books, 2016), pp. 101–2; T. Robinson, *Enemy of the State* (London: Press News, 2015), p. 80.

6. Copsey, *The English Defence League*, p. 10.

7. Stocker, *English Uprising*, pp. 104–6; S. Winlow, S. Hall and J. Treadwell, *The Rise of the Right: English Nationalism and the Transformation of Working-Class Politics* (Bristol: Policy Press, 2017), pp. 75, 149.

8. B. Blake, *Coming Down the Road* (Birmingham: VHC Publishing, 2011), p. 2.

9. J. E. Richardson, 'Ploughing the Same Furrow? Continuity and Change in Britain's Extreme-Right Fringe,' in R. Wodak, M. Khosravinik and B. Mral, *Right-Wing Populism in Europe: Politics and Discourse* (London: Bloomsbury Academic Publishing, 2013), pp. 105–120, 115; J. Elgot, 'EDL dismisses Jewish arm as too extreme,' *Jewish Chronicle*, 25 February 2011: Blake, *Coming Down the Road*, pp. 211, 237.

10. R. O. Paxton, *The Anatomy of Fascism* (London: Allen Lane, 2004), p. 49; C. Holmes, *John Bull's Island: Immigration & British Society 1871–1971* (Basingstoke: Macmillan, 1988), pp. 68-70; K. Theweleit, *Male Fantasies Volume 1: Women, Floods, Bodies, History* (Minneapolis: University of Minneapolis Press, 1987).

11. P. C. Gattinara and A. L. P. Pirro. 'The far right as social movement,' *European Societies*, 24 April 2018; 'Gone boy on the right: How an anti-foreigner, anti-establishment group is changing German politics', *Economist*, 24 January 2015; C. Mudde, 'What the stunning success of AfD means for Germany and Europe,' *Guardian*, 24 September 2017.

12. Blake, *Coming Down the Road*, p. 51; Busher, *The Making*, pp. 5–6; Copsey, *The English Defence League*, p. 31; Robinson, *Enemy of the*

State, pp. 184–5; J. Busher, *The Making of an Anti-Muslim Protest: Grassroots Activism in the English Defence League* (London: Routledge, 2016), p. 115; Bartlett, *Radicals*, pp. 79–90.

13. A. Gilligan, 'Tommy Robinson winds up bigots and the clash floods in,' *Times*, 5 August 2018; L. Dearden, 'Darren Osborne: How Finsbury Park terror attacker became "obsessed" with Muslims in less than a month,' *Independent*, 1 February 2018; 'Former EDL leader Tommy Robinson suspended from Twitter,' *ITV News*, 28 March 2018.

14. F. Perraudin, 'EDL founder Tommy Robinson jailed for contempt of court,' *Guardian*, 29 May 2018; O. Jones, '"Tommy Robinson" is no martyr to freedom of speech,' *Guardian*, 31 May 2018; R. Seymour, 'The Phony Martyrdom of Tommy Robinson,' *Jacobin*, 7 August 2018; *Re Yaxley-Lennon (aka Tommy Robinson)* [2018] EWCA Crim 1856; J. Ruffell, 'Fascism, Populism, Nationalism, Closure and the "Politics of Fantasy",' *Paths and Bridges*, 12 May 2018; P. Walker, 'Ukip toys with lifting ban on Tommy Robinson joining party,' *Guardian*, 6 September 2018.

15. Theweleit, *Male Fantasies volume 1*.

16. K. Bradley, 'Always anti-fascist, always anti-sexist,' *rs21*, 7 August 2018. For earlier fears of paedophilia J. Drury, '"When the mobs are looking for witches to burn, nobody's safe:" talking about the reactionary crowd,' *Discourse and Society* 13/1 (2002), pp. 41–73.

17. Pai, *Angry White People*, p. 100.

18. Copsey, *The English Defence League*, p. 31.

19. M. Coppins, 'Trump's Right-hand Troll,' *The Atlantic*, 28 May 2018.

20. M. Holt, 'The Rise and Fall of the Alt Right,' *American Greatness*, 4 September 2018.

21. S. Burley, 'Anti-Semitism in the White House: Stephen Bannon, Donald Trump and the Alt-Right,' *Truthout*, 20 November 2016.

22. Anti-Defamation League, *Anti-Semitic Targeting of Journalists During the 2016 Presidential Campaign, A report from ADL's Task Force on Harassment and Journalism* (New York: ADL, 2016), p. 6; Anti-Defamation League, *Quantifying Hate: A Year of Anti-Semitism on Twitter* (New York: ADL, 2016), p. 2.

23. '"Get Out of Germany, Jewish Pigs": Jewish Restaurant in Germany Attacked by neo-Nazis,' *Haaretz*, 8 September 2018.

24. T. Phillips 'Brazil's Jair Bolsonaro threatens purge of leftwing "outlaws",' *Guardian*, 22 October 2018.

25. K. Marx, *The Eighteenth Brumaire of Louis Bonaparte* (Moscow: Progress Publishers, 1937).

26. Lanchester, 'After the Fall.'

Conclusion: Stopping the right

1. N. Kapoor. *Deport, Deprive, Extradite: 21ˢᵗ Century State Extremism* (London: Verso, 2018), p. 7.
2. 'Enoch Powell's "Rivers of Blood" speech,' *Telegraph*, 6 November 2007.
3. *R (On the Application of Gureckis and ors) v Secretary of State for the Home Department* [2017] EWHC 3298; A. Gentleman, 'Woman nearly deported after 50 years in UK wins leave to remain,' 11 January 2018'; A. Gentleman, '"They don't tell you why": threatened with removal after 52 years in the UK,' *Guardian*, 1 December 2017; A. Gentleman, 'Man who moved from Antigua 59 years ago told he is in UK illegally,' *Guardian*, 30 March 2018.
4. 'Children separated from parents cry at US detention centre – audio,' *Guardian*, 19 June 2018; F. O'Toole, 'Trial runs for fascism are in full flow,' *Irish Times*, 26 June 2018.
5. C. Arruzza, 'Lessons from Italy: The Dangers of Anti-Trumpism.' *Verso*, 21 November 2016.
6. P. Murphy, 'White nationalist Richard Spencer punched during interview,' *CNN Politics*, 21 January 2017.
7. M. Goodwin and C. Milazzo, *UKIP: Inside the Campaign to Redraw the Map of British Politics* (Oxford: Oxford University Press, 2015), p. 78.
8. R. Seymour, *Corbyn: The Strange Rebirth of Radical Politics* (London: Verso, 2017), p. xxvi; R. Seymour, 'The "youthquake" revisited,' *Patreon*, 31 May 2018; M. Goodwin and O. Heath, *The UK 2017 General Election examined: income, poverty and Brexit* (London: Joseph Rowntree Foundation, 2017), p. 18.
9. G. Eaton, 'How Jeremy Corbyn and the European left are reclaiming populism,' *New Statesman*, 11 July 2018; D. Law, 'Labour's Brexit Policy,' *Duncan Law*, 8 June 2018; T. Lochocki, 'Jeremy Corbyn Doesn't Translate Into German,' *Foreign Policy*, 29 August 2018.
10. E. Platt, 'Comrades at War: the decline and fall of the Socialist Workers Party,' *New Statesman*, 20 May 2014.

Index

About Haymarket Books

Haymarket Books is a radical, independent, nonprofit book publisher based in Chicago.

Our mission is to publish books that contribute to struggles for social and economic justice. We strive to make our books a vibrant and organic part of social movements and the education and development of a critical, engaged, international left.

We take inspiration and courage from our namesakes, the Haymarket martyrs, who gave their lives fighting for a better world. Their 1886 struggle for the eight-hour day—which gave us May Day, the international workers' holiday—reminds workers around the world that ordinary people can organize and struggle for their own liberation. These struggles continue today across the globe—struggles against oppression, exploitation, poverty, and war.

Since our founding in 2001, Haymarket Books has published more than five hundred titles. Radically independent, we seek to drive a wedge into the risk-averse world of corporate book publishing. Our authors include Noam Chomsky, Arundhati Roy, Rebecca Solnit, Angela Y. Davis, Howard Zinn, Amy Goodman, Wallace Shawn, Mike Davis, Winona LaDuke, Ilan Pappé, Richard Wolff, Dave Zirin, Keeanga-Yamahtta Taylor, Nick Turse, Dahr Jamail, David Barsamian, Elizabeth Laird, Amira Hass, Mark Steel, Avi Lewis, Naomi Klein, and Neil Davidson. We are also the trade publishers of the acclaimed Historical Materialism Book Series and of Dispatch Books.